PRAISE FOR *FORTUNE FAVORS THE BRAVE*

"An honest account of the men who fought and died developing First Force Recon."
—W.E.B. Griffin, author of *The Brotherhood of War*, *The Corps*, *Honor Bound*, and *Men at War*

"Everything that force recon is today was built upon the solid foundation laid by Colonel Meyers and his generation. From night parachuting off carrier-based jets to slipping stealthily ashore from submerged subs, they 'wrote the book' for those who followed. Today's recon men owe them a debt of gratitude for their ingenuity, daring, and dedication. My thanks to the author for telling their story so well."
—Maj. John Plaster, U.S. Army Special Forces (Ret.), author of *SOG: The Secret Wars of America's Commanders in Vietnam*

"The danger starts before men ever go to war. *Fortune Favors the Brave* is an intriguing account of men who learned to swim from submerged submarines and others who fell from jets in the sky—and how they came together to create a remarkable fighting force."
—Sherry Sontag, coauthor of *Blind Man's Bluff, The Untold Story of American Submarine Espionage*

"Colonel Meyers has made a major contribution to the nation's reconnaissance capability by perfecting techniques for launch from submarines. Although his book describes these technical issues, it is written in a narrative style filled with excitement—an adventure story in the laboratory."
—Capt. Paul Keenan, USN (Ret.)

"Good slide history that covers the very complex nature of creating something new and different within a culture that is hidebound and conservative."
—Lt. Col. Alex Lee, USMC (Ret.)

FORTUNE FAVORS THE BRAVE

BRUCE F. MEYERS

St. Martin's Paperbacks

Published by arrangement with Naval Institute Press.

FORTUNE FAVORS THE BRAVE

Copyright © 2000 by Bruce F. Meyers.

Cover image of soldiers courtesy of U.S. Marine Corps.

Library of Congress Catalog Card Number: 99-056896

ISBN: 0-312-99680-2
EAN: 80312-99680-2

Printed in the United States of America

Naval Institute Press edition published in 2000
St. Martin's Paperbacks edition / August 2004

St. Martin's Paperbacks are published by St. Martin's Press, 175 Fifth Avenue, New York, NY 10010.

10 9 8 7 6 5 4 3 2 1

CONTENTS

	Foreword	vii
	Introduction	xiii
1	The World War II Experience	1
2	Amphib Recon School	13
3	Training with the Army	32
4	Marine Corps Test Unit 1	37
5	Off-Carrier Capability	53
6	Pathfinding in Test Unit 1	70
7	Anatomy of a Parachute Accident	83
8	Forming 1st Force Recon	100
9	Submarines and Beyond	127
10	Buoyant Ascents	159
11	Shaking Down	180
12	Deployment Overseas	197
13	Methods of Extraction	216
14	Combat Parachuting	234
	Afterword	243
	Notes	251
	Glossary	265
	Bibliography	283
	Index	287

FOREWORD

As the United States enters the twenty-first century, it is vital to remember that we have always been and remain a maritime nation. It is, after all, back and forth across those highways we call oceans that we—and the free world as we know it today—must move for economic and societal well being. Our national purpose, interalia, remains to survive and perchance to flourish. To this end, our navy and marine expeditionary forces remain powerful strategic instruments to project both power and influence in support of national policy.

Today, as in the past, our nation's Marine Corps maintains versatile and adaptable marine expeditionary forces prepared for the full spectrum of potential conflicts worldwide. These organized marine air-ground task forces (MAGTF) include fully integrated force reconnaissance units, which, when used with other specialized capabilities, provide for a broad spectrum of special operations. As they collect vital intelligence on enemy capabilities and other critical information, our force reconnaissance companies are truly the eyes and ears of our forces. They also conduct raids, tactical recovery of downed aircraft personnel, and other direct-action missions. This has not always been the case, however. Our current force reconnaissance capabilities have evolved over the past fifty years. They became possible only after our vast experience with amphibious reconnaissance missions in World War II and the immediate postwar era.

This book tells the fascinating story of the early years of marine deep reconnaissance development carried out by a special breed of courageous, superbly trained and motivated, innovative and persistent marines and sailors who pioneered the tactics, techniques, procedures, and special-equipment testing required to bring new capabilities to the battlefield. Our author, Colonel Bruce F. Meyers USMC(Ret) was the leader of these splendid warriors and thus has firsthand knowledge of their relentless quest for improving the insertion and extraction of deep reconnaissance units. In my view, his well-researched book accurately chronicles the sophisticated, arduous training and experimentation that led to techniques and tactics new to military operations at the time.

Although I had heard about Bruce Meyers through the years, I did not meet him until we served together in Vietnam. Later, when Bruce was chief of the ground combat division at the Marine Corps Development Center at Quantico, I was there as chief of the intelligence, surveillance and reconnaissance division.

Bruce Meyers served in the latter stages of World War II as a young lieutenant and platoon leader in a combat swimming company where he developed his skills in rubber boat operations and combat swimming. Upon return from command of a rifle company in Korea, he served under the legendary General Lewis B. "Chesty" Puller as his reconnaissance officer. General Puller fully supported the use of the parachute as a means of entry and the development of more sophisticated means for inserting personnel from submarines than our Corps had been capable of during the many successful amphibious reconnaissance missions of World War II.

Following training as a parachutist (by both the army

and the navy), then Major Meyers joined Marine Corps Test Unit 1 at Camp Pendleton, California. Test Unit 1 had been established by then Commandant Lemuel C. Shepherd to develop new long-range, helicopterborne assault concepts deemed essential for the potentially "atomic" battlefields of the future. Under the command of Col. Edward N. Rydalch, the unit was an organized MAGTF of combined arms tasked to test these concepts. It conducted operations from the sea using a converted navy ship as a helicopter transport. Early on, Colonel Rydalch and his marines recognized the need for long-range reconnaissance operations deep in hostile territory to provide timely combat intelligence information, particularly as it concerned proposed landing zones and sites. Test Unit 1's recommendations to test and evaluate these new techniques for gathering that intelligence were approved, and the force recon journey was under way.

Major Meyers, along with Capts. Joe Taylor and Don Koelper (Mr. Pathfinder) and their superb marines and navy corpsmen were given a virtual blank check from Lt. Col. Regan Fuller (later Brigadier General) to develop new parachute and submarine techniques for inserting marine reconnaissance teams. These superb professionals wrote the book on pathfinding and guidance procedures that made deep helicopterborne operations on a fluid battlefield possible. They also created new methods for inserting both pathfinders and reconnaissance teams from aircraft and carriers at sea (the first use of parachute personnel from carriers in naval aviation history). To accomplish this task, they had to perfect techniques for exit from many new types of naval aircraft that had never been used for parachute operations. These aircraft included the Grumman TF-1 fighter aircraft such as the Douglas F3D Skyknight, where they jumped from a formation of four aircraft, and the Douglas A3D Skywarrior,

a twin-jet, carrier-based bomber, where they jumped
from the bomb bays. Many of these jumps were made at
night into small drop zones with marginal weather conditions. Though lives were lost during these historic experimental trials, the result was a capability unique among
armed forces worldwide.

Concurrent with the aforementioned developments, reconnaissance swimmers and divers continued to develop
new procedures to improve clandestine entry and recovery techniques from submarines. Operating from the
USS *Perch* (ASSP 313), an older fleet submarine that had
been recommissioned and reconfigured to carry assault
troops, these innovative warriors exploited German
World War II submarine escape experiences. The *Perch*
and her sister boat, the USS *Sealion* (ASSP 315) assigned
to the Atlantic fleet, had their fore and aft torpedo areas
converted to carry troops. Mounted just aft of the conning
tower was a large cylindrical water-tight structure (affectionately known as "the bubble") used for carrying a
launch, rubber boats, and other reconnaissance equipment. Using these reconfigured submarines, reconnaissance marines and corpsmen developed "buoyant ascent"
techniques for nighttime egress and underway recovery.
This too, is an inspiring story.

On a personal note, the story of the submarine operations was especially memory-catching for me. Having
been one of the original noncommissioned officer plank
holders of the First Amphibious Reconnaissance Platoon,
Fleet Marine Force Pacific in 1951, I remember well the
exciting nighttime rubber boat launches and swimmer operations from the USS *Perch*. Our West Coast training operations were under Capt. Francis "Bull" Kraince (now
Col. F. R. Kraince USMC(Ret)), M.Sgt. John W. Slagle
(now Capt. J. W. Slagle USMC(Ret)), the late Gy.Sgt.
Ernie L. DeFazio (Lt. Col. E. L. DeFazio USMC(Ret))

and S.Sgt. Neal D. King (now Sgt. Maj. N.D. King USMC(Ret)). These marines were distinguished professionals and magnificent leaders who patiently taught me so much. They showed me firsthand why staff noncommissioned officers are indeed the backbone of the Corps. For their leadership and encouragement, I will always be eternally grateful.

This splendid book should be read by all military professionals interested in how we developed our current flexible force reconnaissance capabilities. Although Col. Meyers focuses on the early development of First Force Reconnaissance Company, we should not forget the many significant contributions of the Second Force Reconnaissance Company led by warriors such as (then) Capt. Paul X. Kelley (later Gen. P. X. Kelley, our twenty-eighth commandant) and their superb marines. It has been my privilege to serve with and know very well nearly all of the distinguished marines mentioned in *Fortune Favors the Brave*. Thank you all for having the courage, the wisdom, and the perseverance to change the institution of our Corps.

Finally, for all those splendid warriors who served in and supported our force reconnaissance efforts all through the years—and who serve today—our nation owes you so much. Our capabilities today are indeed second to none because of you. Take care of yourselves, take care of each other, God Bless and—Semper Fidelis!

General Al Gray USMC(Ret)
29th Commandant

INTRODUCTION

To my knowledge, there have been no books written about the early pioneers in marine reconnaissance. Just prior to World War II, during the early development of amphibious doctrine by the United States Navy and the Marine Corps, marine scouts were landed in Puerto Rico at night by rubber boats from submarines. These early efforts culminated in the formation of marine amphibious reconnaissance units, which performed with great success during the amphibious landings of World War II.

"Amphibious reconnaissance" became a term denoting—as the *Joint Landing-Force Manual* said—"A directed effort by personnel landed from seaward *by any means* to collect the information on a coastal area required for the planning and conduct of amphibious operations" (emphasis added). Later the *Landing-Force Manual*'s "Doctrine for Amphibious Operations" refined the description to include "a landing conducted by minor elements, involving stealth rather than force of arms for the purpose of securing information, followed by a planned withdrawal."

A number of books have been written about the later years of force reconnaissance, particularly the Vietnam era—*Inside Force Recon: Recon Marines in Vietnam*, by Michael Lanning and Lt. Cdr. Ray W. Stubbe, for example, and Maj. Bruce "Doc" Norton's two books *Force Recon Diary, 1969* and *Force Recon Diary, 1970*. And more recently, the Naval Institute Press has published in its Special Warfare Series *Force Recon Command: A Special Marine Unit in Vietnam, 1969–1970*, written by Lt. Col. Alex Lee.

I was privileged to participate in the creation of the concept of force reconnaissance as the logical enlargement of the doctrine of a unit designed for insertion of recon personnel far deeper inland (or behind enemy lines) than had ever been contemplated or employed by marines during World War II. The idea for such a unit was fleshed out during the period from 1954 through 1957 by a special test and evaluation unit created by the commandant of the Marine Corps for the evaluation of doctrine, tactics, and units for the Marine Corps to employ in the "nuclear age." This was Marine Corps Test Unit 1, located at Camp Horno at Camp Pendleton, California. The Cold War and all of its implications of conducting operations at greater depth inland from the sea or farther beyond what had previously been considered behind enemy lines became significant factors in all of our operations.

At Marine Corps Test Unit 1, I served for three years as "parachute/reconnaissance/pathfinder project officer." Upon the disestablishment of this special test regiment, the only Fleet Marine Force (FMF) unit to emerge was 1st Force Reconnaissance Company. On 18 June 1957, I took over from Capt. Mike Spark the command of the 1st Amphibious Reconnaissance Company, which was operationally attached to the 1st Marine Division at Camp Pendleton. The next day, we commissioned 1st Force Recon Company as an FMF unit. It had its own table of organization and equipment (TOE) and began its separate and unique life within the U.S. Marine Corps. Nearly a year later at Camp Lejeune, North Carolina, my executive officer, Capt. Joseph Z. Taylor (who was later appointed U.S. Assistant Secretary of State), took half of our jumpers and divers and infused them into 2d Amphib

Recon. That company was then transformed into 2d Force Recon. Later, as the Marine Corps expanded for duty in Vietnam, four more force recon companies were organized and trained: the 3d, 4th, 5th, and later the 6th, with the 3d and 4th being deployed and the 5th providing personnel to 3d for its deployment.

The emphasis in Test Unit 1 and during the early days of 1st Force (and to a similar degree, 2d Force on the east coast) was on the development of new operational techniques for insertion, both parachute and submerged submarine, and extraction of reconnaissance and pathfinder personnel deep behind enemy lines (including evasion to pickup sites, or use of special extraction equipment such as SPIE rigs, Fulton Skyhook, trooper's ladders, and so on). We approached all of our operations with the idea of trying to improve on prior methods of insertion and extraction, which up to that time were primarily via submarines and rubber boats. Parachutes and buoyant ascents offered entirely different methods.

I readily acknowledge the fact that a number of other reconnaissance and intelligence personnel within the Marine Corps had ideas that were similar to our own for carrying out deeper reconnaissance than had yet been attempted, as well as ideas for the use of parachutes and more sophisticated methods of entry from submarines. A sizable number of individuals contributed to the development of the methods and tactics that were initiated by Marine Corps Test Unit 1—individuals who range from the officers and men of our unit itself up to the top levels of Marine Corps command.

Help from on High

Much in the formation and development of force reconnaissance within the Fleet Marine Force would not have occurred without significant assistance from senior officers serving at higher headquarters and on higher staffs. In the development of the deep reconnaissance concept, one of the persons who gave us our start was Brig. Gen. Lewis B. Puller. When I approached General Puller to outline my plan for adding the parachute entry capability to reconnaissance within the Marine Corps, he agreed with the potential for the concepts and immediately tasked me to write a letter to the commandant of the Marine Corps outlining our plans and thoughts on deeper reconnaissance and pathfinding. Chesty signed this letter, and months later it led to my being sent to Fort Benning, Georgia, to attend the Army Advanced Infantry School and later to enroll in the parachute course and the jumpmaster course.

Later, at Marine Corps Test Unit 1 at Camp Pendleton, Col. Edward Rydalch, commanding officer, and Lt. Col. Regan Fuller, head of Plans of Development, were always at the fore in presenting our case. After 1st Force was formed, within the 1st Marine Division (to which 1st Force was operationally attached), we had strong supporters in our division commanders: Maj. Gen. David M. Shoup (who would later be named commandant of the Marine Corps) and Maj. Gen. Edward Snedeker. At Fleet Marine Force, Pacific (FMFPac), in Hawaii, 1st Force Recon benefited from Col. Henry W. "Bill" Buse, Col. Herman Nickerson, Lt. Col. Kenny Houghton, and naval aviator Lt. Col. Ralph "Smoke" Spanjer. Within the 1st Marine Air Wing at El Toro was the irrepressible and dynamic marine aviator Lt. Col. Bill Mitchell, helicopter squadron commander and a true believer in guidance by ground teams, or pathfinding, for our helicopter assaults.

Back at Marine Corps Base Quantico, Virginia, in the Intelligence School was Lt. Col. Bob Churley, who asked for copies of everything we were doing and, in turn, kept us abreast of what others were up to that might help us in our missions. CWO Lewis T. Vinson and his successor, CWO L. V. Patinetti, jumpmasters at the U.S. Naval Parachute Unit, El Centro, California, were always ready to offer suggestions. They worked with us continuously to ensure that the new and untried techniques and jumps of all different types of equipment and aircraft were as safe as possible and were operationally compatible with fleet naval aircraft and aircraft carriers.

Influences in Formation

The two officers who were most influential in the formation of 1st Force and who worked with me to create and execute ideas are Lt. Col. Regan Fuller and Capt. Joseph Z. Taylor. Regan Fuller had the acumen, foresight, consummate staff skills, and post-World War II recon command experience to successfully shepherd us through all of the difficulties that arise during the implementation of new techniques in a monolithic organization like the U.S. Marine Corps. It was he who selected Captain Taylor to train the fledgling recon platoon that was Test Unit 1, with the goal of bringing the personnel to a high degree of competence in state-of-the-art amphibious reconnaissance methods and practices. And I must presume that it was Lieutenant Colonel Fuller who chose me to impart the skills related to the parachute reconnaissance and parachute pathfinding innovations that the two of us had discussed for many hours.

I could not have asked for a better leader than Regan Fuller nor a better recon officer and exec than Capt. Joe Taylor, who worked very closely with both Lieutenant Colonel Fuller and me to bring to fruition our ideas for new methods of conducting deep reconnaissance within the Marine Corps. Joe was an experienced recon officer, and as my executive officer when we formed 1st Force Recon, he not only was the ultimate in support for me but was always there to act as a foil when that role was needed. Joe formed the same synergistic relationship with his exec, Capt. Paul Xavier Kelley (who was later named commandant of the Marine Corps), when 2d Force was formed. It was left to 2d Force to amplify what we had started and to carry it even further.

We were given the challenge and the opportunity, first in Test Unit 1 and later when we commissioned 1st Force Recon, to actually form, train, and operate the company with our new concepts. The 1st Force became the place where significant new techniques of reconnaissance insertion were inaugurated: the first instance in naval aviation history of deliberate parachute entry of recon personnel from aircraft launched from aircraft carriers; the first parachute jumps from diverse naval aircraft including jets, both bombers and fighters; the first buoyant ascents from submerged submarines. Along the way, there was resistance to many of the tactics and techniques we sought to establish, but these obstacles were overcome, usually by help from senior officers or the commandant himself.

For anyone who is looking for a primer on force recon, this is not the book. It is, rather, a historical account of the first two years of 1st Force. It is not intended to recap the scouting and patrolling techniques used by patrols operating deep behind the lines. Those tactics and methods were already well established within the Marine Corps. And this is, indeed, the heritage that we in 1st Force Recon were building on: the hundred-plus amphibious reconnaissance patrols of World War II and the many amphib recon operations that were conducted after the war, up to the time of the formation of 1st Force. Where they are germane within history, these techniques will be discussed. The central hope with this account, however, is that the reader will gain some insight into the unique, innovative, and diverse means by which intelligence is gathered and helicopter landings were controlled by marine recon and pathfinder personnel.

The title *Fortune Favors the Brave: The Story of 1st Force Recon* was chosen because of the great verve and dedication that the personnel of 1st Force Recon evidenced during periods of great stress and adversity. Indeed, in many ways this book is the story of the deaths and injuries of those who dared. "Fortune favors the brave" is a quotation attributed to Pliny the Elder, who was commander of the fleet in the Bay of Naples at the time of the eruption of Mount Vesuvius in A.D. 79. Against the advice of others, he left the safety of his vessel and went ashore, toward the flames and hurling rocks, in an attempt to help the terrified citizens of Stabiae, the port of the city of Pompeii. Pliny died in that holocaust.

Each of us in 1st Force Recon was fully aware of the dangerous aspects of this new form of reconnaissance, yet we all felt fortunate to be able to participate in that effort. None of us ever considered ourselves "brave" in the normal context. We simply looked on ourselves as highly trained professionals and approached all of our tasks with that commitment. We had to take risks in order to get the job done. On occasion, we sustained casualties in the testing of new tactics, techniques, and equipment. Improvements in all three of these areas were implemented in every case in the hope that such losses would never happen again.

Those of us who were fortunate enough to have served in 1st Force Recon do not consider ourselves some masochistic "subgroup" within the marine intelligence community. Everyone with whom I dealt in force reconnaissance was of the highest caliber of professional marines and corpsmen. The price of sound intelligence for the landing force commander is high. Modern amphibious warfare requires the emplacement of young, intelligent personnel deep behind enemy lines. They come in at night from jets and submarines to accomplish these perilous and demanding missions. Since the inception of our unit in 1957, the personnel who have served in the many force recon companies that have followed us have distinguished themselves in combat in Southeast Asia in Vietnam, in the Caribbean and Grenada, in Somalia in East Africa, and most recently, in Southwest Asia in the Persian Gulf in Operation Desert Storm.

Recognition must also be given here to our two most indispensable supporters, the submarines, the aircraft, and the crews that took us to our missions. From beneath the sea, the fleet submarines, particularly the USS *Perch* and her "can do" skipper, Lt. Cdr. Elmer V. "Mac" McKeever and executive officer Lt. Paul Keenan deserve our thanks. And speaking for 2d Force Recon after it was formed, I must acknowledge the USS *Sealion* and her officers and crew. Lastly, the pilots and crews of all of our jump aircraft: marines from Night Fighter Squadrons 532 and 513, who flew the F3D Skyknight; marines from the 1st and 3d Marine Air Wings, who flew the R4D-8 Super Skytrains; members of the U.S. Navy's Transport Squadron VR-5 (later redesignated VR-21)—including our primary TF-1 pilot, Lt. Cdr. Roy Taylor—who flew the Grumman TF-1 Trader; and the personnel from the navy's heavy attack squadrons, HATRON 2 and 6, who flew the A3D Skywarrior and who dropped us both when we were in the States and when we were deployed overseas.

No single small unit within the Marine Corps has equaled the total number of commissioned and senior noncommissioned officers who went on from those formative and demanding years in 1st and 2d Force Recon to rise to positions of high command and great responsibility: a future commandant, many general officers, a sergeant major of the Marine Corps, as well as several winners of the Medal of Honor and many Navy Cross awardees. Silver and Bronze Stars and hundreds of Purple Hearts emblazon the chests of those early few. To all who served in force recon—past, present, and future—this chronicle is respectfully dedicated.

Research Sources

In tracing the creation and development of force reconnaissance, I have relied on a number of sources. I had the benefit of interviewing many participants with whom I had served in the Marine Corps. I had twice worked, for example, with Maj. John Bradbeer, first in Korea, where we were both intelligence officers, and later, when we were both officers in charge of schools at Troop Training Unit, Pacific, in Coronado, California. And earlier, as a young lieutenant at the close of World War II, I had a number of the marines from the Tinian operation serving in my combat swimming platoon at Camp Pendleton.

Fortunately, too, I had kept copies of all of my orders (those from World War II and Korea and those regarding El Centro and NAS North Island, for example), as well as copies of many of the special reports and memorandums for the record that we wrote concerning the new types of aircraft. The Marine Corps Historical Center Library at the Navy Yard in Washington, D.C.—under Brig. Gen. Edward Simmons, with chief historian Benis Frank and head archivist Fred Graboske—was a fertile source of relevant documents. In addition, Lt. Cdr. Ray Stubbe, coauthor with Michael Lanning of *Inside Force Recon*, had copies of almost everything written about recon, which he had obtained from the archives at Headquarters, Marine Corps, in Washington. Ray was kind enough to share copies of some documents that I did not already have. I extend my deepest gratitude to all of these individuals and institutions for their assistance.

Let me not forget my outstanding and understanding copy editor Gayle Swanson, Ph.D., Professor of English at the University of South Carolina, who helped make this a better book.

Finally, thanks to my family support group: Our son, Lt. Col. Craig F. Meyers, USMC, born in Coronado when I had the Recon School for Chesty Puller; sons Bruce F. Jr. and Christopher, both born when I was at Test Unit and later commanding 1st Force at Pendleton, and to Jo, my wife of fifty-two years, known to most in Force Recon as a character of great humor and as a loyal, dedicated marine wife.

CHAPTER ONE
The World War II Experience

The Beginnings

The first unit in marine history to be organized and trained specifically for amphibious reconnaissance was created during World War II, in January 1943, under the leadership of Capt. James Logan Jones. Fifteen months later, after a second amphib recon company had been created, casualties and replacement and training problems forced the reorganization of the two companies into a single battalion. Given a small headquarters company, the newly formed unit was designated the Amphibious Reconnaissance Battalion, V Amphibious Corps (VAC).[1]

For the reader to gain a better insight into the events that led to the formation of 1st Force Recon in 1957, it will be helpful to look back at two classic examples of amphibious reconnaissance operations conducted by the Marine Corps in the Pacific during World War II. Out of the roughly one hundred eighty amphibious recon missions that were carried out during the war, these two missions reflect the kinds of tasks that were later assigned to the force reconnaissance companies and that continue to this day in the current Fleet Marine Force. The first of the two examples that I want to examine is the operation conducted by 1st Marine Division scouts on Cape Gloucester, on the southwestern coast of New Britain, the largest island of the Bismarck Archipelago in the southwestern Pacific, September through November 1943. The second is that conducted on Tinian Island, in the Northern Marianas in the Pacific, by the 5th Amphibious Reconnaissance Battalion in July 1944.

Cape Gloucester, September 1943

The island of New Britain was a staging area for the Japanese reinforcing from Rabaul, the island's chief town, through New Britain to their bases at Finschaven, New Guinea. The Japanese had an airstrip on New Britain that was being used to harass Gen. Douglas MacArthur's forces on New Guinea. Three months before the scheduled landings on New Britain, the Marine Landing Force commander, Maj. Gen. William H. Rupertus, needed information on which to base his plans for the seizure of New Britain. He briefed his chief division scout, 1st Lt. John D. Bradbeer, and assigned him the task of obtaining information on the prospective landing areas as well as intelligence on the Japanese defenses.

Using the cover of the rainy night of 24 September 1943, Bradbeer; a member of the Royal Australian Navy, Lt. Kirkwall Smith; several U.S. Marine scouts; and two natives of the region were taken to the Cape Gloucester area by three PT (patrol torpedo) boats (PT-325, PT-327, and PT-110)—one to carry the patrol and two to escort them. Having gone over the side of their patrol PTs into a rubber boat, the party left their PTs lying off the southwestern coast of New Britain. The heavy jungle rain permitted them to avoid being seen from the passing Japanese barges. They made it through the surf and hid their rubber boat in the bush, which came down virtually to the surf line. The rise and fall of the tide was slight, and large jungle trees overhung the water's edge like mangroves, protected by offshore reefs from the action of the waves.

The mission was to last ten days. The patrol was to be picked up again at night by the PT boats. Bradbeer, having found the initial size of the patrol to be too cumbersome for the mission, left several marines in a base camp to guard their hidden boat. Bradbeer, Lieutenant Smith, and the two natives completed the bulk of patrolling. With assistance from friendly locals, they made sketches of the beaches, located the coastal defense guns, and determined the timing and routes of Japanese patrols. They formed an opinion as to the discipline and logistic support of the local Japanese. As the patrol arrived back at their base camp ten days later, friendly natives warned of an approaching Japanese patrol.

Unable to contact their PTs, Bradbeer decided to take their rubber boat to sea and attempt to evade offshore to Siassi Island in Dampier Strait. They again attempted to contact their PT boats, and being successful this time, they were picked up. Bradbeer and his men operated on this enemy beach in an area that esteemed naval historian Samuel Eliot Morison has described as having "about 7,500 [Japanese] troops" at the time.[2]

Some forty-five days later, on 30 November 1943, Bradbeer accompanied another patrol from the PTs, this time led by marine lieutenant R. B. Firm; a navy hydrographer for beach information, Ens. A. E. Gipe; marine corporal A. M. Wociesjes; marine sergeant Elmer Potts; and two natives. Bradbeer remained as a standby in the PTs during the landing. Information attained by this second patrol made it clear that the planned invasion on this particular beach would have been a disaster—the shore was backed by high cliffs with only one narrow exit. The patrol was recovered shortly thereafter.

On 21 December 1943, six days before D-day, Lt. Bradbeer led a third and final reconnaissance at Cape Gloucester. Using three PT boats again, they landed, this time employing three rubber boats to go ashore. Once on the beach, they split into two parties. Bradbeer took the south patrol with six of his marine scouts, while 1st Lt. J. P. Fornier took the north patrol, consisting of six of the remaining scouts. In just a matter of hours, both patrols confirmed the usability of the scheduled landing beach. Importantly, they determined that all the beaches continued to be lightly defended. After the patrols were picked up by their PT boats, the PT with Bradbeer's team aboard came upon an armed Japanese barge, which took them under fire, wounding three of the PT's crew. The skipper, naval lieutenant Paul Rennel, was able to break contact and escape to return the patrol with its vital information to I Amphibious Corps.[3]

It is important to note at this point that in every marine division prior to and during World War II, there were scouts who had undergone much the same training, selection, and assigned missions as had the marines in the two actual amphibious reconnaissance companies. The chief scout of the 1st Marine Division, 1st Lt. John D. Bradbeer, was certainly one of the innovators and early practitioners of amphibious reconnaissance. Interestingly, Bradbeer was given the army's Soldier's Medal (the equivalent of the navy's Marine Corps Medal, which is awarded for noncombat heroism) for his patrol exploits on New Britain, for lifesaving valor in a "noncombat" situation—something John Bradbeer confided to me that he never understood, considering the patrol's encounters.[4]

Tinian, July 1944

Of the twenty-two islands constituting the Marianas, the four largest islands—Guam, Rota, Saipan, and Tinian—

were the logical strategic targets. The northernmost two, Saipan and Tinian, became the landing sites in June 1944 for Lt. Gen. Holland M. "Howling Mad" Smith's V Amphibious Corps, consisting of the 2d and 4th Marine Divisions and the 27th Army Division. Seizure of Guam in the southern Marianas was at this same time tasked to Maj. Gen. Roy S. Geiger, whose III Amphibious Corps was composed of the 3d Marine Division, the 1st Provisional Marine Brigade, and the 77th Army Division.[5] On 15 June 1944, the 2d and 4th Marine Divisions made an assault landing on Saipan. Complete seizure of Saipan took thirty-nine days of heavy fighting against a determined enemy. On 9 July 1944 the island was declared secure. Of the twenty-four thousand Japanese defenders, some twenty-three thousand had died and one thousand were taken prisoners.

Two and one-half miles across Saipan Channel to the south lay the island of Tinian. Only twenty-one thousand yards from north to south, Tinian was the site of airfields that were to figure importantly in the ultimate conquest of Japan (it was from Tinian that, in August 1945, two B-29s took off to drop atomic weapons on Hiroshima and Nagasaki). Some nine thousand Japanese defenders, under Japanese commander Col. Kiochi Ogata, were to oppose the expected landing on Tinian by the marines now based on Saipan.

Tinian was a complex plateau of relatively flat terrain arising from cliffs from the sea. There were only two major terrain features, Mount Lasso (five hundred feet) to the north and another unnamed peak (some five hundred eighty feet high) to the south. The terrain in between the two was mostly level fields of sugarcane. The cliffs in the south, some as high as one hundred fifty feet, were rough and undercut rusty-brown lava and water-carved coral. In contrast, most of the northern beaches were backed by cliffs of only three to ten feet. Few beaches breached these natural barriers to an amphibious assault. Yellow Beach 1, at Asiga Bay on Tinian's east coast, was only four hundred yards wide. Backed by twenty-three pill-boxes, the beach was, from the outset, considered probably too narrow and too heavily defended to be the site of the 2d and 4th Marine Divisions' planned assault.[6]

The beaches at Sunharon Bay, on the southwest side of the island in front of Tinian Town (the island's major city), were the best and, logically, the most heavily defended ones. In initial planning, these beaches were given the code names Orange, Red, Green, and Blue. It was here that the Japanese had concentrated their major defenses, which included six-inch guns captured from the British in the fall of Singapore as well as 140-mm, 120-mm, and 76.2-mm guns.[7] The Japanese located their mobile reserve in the south, anticipating that the marines would land near Tinian Town or at what they believed to be the only other usable site, Yellow Beach 1.

The two most difficult and smallest beaches lay on the northwest tip of Tinian, called Hagoi—White Beach 1, which was a mere sixty yards wide, and White Beach 2, one hundred sixty yards wide. The landing force commander had to make a decision regarding which beaches to use for his assault. A and B Companies of the Amphibious Reconnaissance Battalion, under Capt. James Jones, were tasked by the V Amphibious Corps, under Lt. Gen. Holland Smith, to do the preassault amphibious reconnaissance on Tinian's northern beaches on the nights of 10 and 11 July. Capt. Merwin H. Silverthorn's A Company was assigned to do Yellow Beach 1 at Asiga Bay on the east coast of Tinian. Accompanied by a detachment from underwater demolition team (UDT) 7, under Lt. Richard F. Burke, USNR, they were to debark at 2100 from the USS *Stringham* (APD-6), a converted World War I four-stacker destroyer transport.[8] Their operation order directed them to land "in rubber boats and proceed to a point four hundred yards off Yellow Beach 1, then launch swimmers to that beach and approaching from the flanks reconnoiter that beach. Upon completion of the reconnaissance but not later than 0200 return to the assigned APD [high-speed destroyer transport]."[9]

B Company, commanded by 1st Lt. Leo B. Shinn, was aboard the USS *Gilmer* (APD-11). Accompanied by a detachment from UDT 5, under Lt. Cdr. Draper Kaufman, B Company was assigned identical missions for the amphibious reconnaissance of both White 1 and White 2 near Hagoi, on the northwest side of the island. They were to debark at 2130. Rubber boats were put over the afterdecks (referred to as fantails) of both APDs, and small landing craft towed the respective patrols in ten rubber boats (eight for recon, two for the UDT) to about five hundred yards off their respective beaches. The patrols paddled in to a point just outside the surf zone.

Here the reconnaissance marines, faces blackened, slipped over the sides of their boats. They carried no weapons other than their "K-Bar" or Fairbairn fighting knives.[10] Dressed for swimming, everyone carried small inflatable bladders (deflated) in their sweaters or camouflaged dungarees, to provide buoyancy when needed. They wore boondockers or tennis shoes to prevent being cut by the coral. Two marines were left in each rubber boat to hold their position off the beaches for later recovery of the swimmers. UDT officers and men accompanied the marines to the beach, where the UDT remained in the water to conduct hydrographic surveys.

B Company's team for White 1 was swept north some distance by strong currents and never made their beach, landing instead on a small reef just to the north of Tinian.

The team for White 2 was also swept northward by the same ocean currents but managed to reach White 1 successfully.[11] Their recovery by their rubber boats was spotty: some missed their pickup and had to swim into Tinian Channel for early morning recovery by several of the picketboats (craft used for harbor patrol).

Captain Silverthorn's amphib recon of Yellow 1 (Asiga Beach) confirmed the heavy Japanese defenses inland from Yellow Beach. Offshore UDT found anchored mines. Over the reef UDT found numerous potholes, boulders, and coral heads. Second Lt. Donald Neff and several of his marines worked their way inland about thirty yards, attempting to locate exits for wheeled vehicles. Barbed wire had been laid along the beaches, which were flanked by twenty-five-foot cliffs.[12] Silverthorn's negative report on Yellow killed any further consideration of this beach, although the amphibious task force commanders continued for a time to argue for landing on Yellow Beach.

The second night, 10 July, Captain Silverthorn's A Company was tasked to make another attempt at a recon of Hagoi's White 2—an effort in which the heavy northward currents and tides had frustrated B Company the previous night. Captain Silverthorn (call sign "Silver") took with him eight of his company's swimmers and one swimmer from B Company, MGy.Sgt. Charles "Pat" Patrick, and they successfully performed the amphibious reconnaissance on White 2. This time the *Stringham* was able to control its course by using an SCR300 radio to make radar-course corrections to the shoreward-bound rubber boats.[13]

The hydrographic survey of beaches White 1 and White 2 confirmed their compatibility for the use of landing craft, amphibious tractors (LVTs), and tanks. Capt. Silverthorn's briefed both Lt. Gen. Holland Smith and the amphibious task force commander, Rear Adm. "Handsome Harry"

Hill, on the results of their recon. Admiral Hill kept pressing Captain Silverthorn for his opinion on the two beaches. Finally, in exasperation "Silver" emphatically told the admiral, "They were as flat as a billiard table!"[14] That did it: Admirals Turner and Spruance agreed with Lieutenant General Smith to use White 1 and White 2 instead.[15]

As a result of these two night-reconnaissance explorations of possible beaches on Tinian, the landing force commander made the decision to take the gamble to use White 1 and White 2. Never before in the history of amphibious operations had an attempt been made to land over such narrow beaches. On 24 July 1944, the 4th Marine Division arrived at White 1 and White 2, the northernmost Hagoi beaches, behind the major Japanese defenses, catching the enemy completely off guard.[16]

Simultaneously the amphibious force, using the 2d Marine Division, made a major effort in a feint off Tinian Town. This diversionary landing included lowering of boats, which twice started toward the beaches, drawing heavy fire. It also involved the demolition of several offshore reefs by some of the UDT teams. The Japanese were convinced by the decoy landing to keep their reserves in the south for the expected landing over the Tinian Town beaches. They continued to reinforce behind the beaches that were not used. This permitted the major elements of both the 2d and the 4th Marine Divisions to get ashore and move inland before any significant Japanese response could be initiated. The entire 4th Marine Division was landed the first day over these beaches in just over nine hours, with only fifteen killed. They did not sustain their first casualty until they were nearly fifteen hundred yards inland. The 2d Division landed the next day.[17]

The assault—given long-range artillery-fire support from Saipan, supplemented by naval gunfire—went almost like clockwork. Special LVT steel and wooden ramps were laid by the first waves to ease passage over the five-foot cliffs behind White 1 and White 2. Preloaded trucks, amphibious tractors, and medium tanks were able to drive from the beach directly inland. This eliminated much of the usual beach congestion of off-loading and reloading onto land carriers for transfer inland. The entire operation on Tinian took two weeks. The island was declared secure on 1 August 1944.

Some naval historians attribute the low casualties and relatively short length of the Tinian operation to its location contiguous to Saipan. Certainly that, coupled with the ability of the landing force to concentrate a large amount of preassault air strikes and naval gunfire and the ability of the marine troops to use artillery in a direct-fire support role across the Saipan Channel, made a significant difference. However, most military historians—including the eminent Samuel Eliot Morison, attribute the lighter-than-expected marine casualties to the marines' unexpected

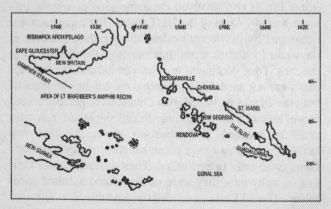

Solomon Islands
Map by author

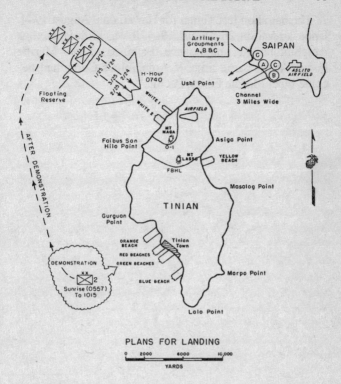

Plans for Tinian landing

Courtesy of Marine Corps Historical Center, from Harwood, *A Close Encounter: The Marine Landing at Tinian*, 8

use of White 1 and White 2, permitting the landing behind the enemy defenses.[18] Clearly, this surprise for the Japanese would not have been possible without the success of the amphib recon marines from A and B Companies, Amphibious Reconnaissance Battalion, VAC.

The battalion left Tinian for Hawaii on 9 August 1944. Upon arrival on 26 August 1944, it was redesignated as Amphibious Reconnaissance Battalion, Fleet Marine Force. At the same time, V Amphibious Corps had become Fleet Marine Force, Pacific.[19]

CHAPTER TWO
Amphib Recon School

The California sun in winter 1952 was bright as we jogged along the Coronado Strand, south of the majestic old Del Coronado Hotel, dressed in running shorts, T-shirts, and marine boondockers. I had been assigned as the officer in charge (OIC) of the Amphibious Reconnaissance School at the Naval Amphibious Base at Coronado on my return from Korea in January. At the school we taught tactics and techniques for conducting amphibious reconnaissance operations on enemy beaches. And today we had just completed training a group of Chinese Nationalist officers in from Taiwan.

As a twenty-six-year-old captain in the U.S. Marine Corps, I was able to draw upon my recent year's worth of combat experience in Korea in training these reconnaissance officers. Initially, in the spring of 1951, while working as an assistant division intelligence officer (assistant G-2), I teamed with an army warrant officer named Dubois in running a group of indigenous Korean line-crossers to the north, into country teeming with North Korean and Chinese, to bring back valuable intelligence information on enemy troop dispositions and troop movements. Later, as a rifle company commander in the 5th Marines on the east coast of Korea, above the 38th parallel, I found both myself and my troops to be vitally interested users of this "intelligence from across the lines."

As I now jogged north along the plunging surf, various kinds of naval aircraft were flying over me, making their final approaches to runway 28 at the NAS (Naval Air Station) North Island in San Diego. I had been thinking of our current methods of submarine and rubber boat insertion of marines onto enemy-held beaches. I knew there had to be better ways. Seeing the Douglas AD Skyraiders and the Grumman TF-1 Traders on final approach, I was reminded of a shipboard tour I made in 1944 during World War II as a midshipman aboard an escort aircraft carrier (CVE). I said to myself, jet aircraft must slow down and "dirty up" (extend their flaps and landing gear and/or speed brakes) for shipboard arrests. If they can slow down for this, why can't they slow enough to drop parachutists safely?

I began to develop the idea of having a marine reconnaissance unit with the capability of launching from a carrier far at sea. We could come in under the cover of the normal air activity that is always present in an objective area. We would be able to insert a marine reconnaissance team far deeper inland from the beach than had ever been done in any amphibious landing in the Pacific. We would supplement the normal beach reconnaissance by seaward means.

As a nineteen-year-old lieutenant during the latter part of World War II, I had the good fortune to be assigned as a platoon commander of a combat swimming company in the staging regiment at Camp Pendleton. The staging regiment was the final departure point for all marines headed for the Pacific Theater. Within this regiment, the combat swimming company taught sea, surf, and land survival to all marines then bound for the Pacific for occupation duty in Japan and North China. In addition, we ran specialized surf survival courses for marine aviators from the El Toro Marine Corps Air Station. The company and my platoon had also become a haven for a number of reconnaissance marines just back from the Pacific. These were the young marines who had served either in the Amphibious Reconnaissance Battalion, FMF, or within one of the marine division's scout units. They had landed by rubber boats from submarines, PT boats, and PBY Catalina flying boats in their missions throughout the South Pacific and the western Pacific region. They were skilled in surf and sea survival and the vagaries of rubber boat launchings and recoveries at night from submarine decks awash.

Our regimental commander was the colorful Col. Herman Hannekan, who had been awarded the Medal of Honor as a sergeant in Haiti in 1919.[1] My company commander was Capt. Harold "Dutch" Smith, who, because of his swimming ability, had been directly commissioned into the Marine Corps to head the marine swimming programs. Dutch had been awarded the Olympic Gold Medal for diving in the 1932 Olympics in Los Angeles.[2] In addition to the recon marines recently returned from the Pacific, we had a diverse group of instructors. Actor Robert Ryan was in our company, as well as Sgt. "Lug" Carlusi, formerly chief lifeguard at Santa Monica. I have never known a marine more at home in the surf than Lug Carlusi, and we all learned much from him.

Having grown up on the water in Seattle, I was a strong swimmer. By around the age of thirteen I had built my own diving helmet and was salvage diving for outboard motors and articles dropped alongside docks. Although I was not a competitive swimmer at the University of Washington, later as a midshipman I was taught survival swimming. Commanding the combat swimming platoon,

I learned a great deal very quickly from these practical, hands-on marine combat swimming instructors.

Troop training units (TTUs) were located on both coasts, Troop Training Unit, Pacific (TTUPac) at Coronado, California, and Troop Training Unit, Atlantic (TTULant) at Little Creek, near Norfolk, Virginia. Both were commanded by brigadier generals. At Coronado, our commanding general was Brig. Gen. Chesty Puller. Chesty was already an icon within the Marine Corps. He was the marines' most decorated officer, wearing five Navy Crosses for heroism in combat.[3] Schools within TTUs were titled with generic names representing the subjects taught: Logistics School, Communications School, Artillery and Naval Gunfire School, Intelligence School, and my Amphibious Reconnaissance School. Officers from each of the schools would be task-organized in teams to deploy throughout the Orient to conduct amphibious warfare training.

The Amphib Recon School usually had one officer and three enlisted assigned besides the officer in charge (OIC) to do the instruction in amphibious reconnaissance. We were sequentially blessed with two very experienced recon officers, 1st Lt. Dana Cashion and 1st Lt. Robert "Mumbles" Maiden. Cashion had been with Capt. Kenny Houghton's 1st Marine Division reconnaissance company in Korea. Bob Maiden had been in amphib recon at Camp Lejeune, North Carolina. While serving in Korea, Maiden had taken shrapnel in the lower part of his face. As a consequence, navy doctors wired up his jaw, and for a number of weeks while in the hospital, Maiden could only mumble when trying to talk—it was hence that he earned the nickname "Mumbles." As often happens when very tough individuals have been given unflattering monikers, a person had to know Bob Maiden pretty well to get by with calling him Mumbles. Maiden was always in top physical condition, having played and coached football, and was always eager for any project. At Camp Lejeune, our recon peers advised us that Bob Maiden was also called "Go! Go!" because of his enthusiasm and his football-coach approach to leading his recon troops.

Recon School's senior noncommissioned officer, T.Sgt. (technical sergeant—a rank later changed within the Marine Corps to gunnery sergeant) George F. Evans, was a laid-back pipe smoker who looked on our required runs and rubber boat exercises in the surf with a somewhat diminished enthusiasm. He proved to be a very competent instructor and was one of the best scroungers on the Amphibious Base, a real asset. Technical Sergeant Evans's hobby of fishing became apparent when we would be returning from a submarine exercise, running on the surface (not submerged) coming back in to San Diego. On the fantail of the submarine, George would put a heavy-duty line over the side, mindful of the submarine's propellers, and would invariably hook onto and land a good-sized shark (usually about a six-footer). In contrast to Evans was Sgt. John W. Opsal, a movie double for the early 1940s star Wayne Morris, who played the roles of navy pilots or other similar action heroes.[4] Sergeant Opsal, who coupled energy and dedication with his Korean War recon experience, was in superb physical condition and always eager for us to hit the surf with the rubber boats. He proved to be an absolutely outstanding instructor. His enthusiasm was totally infectious.

During my thirty-month tour as officer in charge of the Amphibious Reconnaissance School, we made two four-month deployments to the Far East. We trained the army reconnaissance units from the 1st Cavalry Division on Hokkaido and the 24th Army Division at Sendai, Japan. The Korean War was still raging, and on occasion, MIG contrails could be seen in the straits north and east of

Hokkaido. On Hokkaido, our TTUPac training team was billeted at Chitose Air Force Base (AFB). Our officers' mess was located immediately adjacent to the "strip alert" aircraft (usually two air force F-86s). Most mornings we would ingest the fumes of JP-4 jet fuel exhaust along with our breakfast eggs as the aircraft were launched. One of our supporting arms instructors, marine aviator Capt. Leo Corboy, a tall, slim jet pilot, would inhale deeply and remind all of us how it was a fighter pilot's dream to be served jet engine exhaust with his food.

Our TTU Far East detachment headquarters was at Camp McGill, Japan. This was about ten miles east of the main U.S. naval base at Yokosuka and some thirty miles south of Tokyo. Our team usually spent time at Camp McGill only when arriving from Coronado or departing from Japan back to California. We did take a training team into the rear areas of the 1st Marine Division on the lines in Korea and provided instruction for assorted elements of the division and its attached units.

Beach Reconnaissance, Hokkaido, Japan

While deployed on Hokkaido, the northernmost island of Japan, my amphib recon detachment received a rather unusual request for a beach reconnaissance. Our colonel, John C. Miller, called me into his office at Chitose AFB (located east-southeast of Sapporo, the capital of Hokkaido) and handed me a dispatch that had come in from the intelligence section at Yokosuka. The commander of U.S. naval forces in the Far East (ComNavFE) had asked if we could conduct a hasty reconnaissance of several beaches at the very northern tip of Hokkaido up east of Wakkanai and Point Soya, on Russia's Sea of Okhotsk. The area was twelve miles to the west of Russia's Sakhalin Island and just south of the chain of the Kuril Islands, across the La Pérouse Strait. Although the beaches that U.S. intelligence wanted information on were in Japan, we were cautioned by Japan Self-Defense Force intelligence that Russian radar covered the area. The Russians had the reputation of being less than meticulous in their flights around the Kurils (as was evidenced years later when Korean Air Lines flight 007 flew into Soviet airspace and was shot down). We were cautioned to be wary in the conduct of the recon.

The thrust of the U.S. intelligence inquiry was to have a "visual recon" of the two beaches to determine, if possible, the beach composition and the gradient of the foreshore and back shore (the area immediately inland from the foreshore, marked by the high-water line). After making a map reconnaissance of the designated beaches, we determined that within the time frame of their request, the only possible way to get a "quick and dirty" beach recon was by low-level air.

We contacted one of the aviators from the army division that we were training and briefed him on the mission. He felt that an observation aircraft, an army Stinson L-5 Sentinel (almost identical to the marine Convair OY-1 Sentinel) with full fuel could fly from our location at Chitose to the northeastern end of Hokkaido and handle the mission. Their division air officer approved our joint request, and the next day I flew with a young pilot, an army captain whom we knew as "Alabama," to the beaches. We had not been briefed on the reason that ComNavFE wanted this reconnaissance, but we surmised that it must have had some relation to a threat of Cold War activity by the Russians from either the Kurils or Sakhalin.

We flew at low altitude as we approached the beach. About five miles from the coastline, we dropped down on the deck, literally flying the rice paddies and skirting the small pine trees in between. Although we were in Japanese airspace, neither of us wanted to present Russian radar any indication of our activity in the area. The first beach we quickly determined to be unsuitable for amphibious operations because of the lack of adequate exits from the shore inland. In addition, the beach gradient was very steep, and the beach itself was exposed laterally to the northeast on the Sea of Okhotsk. The seas would have broached any landing craft making an extended operation in the area.

The second beach had a more gentle gradient, and it did have exits. It appeared to be usable. Alabama was getting edgy. Both of us were watching our fuel gauge, which was indicating that we did not have much time left to be flying over the beaches. We were going to be forced to return in just a few minutes, but we still wanted to assure ourselves as to the composition of the beach sand. It looked soft, coarse, and loose, which would have been poor for supporting amphibious vehicles, LVTs, and trucks. Short of landing the aircraft, which would have been dangerous if the beach was as soft as we both believed, we had to come up with some method of evaluating the beach's density. We had to know whether it would hold amphibious vehicles, whether trucks would bog down in it, and so on.

Fortune smiled on us that windy, sunny afternoon on northern Hokkaido. After we had make several very low passes (eight to ten feet above the surf), a large German Shepherd came out to chase our plane. We had throttled back and were in slow flight, and with the side window open, we could hear him barking as he was running with the aircraft. Then suddenly we realized he was having difficulty running. His feet were sinking into the sand. That proved to us this beach would be too soft for an amphibious landing unless extensive matting or some form of stabilization were used. Sinking deeper with every step

he made, the dog was finally up to his forelegs in the soft
sand.

Satisfied that we now had the information that Com-
NavFE wanted, we flew back to Chitose AFB, landing
with a good half hour's fuel left. I framed a dispatch report and marked the maps and sent a follow-up written
report and sketches to ComNavFE at Yokosuka. Apparently we had given U.S. intelligence what it needed: later,
through channels, we received a classified "well done"
message.

I relate this incident only to illustrate the point that in
amphibious reconnaissance, one may employ any means
at hand to acquire the necessary information. There
is nothing that can equal an on-site recon, however. Our
report in this instance was sufficiently clear—and
negative—so that the need to physically walk the same
beaches was unnecessary.

In my research for this book, I came across another example of the ingenuity of reconnaissance marines in performing their assigned tasks that is worth recounting
here. The story is reminiscent of the legends of Lt. Col.
Pete Ellis in his pre-World War II travels throughout the
southwestern Pacific. Ellis corroborated the information
that later became the basic war plan of the reconquest of
the Pacific by Adm. Chester Nimitz and Gen. Douglas
MacArthur.[5] The particular marine reconnaissance to
which I refer took place in the summer of 1948, at the
time when the British were contemplating the return of
Palestine to the Jews, creating what later was to become
the State of Israel.

Naval intelligence was concerned about the possibility
of the United States having to project itself ashore in the
Persian Gulf (this was indeed clairvoyant, in light of Operation Desert Storm). There was no force-level reconnaissance in existence in 1948, so the Office of Naval

Intelligence (ONI) turned to both the 1st and the 2d Marine Divisions for reconnaissance assets. Capt. Merwin H. Silverthorn, commander of 2d Division Recon Company (who had done the very successful amphib recons on Tinian six years before), was called to Washington, D.C., for two weeks of intensive briefings. Captain Silverthorn was given an attached recon platoon from 1st Marine Division, Recon Company. The composite company was given the mission of reconning the beaches of Kuwait and Bahrain Island in the Persian Gulf.

Silverthorn took his provisional reconnaissance unit to Naval Amphibious Base Little Creek, in Virginia, for two weeks of refresher training at TTULant. His executive officer was the very experienced recon officer 1st Lt. Francis X. "Bull" Kraince. Embarking on two APDs, accompanied by UDT elements, they were quickly en route to the Persian Gulf. Entering the Mediterranean, they had a brief liberty stop in Naples before continuing on through the Suez Canal. Captain Silverthorn, as task force reconnaissance officer, initially rode the command ship, an AGC (amphibious force flagship). The task force was accompanied by one of our carriers and several destroyers.

On arrival in the Persian Gulf, Captain Silverthorn took one platoon from 2d Marine Division, led by a Lieutenant Glover, and one platoon from 1st Marine Division, led by a Lieutenant Alexander, under his personal command to recon the beaches in the vicinity of Kuwait City. He assigned Lt. Donald Swanda from his own 2d Marine Division's recon company to do the beaches of Bahrain Island. Working with their UDT counterparts, each of the two teams spent portions of three days on their assigned beaches, returning to their respective APDs by mid-morning each day. The marines had the mission of mapping and obtaining data on their beaches out to the one-fathom line. UDT took it from the one-fathom line out.

Both marine recon units went ashore before dawn (at about 0430), each team landing with a jeep. Silverthorn's jeep was quite plain; he had simply had all its marine markings painted over. Lieutenant Swanda, on the other hand, had gone a step further: his jeep had been completely repainted—disguised to represent a civilian oil exploration jeep, with the markings of Standard Oil Company. Pith helmets were issued, and everyone wore khaki long-sleeved shirts and trousers, the typical field dress of Standard Oil's seismic oil crews. Wearing nothing with insignia on it, they made every attempt to look as "civilian" as possible.

Setting up the old pre-war mahogany sketching tables on tripods, the teams began to take photographs. Suddenly, Silverthorn's team was approached by a group of eight to ten Kuwaitis or Arabs in Bedouin dress, armed with traditional desert knives. Since the marines had no weapons, they were greatly relieved when the natives appeared to be merely curious and even offered them a bitter Arab coffee. After this brief encounter, the Americans were never again in contact with any of the indigenous people, though one of the beaches they mapped was quite close to Kuwait City. Able to complete their work in the allotted three days, they prepared their maps, charts, and photographs for naval intelligence and returned to the United States.[6]

By use of ingenuity and camouflage, these reconnaissance marines were able to pass themselves off as an oilfield survey team and thus fully to accomplish their mission. In light of Operation Desert Storm and the situation in the Persian Gulf region today, however, it is highly improbable that this tactic would ever work again.

Training with the UDT

At the Amphibious Reconnaissance School at Coronado, we were able periodically to train with underwater demolition specialists. Underwater Demolition Unit 1 (UDU 1) was located just across the road from us on the strand, south of the Hotel Del Coronado. Several of us had the opportunity to go through UDU 1's scuba course, which included the usual open-water bounce dive to one hundred ten feet. We did our diving off Point Loma and our one-mile underwater compass swims in lower San Diego Bay. Later our Amphib Recon School worked together with UDT aboard submarine. UDT and our Recon School would share one of the fleet diesel submarines from Submarine Flotilla 1.[7] We would have some of our recon marines aboard, and we would share spaces in the forward torpedo room while we did our respective submarine operations.

UDU 1 was composed of four teams—UDT 3, UDT 5, UDT 7, and UDT 11—with one team always deployed to the Far East, one getting ready to deploy, and one just returning. UDU 1 was commanded by Lt. Cdr. Francis Douglas Fane, one of the foremost experts within the navy on underwater demolition. Commander Fane, together with Don Moore, is the author of the book *The Naked Warriors*, which was made into the 1958 motion picture *Underwater Warrior*, with Fane played by actor Dan Dailey.[8]

We found Fane was prickly to deal with, but he had a wealth of experience. He did not support our amphib recon marines' doing hydrographic surveys of beaches. Commander Fane felt anything dealing with the hydrographic reconnaissance of beaches was strictly the province of his navy UDT teams. We argued that past experience had shown that whenever the landing force needed the hydrographic information, UDT was committed to other tasks and frequently was unavailable. We felt that Fane was "protecting his turf." Finally we reached a compromise with Fane, and he grudgingly acknowledged that it made sense for my marines to know how to do the hydrographic work. We also "happened" to show Commander Fane the *Landing-Force Manual*, which outlined hydrographic surveys as part of our assigned Marine Corps reconnaissance mission.

Frequently Fane's UDT and my recon team worked off the same submarine. Despite the normal bantering between the recon marines and UDT sailors, each group respected the other for what it did, and we had no major problems in that regard. We were able to set up a number of periods of cross-training for students in each of our classes—amphibious reconnaissance and underwater demolition—for hydrographic recon. Marines trained UDTs in movement on the beach, and navy UDTs trained us for specialized tasks in the water. We marine students learned to use plastic slates with wax underwater pencils and lead lines marked for depth to chart the hydrographic features of any beach. It was a strictly hands-on type of instruction. We learned, for example, how to be dropped off at a target beach from a small, fast LCPR (landing craft, personnel, ramp) making a high-speed pass and to form in a line when we hit the water. We also learned how to be picked up "on the fly" by the same high-speed naval craft after we had completed our beach recon. Each swimmer would be treading water in a line, parallel to and about seventy-five yards off the beach, and each would be holding one arm in the air. The navy coxswain would then aim the LCPR at the line of swimmers' upraised arms.

UDT had a very large ship's cook, a man named Tiz Morrison, who enjoyed the reputation in the navy as the best swimmer "pickup man" in UDT. I talked to Tiz recently, and he confirmed what my UDT friends had told me—that after his retirement, he ran a bar in San Diego that had become the haven of UDT team members and navy SEALs (sea, air, land). Tiz's teammates at Coronado nicknamed him "King of the Frogmen." Tiz, as pickup man, had a large padded rubber ring, about two feet in diameter, that was attached to a long piece of bungee cord. As the coxswain would aim toward the swimmer awaiting pickup, Tiz would very precisely drop the ring over the swimmer's upraised arm. Instantly the swimmer would clasp the ring, locking the upraised arm with the other wrist. Tiz, with an effortless tug, taking advantage of the speed of the boat, would then roll the swimmer into the rubber boat—and all of this at a speed of about fifteen knots. As the swimmer rolled up over the gunwale of the rubber boat, which was lashed to the side of the high-speed landing craft, he would instantly unhook his arm from the ring and roll over the side into the landing craft. Tiz would simultaneously turn and drop the ring over the next swimmer in line. The technique worked most effectively. UDT would pick up a line of eight of our swimmers in a matter of thirty to forty-five seconds. Once we had learned how to do drop and pickup, we wanted to put it into operational use as recon marines. We liked to practice the technique whenever possible. Tiz had almost made a game out of it for us.

Later we used marine rubber boats to do this same type of training at Camp Pendleton. We would use inflatable boats with large outboard motors—it worked beautifully. In the context of the swimmer pickup training that we did at Coronado with UDU, months later, while deployed to the Far East with a troop training unit detachment at Camp McGill, Japan, we all had the chance to learn a new technique of drop and pickup. The deployed UDT team from Coronado was stationed near Camp McGill. They invited several of us to do some helicopter drops into the Sagami Wan at the lower end of Tokyo Bay with our former UDT classmates from scuba school. A helicopter drop was a much more rapid means of insertion of reconnaissance swimmers (be they UDT or marine recon) into an offshore area than was insertion from boats. However, helicopter insertion was a bit trickier than the boat because of the aircraft's greater speed. We learned that a drop from about eight feet while the chopper was flying at fifteen knots could rip one's face mask off unless we held onto them. Our drops went well, and so we acquired a new method of entry for evaluation.

Training Marine and Navy Units

In addition to training elements from the Chinese Nationalist Army and Navy, we trained three major U.S. units during my tenure as officer in charge. In February 1953 we trained the 3d Marine Division's reconnaissance company, commanded by Maj. Martin J. "Stormy" Sexton (who later commanded a division reconnaissance battalion). Stormy and his officers made the course a pleasurable, intense learning experience for all hands. A month later, we trained elements of the 1st Provisional Reconnaissance Battalion from Camp Pendleton. And the final U.S. unit that trained while I was serving as OIC of the Amphib Recon School was the navy's Beach Jumper Unit 1 (BJU 1).

At the time, the Beach Jumpers were a hush-hush outfit with a classified mission: tactical deception. They were capable of simulating all the sights, sounds, and communications of an amphibious landing. They had all kinds of pyrotechnics, radios, tape recordings of battle sounds and activity, and noise-transmitting gear to conduct an imitation of a full-scale amphibious landing. The Beach Jumpers had been formed in 1943 and operated with great success in faking diversionary landings in Salerno, Italy, and later in the Allied landings in southern France and on the island of Elba.[9]

We trained the Beach Jumpers in rubber boat and hydrographic techniques and in scouting and patrolling. Whenever our amphib recon school had to do any training on land, we used the rugged backcountry north and east of San Diego at what had been Camp Elliot during World War II. During these periods of training, on our night patrols we always apprehended a number of Mexican immigrants who were attempting to gain access to California via the backcountry, bypassing San Diego. We gained practical experience in snatching "prisoners," and the Border Patrol was always grateful for our call to come and pick up our catch. We usually would quietly grab the last immigrant in the column; then, one by one, we would seize them all in the same stealthy manner. (This same tactic of snatching the last one in the column was later used by U.S. forces taking prisoners in Vietnam.)

The Beach Jumpers had their own high-speed boats, which appeared to be converted PT boats. We used these and combined them with the use of rubber boats for the simulation of pre-D-day UDT operations and beach reconnaissance. We made several joint reconnaissance operations off San Clemente Island.

Inherent Dangers

Reconnaissance can be an extremely hazardous undertaking. Recon units operate at night, frequently under adverse surf, seas, and (after formation of force recon) flying conditions. We used submarines, swimming, rubber boats, and parachutes for the insertion of small teams onto unknown shores with sometimes treacherous coastal reefs, beaches, and tides—and, with parachuting, into very small drop zones (DZs) at night with unknown wind conditions.

With these facts as background, one can more fully comprehend the type of tragedy that can strike during recon training or operations. Anyone who has been around the West Coast knows the unpredictability of the Pacific's heavy surf. Plunging breakers can kill without warning. Unless a coxswain is very alert and very experienced with regard to the timing of the crests of incoming surf, a breaker can flip a rubber boat, sending all hands and any equipment aboard flying. Darkness compounds the problem.

Shortly after we finished our work with Beach Jumper Unit 1, some members of that unit were on a daylight rubber boat exercise along the Coronado Strand. One of their boats, caught by a wave, was flipped, and two excellent swimmers were dumped headfirst onto the sand bottom in the surf zone. Knocked unconscious, they drowned before anyone could get to them—despite the fact that they were wearing the small UDT-type inflatable jackets that all of us wore during rubber boat and submarine operations. Several of us from the Amphib Recon School assisted in the recovery of the Beach Jumpers' bodies. Reconnaissance is a skill, and one must constantly be alert to its nature, or it, like the sea, can be terribly unforgiving.

Parachutes Ahead

As I have mentioned, during my runs on the beach in Coronado, during the winter of 1952, I came up with some ideas for deeper insertion by parachute entry from aircraft taking off from carriers. I presented these ideas to

Gen. Chesty Puller, who agreed that I was onto something valuable. Later he sent a request to the commandant of the Marine Corps for my training as a parachutist. I thus spent two weeks TAD (temporary additional duty) as a student at the Naval Parachute Loft at NAS North Island in San Diego, learning to pack several different kinds of parachutes—back packs, seat packs, and chest packs. At the end of the two weeks of what riggers call "whipping silk," I live-jumped five of the parachutes that I had packed. Mindful of my limited experience in packing, I always wore a reserve chute that had been packed by a fully certified navy parachute rigger.

Having already done five free falls with the navy, I had an advantage over most of the army instructors and my classmates when I finally did arrive at army jump school at Fort Benning, Georgia. At Benning, I did seven static-line jumps (five in jump school and two in jumpmaster school). These army instructors and students had never been given the opportunity to do free falls—a situation that changed several years later when the army's Special Forces began to evaluate free-fall training.

When my orders for Fort Benning came in to TTUPac, I was called into Chesty Puller's office. Within the Marine Corps, General Puller had never had a very big reputation for having a sense humor. So when the chief of staff, Col. Lewis Plain, took me in to see General Puller, I stood tall at attention, two paces in front of his desk, my eyes straight to the front—ten inches over Chesty's head. I was quietly apprehensive, trying to anticipate what he was going to say to me. I was really expecting some sort of "four freedoms" speech and "Do your best for the Corps" words of encouragement. Chesty pulled on his pipe and, in his own taciturn way, said, "Meyers, I hear you are going to Fort Benning." I responded with a cheery "Yes, Sir," well knowing that he had signed the request to the commandant to send me there. He continued: "You know I spent a year with the army down there in 1931. They have good people there, you know." "Yes, Sir," I again responded, aware that Col. George C. Marshall, Maj. Omar Bradley, and Maj. Joseph Stillwell had been Chesty's instructors and that his marine classmates at Benning were marine captains Oliver P. Smith and Gilder Jackson and marine lieutenant Gerald C. Thomas— all of whom had later become general officers.[10]

At this point I was keenly aware of the great pressure put on the one or two marines who are sent each year to the infantry school at Fort Benning. Each is expected to do well and to uphold the high reputation of the Marine Corps at this other service school. I was also aware that one of my recent predecessors at Benning was Capt. Kenny J. Houghton—who had participated in 1st Marine Division's night crossing of the Han River in Korea—and that he had stood among the top ten of his class. Finally, Chesty took another pull on his pipe and said, "Meyers, I am going to give you some advice. . . ."

By this time, I was really beginning to be a bit concerned. Chesty finished, however, with words to this effect: "Do the best that you can, and watch your hat and your ass!" At that point I realized General Puller did have a sense of humor after all. I smiled, gave him a hearty "Aye, aye, Sir," stepped one pace back, did an about-face, and went off for Fort Benning and a year with the army.

CHAPTER THREE
Training with the Army

My year at Fort Benning went quickly. I attended the Advanced Infantry Officer's Course for ten months and then completed the basic four-week airborne (parachute) course and the one-week jumpmaster course. The other marine in the class was Maj. Frank Caldwell, who had earned the Navy Cross on Iwo Jima. He and I studied together, and both of us did well in the class. We made a number of friendships that were to last for many years.

There was a good balance between classroom work and field exercises, which made the time pass quickly. Our class became very familiar with the maneuver and exercise areas of Fort Benning: Kelly Hill, the rolling, sandy terrain with its Southern pines, the perpetually dusty roads to the demonstration or maneuver areas, the Civil War graves spotted throughout the reservation, and the Chatahoochee River on the western flank of the post. And, with only a couple of exceptions, the teaching at Benning was excellent, particularly with regard to tactics and logistics.

As happens in any military professional school, we students were thrust from our experience at the battalion level (the preponderance of us having been company commanders in combat in Korea) to either the division or the corps level. Throughout most of the instruction, however, Frank Caldwell and I found ourselves transposing the tactics and techniques of the infantry school back down to what we knew our next Marine Corps experience would be in the Fleet Marine Force at the battalion, regimental, and division levels.

During the last month of the infantry officer's course, those of us going on to airborne (basic jump school and jumpmaster training) stepped up our long runs, pull-ups, and push-ups to get ready for the airborne course. Our classmates, who were already parachute qualified, had warned us that the pull-ups were the physical requirement that washed more people out of the airborne course than any other. Having come this far, though, and with so much at stake, there was no way any of us would let that happen.

My prior experience of five navy free falls was helpful to me in jump school, but the army's instruction on static-line jumping (where the parachute is attached to the aircraft and is literally pulled out of the parachute pack on one's back) was precise and demanding. We had to learn "the army way" for PLFs (parachute landing falls) for exit, from both the thirty-four-foot towers and the two-hundred-fifty-foot towers, and for our body position on exit. The airborne department had been giving instruction in parachuting since the early 1940s in World War II. The department had it down to a true science, and the instructors were superb. Each of us gained a great deal from this three-week course.

The jumpmaster course was short and intense, teaching us—officers and noncommissioned officers (NCOs) serving in an airborne unit—all the techniques and safety procedures for unit jumps, as well as giving us an overview of the requirements for guiding the follow-on units in the basics of pathfinding. We learned how to "spot" for the exit point for a stick of jumpers and how to judge winds, those aloft and those on the deck. And we learned about beacon markers and panels and about DZ control—something that was to prove invaluable when we actually began pathfinding in the Marine Corps. As always, safety and equipment checks had a high priority.

Our last official acts at Fort Benning were to go through graduation at jump school, get our parachute wings pinned on, and (in my case) depart for Camp Pendleton and the new set of orders for duty at Marine Corps Test Unit 1. I am forever grateful to Chesty Puller for permitting me to share his experience with the army at Fort Benning, some twenty-three years after his completion of the advanced infantry course. I am sure when he sent the letter to the commandant, he had no idea that it would really lead to the beginning of a whole new method and concept of reconnaissance within the Marine Corps.

The Value of Cross-Service Schooling

In July 1958, four years after I left Fort Benning and had returned to Camp Pendleton, California, both force recon commanders—Maj. Joe Taylor (CO of 2d Force) and I (CO of 1st Force)—were ordered to Fort Bragg, North Carolina, for a CIA-sponsored special warfare course of nine days conducted at the Special Forces Warfare Center at Smoke Bomb Hill. Upon reporting in, we were met by one of my former Fort Benning classmates, West Pointer Capt. Clint Norman, who was now serving in Special Forces.

The course was an excellent overview of Special Forces operations. There were demonstrations where we learned the latest in demolition techniques including the use of indigenous materials to blow up boxcars, electric transmission stations, and a wrecked F-86 fighter. In addition to Joe Taylor and me from Marine Corps force recon, our class included representatives from Special Forces, "The Company" (CIA), several of Col. Harry "Heinie" Alderholt's air commandos, and UDT (the SEALs were not formed until January of 1962). All of us were in units whose missions required operations deep behind enemy lines.

While we were at the Special Warfare School, Captain Norman introduced us to another army Special Forces officer, Maj. Lucien E. Conein. Lou was an interesting character who was referred to by his Special Forces friends as "Three-Finger Louie" (one of his hands had two fingers missing). As a young lieutenant, Lou had served with Brig. General Bill Donovan's Office of Strategic Services (OSS). Just prior to the end of World War II, Lou had parachuted with the OSS into Indochina to work with the resistance against the Japanese occupying forces. While there, he met Elyette, the daughter of one of his contacts, and fell in love as she nursed him back to health from his Japanese-inflicted wounds. After the war, Lou came back to Vietnam and married her.

At Fort Bragg, he became very interested in the unique type of parachuting that we were doing within the Marine Corps in both force recon companies. He was surprised to find out that we were jumping free fall from carrier aircraft and particularly from jets. He and his jumpers in Special Forces had just begun working on HALO (high-altitude, low-opening) parachute entry for small teams of Special Forces. Lou was OIC of the initial army tests on HALO and had worked with Parachutes, Inc., a civilian corporation hired to train Special Forces in "stabilized free fall."[1]

The president of Parachutes, Inc. was Jacques Istell, a marine reserve captain with Korean War service. Istell sold the army seven of his "Sky Diver" free-fall para-chutes, and he and a former army paratrooper, civilian Lew Sanborn, trained Conein and six other Special Forces personnel as free-fall instructors. (We were later able to have Istell come on TAD with the Marine Corps and come to Camp Pendleton with 1st Force to instruct our personnel in stabilized free fall.)

After we exchanged information on our respective techniques, Major Conein arranged to come out to 1st Force to see how we were using the parachute to insert small teams. We were able to jump him from the navy Grumman TF-1 Trader, as well as get him his first jet jump from a marine F3D Douglas Skyknight. From the Marine Corps side, we were able to pick his brains on both equipment and techniques for our later force recon HALO operations.

We had surmised that Three-Finger Louie's moniker was the result of some OSS clandestine operation in Southeast Asia. But we were wrong. One night over a beer, Lou confided that he had lost his two digits while being a Good Samaritan to a gray-haired lady with car problems. He was under the hood of her vintage car, and despite his warning to her not to hit the starter, that is exactly what she did. Unfortunately, Lou's hand was within striking distance of the fan blades. The loss had no effect on his ability to use his weapons or his hands, however—a fact to which his illustrious subsequent career in Special Forces attested.

With Lou Conein's experience in Indochina going back to his World War II days, we were somehow not surprised, years later, to see him interviewed on American television when the Republic of Vietnam finally fell. He was one of the last Americans with President Ngo Dinh Diem, just prior to his and his brother's assassination by the cabal of South Vietnamese generals.

CHAPTER FOUR
Marine Corps Test Unit 1

Many marines serving in force recon units today, and even many that served in recon in Vietnam, have no idea of the central role that Marine Corps Test Unit 1 played in the evolution of force reconnaissance. Test Unit 1 was the crucible within which many of the methods of parachute employment and specialized equipment were developed, tested, and evaluated for later employment within the FMF. Tangible evidence of this role exists, for example, in such operations as the one in which Test Unit 1 participated at Case Springs at Camp Pendleton in 1957, after three marines died when they were dragged along the ground by wind inflating their parachute canopies after they had landed. As a result of the unit's work, there was a servicewide adoption of the Capewell canopy-release assembly, with which all military parachutes are now equipped.

With the lessons of the use of nuclear weapons that ended World War II still fresh in the minds of Marine Corps planners, Col. Robert Cushman (later commandant of the Marine Corps) authored a staff report in December 1946 to Commandant Archibald Vandegrift that questioned the viability of massive World War II-type amphibious landings over small areas subject to potential tactical nuclear weapons. Colonel Cushman's report concluded that no longer could the Marine Corps think small: "The tiny island, the single port, the small area . . . these will no longer be proper objectives. We must think in terms of 200 miles in width and depth."[1] The staff study recommended planning for greater mobility and greater dispersion and, implicitly, for greater distances inland from the sea. Until the helicopter experience of Korea in 1951 with the first U.S. forces combat helilifts of companies and battalions in combat, however, the Marine Corps did not possess the capability (either in terms of numbers of choppers or in terms of individual helicopter lift capability) of carrying out the tactics necessary to implement Colonel Cushman's concepts of dispersion.[2]

In 1954, Commandant Lemuel C. Shepherd Jr. decided that the Marine Corps required a special unit outside the FMF to develop specialized tactics, techniques, and organizational concepts for Marine Corps operations in the nuclear age. He approved his staff's recommendation to activate such a unit, Marine Corps Test Unit 1.[3] The decision was made to establish this test unit outside the FMF because the FMF was considered to be far too committed operationally to be able to perform in the orderly and scholarly manner necessary for the development of the new tactics that the commandant desired.

Initially, Test Unit 1 was to be composed of a regimental headquarters and service company, a four-company infantry battalion, a 75-mm antitank platoon, a 4.2-inch mortar platoon, and one 75-mm pack howitzer artillery battery. It was to be located at Camp Pendleton and was to be operationally under the control of the commandant. Administrative and logistic support was tasked to Marine Corps Base (MCB), Camp Pendleton. Initial plans for air elements included a medium helicopter squadron, augmented with three observation helicopters. Six attack aircraft (Grumman F9F-2 Panthers) were to support Test

Unit 1 during its development of these new concepts and tactics.[4] This organization was considered to be a "point of departure," and with future approval by the commandant, Test Unit 1 could recommend changes in its own organization. The organization of the unit, in other words, was not cast in concrete.

The air elements scheduled to support Test Unit 1 reacted with very significant opposition and resistance to the proposed tasking of marine aviation personnel to this new unit. After several attempts by marine aviation staff to shoot down this idea with the claim of "heavy operational commitments," a compromise was reached with marine air units and the commander of the Pacific Fleet, whose operational air assets encompassed the requested air support. The commandant delegated his authority to FMFPac to conclude arrangements with the commanding general of AirFMFPac (at El Toro and Santa Ana) to provide the air on a "request basis."[5] This solved the problems, and the aviators came on board and participated fully in the development of the new tactics and employment of marine air.

The broad mission objectives for Test Unit 1 issued by the commandant were that the unit (1) evolve organizational concepts for the marine landing force under conditions of nuclear warfare, (2) determine requirements for light weight weapons and equipment to permit maximum tactical exploitation of nuclear weapons, (3) develop tactics and techniques responsive to the full employment of nuclear weapons, and (4) evolve operational concepts, transportation requirements, and techniques to enable fast task force ships and submarines, or a combination of such shipping and airlift, for movement to the objective area and the ship-to-shore movement.

This mission statement was followed up with a series of thirty-three specific questions to be answered by Test

Unit 1. Somewhat down this task list—following the expected questions regarding future organization and employment of the marine infantry battalion landing team and its logistical requirements—were questions relating to the intelligence requirements under the deeper (from the beach) operations. The commandant wanted to know the types of reconnaissance needed to accomplish the new tactics of greater dispersion and the impact of helicopter mobility on reconnaissance.[6]

Test Unit 1 was activated on 1 July 1954 at Camp Horno, close by Basilone Road, halfway between the main side of Camp Pendleton and the north gate near San Clemente (a distance of some forty miles). Troop strength was initially set at 104 marine officers (many of whom were marine aviators), 1,412 enlisted marine personnel, 7 naval officers (doctors and chaplains), and 51 bluejackets (predominantly hospital corpsmen).[7]

The four-company infantry battalion progressed rapidly with the acquisition of some of the more specialized equipment—for example, 75mm pack howitzers and the "mechanical mule," a small helicopter-transportable, low-silhouette, flatbed replacement for the jeep. With the high experience level of the battalion's officers under Lt. Col. Stanley Nelson, executive officer Maj. Willmar "Bill" Bledsoe, and the S-3, Maj. Dewey "Bob" Bohn, the battalion commenced infantry training by Thanksgiving. By early 1955, it had become fully operational. Modest wooden mockups of Sikorsky helicopters and repetitive troop exercises soon made the unit fully helicopter transportable.

In March 1955, Test Unit 1 participated in Desert Rock VI, a tactical nuclear weapons test in the Atomic Energy Commission's Nevada test site. Test Unit became airborne seconds after the atomic blast and completed a successful maneuver that contributed many new ideas about operations in a nuclear environment.[8] Little was done during the unit's first year of organization with respect to reconnaissance, but after its return from Desert Rock VI, attention was directed toward the special reconnaissance requirements for operating in the dispersal and mobility environment envisioned by our commandant, General Shepherd.

I reported in to MCB Camp Pendleton in early April 1955, fresh from parachute and pathfinder training and the year with the army at Fort Benning. There was a hush-hush atmosphere when I asked about my orders to Test Unit 1. The administrators put me off with references to classified missions and statements like "You will find out when you get there." This secrecy only intensified my curiosity.

Upon reporting in to Col. Edward Rydalch, CO of Test Unit 1, and to his executive officer, Lt. Col. Regan Fuller, I was assigned initially as assistant operations officer for the regiment. Immediately Maj. Bob Bohn, operations officer of Test Unit's infantry battalion, took me under his wing and gave me the opportunity to gain rapid insight into the integrated aspects of supporting arms and his battalion's full helicopter capability. Simultaneous to my arrival, Colonel Rydalch was making a series of organizational changes for Test Unit to the commandant. These included reorganization with a separate plans and development (P&D) section. Included also was the recommendation for the formation of a reconnaissance platoon: an officer and thirteen enlisted men. It was intended that this element be employed almost exclusively in training, testing, and exercises designed to validate reconnaissance theories and techniques of all-helicopter assault, not only as they apply to the battalion landing team (BLT) level but to higher levels as well.[9]

Some ten days later, the commandant approved a major reorganization, which established the P&D section. The section operated much like a subsidiary of G-3 HQMC (Headquarters, Marine Corps)—albeit with nominal independence within Test Unit 1. A separate "war room" was established in a newly constructed Butler Building, completely surrounded by barbed wire with an armed guard. Colonel Rydalch assumed additional duties as titular head of P&D. He assigned Lt. Cols. Regan Fuller and Chuck Bailey as his "execs" and supervisors of the day-to-day tests and evaluation that were generated by P&D.

Among other officers assigned were Lt. Col. Sam Jaskilka and aviators Maj. Claude "Barney" Barnhill and Maj. Curtis "Red Dog" Jernigan, both fighter pilots. Prominently posted around the war room were three inspirational signs: "We are in the 'How' Business," "All of Us Are Smarter Than Any One of Us," and "The More You Sweat in Peace, the Less You Bleed in War."[10] P&D's mission was to author staff studies for various tests by subordinate units of Test Unit 1 and then make evaluations and reports to the commandant on the progress on the thirty-three questions asked of Test Unit 1.

Helicopter Assault Airborne Techniques Officer

I was initially assigned in May 1955 to the war room as "reconnaissance/pathfinder project officer." To reflect our helicopter-borne capability within the infantry battalion, this title was later changed to "helicopter assault airborne techniques officer." The title changed, but the duties remained essentially the same.

Initially working with Maj. Bob Bohn, I set up an SOP (standard operating procedure) for organizing all of the elements of Test Unit (not only the infantry battalion but the supporting arms and logistics elements as well) for

rapid breakdown into "heli-teams," a name coined from
the World War II term "boat team." The term denotes a
group of persons chosen because they fit into specific
types of boats and helicopters. Shortly thereafter, Lt. Col.
Regan Fuller and I prepared a detailed recommendation,
to be signed by Colonel Rydalch and sent to the commandant, for the formation and training of the reconnaissance
platoon.[11]

Lieutenant Colonel Fuller had personally requested assignment of Capt. Joseph Z. Taylor, newly returned from
duty in Japan as a recon company commander with 3d
Recon Battalion. Joe Taylor had been in Fuller's 2d Amphibious Reconnaissance Battalion at Camp Lejeune in
1950. Joe was initially distressed at now being made a reconnaissance platoon commander, after having served as
a company commander and having attained the rank of
captain. Regan Fuller and I both attempted to reassure Joe
of the importance of his new assignment.

Rapid approval came from the commandant, and in
September of 1955 the new reconnaissance platoon was
established. Because of the operations and tests envis-
aged for the recon platoon, the selection criteria for personnel mandated "highly motivated non-commissioned
officer volunteers for parachuting and other operations
involving extra-hazardous duty . . . temperamentally and
physically suited for vigorous training . . . [with] demonstrated initiative, self reliance and demonstrated maturity
and interest in the Marine Corps."[12] Generally, individuals only from the rank of corporal through that of staff
sergeant were accepted; however, we did admit a few outstanding PFCs and lance corporals. All had to be second-
class swimmers at a minimum, volunteers for parachute
duty, unmarried (except for staff sergeants), and have a
minimum general classification test score of ninety.

At Test Unit 1, Captain Taylor assumed duty as pla-

toon leader and began to assemble and train the personnel
who were to become the nucleus of 1st Force Recon. He
had just successfully completed a submarine exercise
with fifty-seven of his 3d Recon Battalion Marines landing by rubber boat from the USS *Perch* (APSS-313) on
the island of Iwo Jima during RECONEX (reconnaissance exercise) 551 conducted during February-March
1955. He thus brought fresh submarine experience to his
command. Both Joe Taylor and I have to credit Lt. Col.
Regan Fuller with being the real "father" of force reconnaissance, however.

Joe and I spent many hours reflecting on Regan
Fuller—his foresight, perseverance, and ability—and his
impact on the marines and the effect he had on both of us
and our subsequent careers. Regan Fuller tasked Joe Taylor, who was fresh from the state of the art in modern amphibious reconnaissance in the FMF, to mold and whip
the brand new reconnaissance platoon of Test Unit into a
highly trained and skilled amphib recon unit—one that
was fully capable of adding on and assimilating new and
diverse methods of entry and operation. Lieutenant Colonel Fuller gave me, as a major, the freedom to exercise
my ideas for parachute reconnaissance and pathfinding.
He turned Joe and me loose as innovators to find practical
new aircraft, equipment, and methods to enhance and develop our emerging deep reconnaissance capability
within the Marine Corps.

Reconnaissance Training for Test Unit 1

Test Unit 1 was able to set up basic and advanced amphib
recon training with the Amphibious Reconnaissance
School at Coronado, TTUPac. Terrestrial reconnaissance
was taught using the ample and experienced infantry and
recon assets already within Test Unit 1. Liaison was es-

tablished with ComNavAirPac at NAS North Island, and the platoon was able to go through SERE (survival, evasion, resistance, and escape) training at Warner Springs, California. This was a course that had been designed for navy pilots, who faced the possibility of being shot down over enemy territory. It was a reasonable conclusion that reconnaissance marines would be operating deep behind enemy lines and would require the same kind of training. The course was taught on a very practical level by faculty who usually included a former Korean War POW. Individually and as a marine unit, the members of Test Unit 1 stood out in both the navy SERE school and the air force E&E (escape and evasion) school.

During the E&E desert survival course, a humorous incident occurred that displays the kind of initiative that was somehow common to all of these recon marines. The air force personnel had been broken up into administrative bomber crews of about ten men each. In one of these crews, Cpl. Harry R. Lefthand, a Native American, was teamed with a corporal from Brooklyn—an improbable pair, to say the least—for the land survival exercise. Marine corporal Lefthand kept his crew in food by tickling trout from the local streams, a technique that amazed his urban pilot classmates. On one occasion Lefthand spotted a porcupine, and as they chased it, the animal climbed a large desert pine tree. Lefthand himself climbed some forty feet up the tree and followed the porcupine out onto a limb. Carrying a stick, the corporal forced the porcupine off its perch, and it plummeted to the ground. Waiting on the ground was the corporal from Brooklyn, armed with a large rock. As the animal hit the ground, the city lad finished him off by dropping his rock on the porcupine's head. The crew ate cooked porcupine that night, though they complained it was pretty gamey. The air force colonel commanding that crew boasted to all who would listen that during the living-off-the-land portion of the survival exercise, his men had gained weight.

Meanwhile, Test Unit 1's recon platoon was beginning to get hands-on recon training, honing many of their acquired skills. It was not until April 1956, however, that Test Unit 1 was able to get the necessary quotas to send Capt. Joe Taylor, Lts. Don Koelper and Kenneth Ball, and twenty enlisted marines to Ft. Benning to jump school.[13]

My recent parachute schooling at Ft. Benning had made me aware of the peril of not being properly prepared for jump school. At Test Unit 1, therefore, we set up a "pre-jump school" to prepare our marines so that all of them would graduate and get their wings. Capt. Joe Taylor was able to get the services of Sgt. Robert Zwiener, a parachute rigger in the air delivery platoon located at the Camp Pendleton airstrip, to run our school. Zwiener ran a tough, demanding course for us. By the time our Test Unit 1 marines went to actual jump school, they had all become proficient in PLFs, body positioning, and positive exits. And all of them could pass the dreaded pull-up physicals and complete the long runs with ease. We quickly recruited Sergeant Zwiener and had him transferred into Test Unit 1, where he became the founder and head of our parachute loft. Importantly, Bob Zwiener also became a proficient test parachutist. Later he and I together made experimental high-speed (over two hundred knots) exits as well as HALO jumps with delays of over sixty-seconds from two marine F3D Skyknights.

All of the recon platoon marines passed jump school with flying colors and returned to Camp Pendleton. Shortly thereafter, Captain Taylor, Lieutenant Koelper, Lieutenant Ball, and I (I had been promoted to major in January) were placed on jump status as of 1 July 1956, "to perform extra-hazardous duty."[14]

Our jumpers were now static-line qualified with the T-10, the standard thirty-four-foot nominal diameter troop parachute. In a static-line jump, the main parachute is opened automatically by a line that is hooked to the airplane and to the parachute pack—hence the familiar parachutist command for jumping static-line aircraft, "Stand up, and hook up." At the time, however, I was the only person in Test Unit 1 with free-fall experience. We now had to turn the majority of our jumpers into free-fall parachutists.

The U.S. Naval Parachute Unit at Naval Auxiliary Air Station (NAAS) El Centro, California, was the logical place for them to obtain this training. Beginning in July 1956, a number of us were sent TAD to the Naval Parachute Unit and began a rapid immersion into the art of free fall and parachute testing. CWO (chief warrant officer) Lewis T. "Lew" Vinson, the jumpmaster at the Naval Parachute Unit at El Centro, was the highly qualified mentor who gave us our instruction. And for some of us, he was the reason for our ultimate parachute qualification as "test parachutists."

NAAS El Centro was also the location of the air force counterpart of the U.S. Naval Parachute Unit, the 6511th Test Squadron, whose parent squadron was headquartered at Edwards Air Force Base. Air force warrant officer Larry Lambert and his test jumpers were all highly qualified. And on occasion navy, air force, and marine parachutists would all be jumping the same aircraft; on other occasions, they would be test jumping other services' specialized parachute rigs. There was always a free exchange and cross-service cooperation in these efforts. On one jump Capt. Joseph Kittinger, USAF, came out from Wright Patterson Test Center and made several jumps with us. "Kitt" later made, and still holds, the world record for the highest free-fall parachute jump: 102,800 feet from the gondola of a high-altitude balloon.[15]

In addition to jumpers from the air force, we had some from the army on occasion at El Centro; however, they did the majority of their parachute testing at Fort Benning and at Fort Bragg. Also the navy's Blue Angels aerobatic squadron would winter-over at El Centro and practice its routines in some of the remote areas west of Mount Signal, the area of our primary DZs, out toward the Chocolate Mountains. Our jumpers established a good rapport with the "Blues," and on liberty, at dinner, or in the BOQ (bachelor officer quarters) we would banter with each other in a good-natured way. The Blues would bemoan the fact that we recon jumpers had the lack of intelligence to jump out of perfectly good airplanes. In response, we in recon would denigrate their highly skilled flying to a level of "air-show showing off." All of this was in good fun, and no one took it seriously.

El Centro is in the desert south and east of the Salton Sea, about a hundred miles due east of San Diego. The winds there would usually pick up in velocity early mid-morning—a fact that dictated an early reveille, usually between 0500 and 0530. We would eat a hasty breakfast and then suit up for the two or three jumps we made each day, contingent on the winds and our ability to get back to the NAF from the Mount Signal DZ by ground transportation. After every jump, we would get back to the flight line, suit up with yet a different type of parachute, and get aboard whatever aircraft was available for the next jump—usually a navy R4D or P2V or an air force C-119.

It became clear both to us at Test Unit 1 and to the Naval Parachute Unit that, because of the increasing sophistication of our types of jumping and the types of parachutes themselves, some of us should try to become qualified as "navy test parachutists." And indeed, over the next year Capt. Joe Taylor, S.Sgt. (meritoriously promoted because of his superior performance) Bob

Zwiener, and I, along with several other of our more qualified jumpers, were able complete the twenty-two jump syllabus to gain that qualification.

The test jumper syllabus consisted of a series of delays (delays of ten, fifteen, twenty, twenty-five, or more seconds in opening the parachute, once one has exited the aircraft), day and night free falls, and a variety of different types and models of parachutes. We jumped the navy QFB (quick fit, back) chute, the QAC (quick attachable, chest) pack, seat packs, and the conical (named for the small conical shape of the canopy). The conical was a twenty-six-foot nominal diameter canopy (in contrast to the thirty and thirty-five feet canopies that we normally jumped), which made for a very fast descent. This caused those of us who weighed over two hundred pounds to have pretty hard landings because of the conical's tendency to have severe oscillations and its higher rate of descent.

Each of us was required to have one jump with the space, or pressurized, suit. The space-suit jump was a little hairy because of the full metal helmet with a Plexiglas face piece (much like a diving helmet), which screwed on one-quarter turn onto a metal neck ring. There were pressure cuffs and metal rings at the wrists as well. The sheer bulk of the space suit made it almost impossible to get one's arms up to undo the helmet once one had landed. We jumped the pressure suit without the normal bail-out oxygen bottle that is used with the suit. Once the helmet was screwed on, it was a bit claustrophobic until we got onto the deck. As a consequence, when it was my turn to jump the space suit, after taking a ten-second delay, I opened and checked to see that I had a good canopy (no line-over or panels blown out). I slipped my chute toward the ambulance on the DZ, and when I had landed, the corpsmen unscrewed my helmet. The jump worked out fine, and we had no problems. Admittedly, however, our space-suit jump caused us more anxiety than any of the different kinds of parachutes or other equipment that we jumped.

Because we were jumping so many different kinds of parachutes, it became something of a mental exercise for us, as we launched from the door of the aircraft, to concentrate on where a particular parachute's ripcord was located. On the QACs and the T-7As (standard troop reserve parachutes), the cords pulled across the chest. The conicals and QFBs had their ripcords up over the left shoulder. The seat pack had its ripcord down below the waist on the left side. We never really had any problem with this, but we did think about it a bit.

To the casual observer, it might appear that we were all "stacking jumps" to build up an impressive number of jumps for ourselves. This was emphatically not the case, however. Experience had shown us that a diversity in the types of parachutes jumped and in the types of aircraft used gave the parachutists the extra bit of indefinable knowledge and expertise that set them apart from other jumpers. We found that after making about ten to fifteen free falls, jumpers could more easily record and marshal their observations on their position at exit, the distance from the aircraft until stabilization or pull, and the relative positions that caused partial malfunctions such as line-overs or blown panels of the parachute or with hard G force (gravitational force)—a chute opens normally in the 3G range, but a hard, or high-speed, opening can go up to 8Gs or 9Gs. The extra and diversified training paid off manyfold.

The Marine Corps had disbanded its paramarines in 1944. Although they were used in a number of landing operations, it was always in an infantry ground mode (that is, parachutes were not used for entry). They never made a combat parachute jump.[16] At the time in 1956 that we in Test Unit 1 started parachuting as a regular duty, the only other units that maintained personnel on jump status were the air delivery platoons (in the event someone slipped or was inadvertently carried out while making cargo air-delivery drops, we were told). Interestingly, resistance to our parachute operations surfaced from several of the older, former paramarines. Although they themselves had not jumped for sixteen years, for reasons unknown to us several of them came forward to advise the commanding general of the 1st Marine Division, Maj. Gen. David M. Shoup, on what we were doing wrong. Few of the paramarines had any extensive free-fall experience and thus had no experience in the more sophisticated type of parachuting that we were doing. General Shoup quickly moved to quiet these few critics on the division staff by appointing me as his "division parachute officer." That ended the resistance and permitted us to go on with our developmental work.

Parachutist Insignia

In 1963, years after General Shoup's deferral to us on parachute matters, I was serving as a lieutenant colonel in the office of the secretary of defense. Having now been named commandant of the Marine Corps, David Shoup called me over to Marine Corps Headquarters and asked for my input on two recommendations on parachuting that had come to him for decision: a recommendation from 2d Force Recon to adopt the army senior and master parachutist silver insignia to indicate the experience of the parachutist, and a recommendation from the SEALs to the chief of naval operations, Adm. George W. Anderson, for readoption of the "old" gold naval aviation insignia, similar to naval aviator wings but with a parachute instead of an anchor and shield superimposed on the aviator's wings. The newly formed navy SEALs were considering adoption of the gold wings. General Shoup asked my opinion on the matter.

I recommended that it would be historically more appropriate for us to readopt the "old" (gold) navy-marine parachute wings worn by our paramarines and marine riggers in early Marine Corps squadrons rather than go with 2d Force Recon's army-type silver wings suggestion. General Shoup liked the idea of a joint adoption—that is, by both the U.S. Navy and the Marine Corps—of the gold wings. He tasked me to write a letter to Admiral Anderson to that effect. So I went home that night to Alexandria and sat down at our kitchen table and composed a short personal note from the commandant of the Marine Corps to the chief of naval operations, and General Shoup signed it the next day. The decorations and awards branches of the navy and the marines simultaneously readopted the navy gold jump wings as a result of General Shoup's letter.[17] Thus the SEALs, air delivery, and force recon started wearing the insignia a few months later.

Not long after the readoption of the gold wings, I received a call from Hilborn-Hamburger, the military insignia supplier in New York. It seems they no longer had the die for the old insignia, so they asked if we could send them a set of the original wings. I called a former paramarine who had been my chief communicator in 1st Force, M.Sgt. Harry Walters, who loaned me his. I sent them to Hilborn-Hamburger, and they recast the mold and made up three sets, which they returned to me along with Master Sergeant Walters's wings. I returned Walters's wings to him, and I presented one of the new sets to the decorations and medals section and one to Bob Zwiener for his dedicated and innovative efforts for force recon. I kept the third set, which I have to this day.

CHAPTER FIVE
Off-Carrier Capability

In tracing the next level of development in force reconnaissance—which is the year 1956–57 in Test Unit 1 and the next two years (1957–59) after we formed 1st Force Recon—I rely heavily on the jump logs from both of these units. A jump log is similar in intent and purpose to a pilot's flight log. It records the date, the unit or organization making the jump, the location of the jump, the type of aircraft used, the type of parachute, the type of jump (static-line, free-fall, night, combat jump, and so on). The log is certified with the name and rank of the senior person on the jump, and it ends with a place for this person's remarks. With our type of "on the edge parachuting" these remarks ran the gamut from "hard opening" to "line-over" to "blew out two panels."

A line-over is a condition in which one of the suspension lines ends up riding over the top of the parachute. This condition can be dangerous because the suspension line can, by rubbing (if the parachute is oscillating), create enough friction to melt through the nylon canopy and cut the parachute in half, sending the parachutist to his or her death if there is not enough time to activate the reserve parachute. If a jumper gets a line-over, he or she can attempt to correct the situation by climbing the suspension lines and whipping the entangled line to one side or the other. Frequently line-overs will correct themselves.

The condition of blown-out panels decreases the amount of the canopy that provides the lift needed to slow a jumper's descent. If one or more panels are lost, the parachutist's rate of descent increases, and landing can result in injury. Our rule in both Test Unit 1 and 1st Force Recon was that if the hole in the canopy was big enough to throw your helmet through, then it was time to activate your reserve parachute to slow your descent to an acceptable rate.

Lt. Col. Pat Carothers, now retired and living in Alaska, recently reminded me of an incident at El Centro when he was a captain going through free-fall training. He had a bad opening, and several panels on his canopy blew out. Having gone out on the previous stick, my group and I were already on the DZ watching the other jumpers come down. We saw Pat dropping below the other parachutists in the air as we spotted several panels blown in his parachute. We yelled up to him, "Pull your reserve!" Either he did not hear us or he reasoned he was too low for it to do much good. In any event, when he landed, he was a bit stunned from a harder-than-usual PLF. Pat laughingly recalled that while he was still on the ground, I ended up astride his body with my feet planted on either side of his helmet, where I proceeded in no uncertain terms to hold school on why, after checking his canopy and noting any blown panels, he should have activated his reserve. Pat never forgot this incident, and he was equally forceful with his jumpers regarding this safety procedure when he became commanding officer of 2d Force Recon.

The jump logs for Test Unit 1 and the first twenty months of 1st Force Recon reflect the use of a wide variety of types of aircraft: air force Fairchild C-119 Flying

Boxcars, navy Douglas R4D-6 Skytrains, navy Lockheed P2V Neptunes (which are a combination turboprop and jet twin-engine ASW [antisubmarine warfare] aircraft), army and air force DeHavilland L-20 Beavers, navy North American AJ-2 Savages, navy (and later marine) Douglas F3D-2s Skyknights, and (with memories of my runs along the strand at Coronado) probably the most important aircraft at the time, the navy Grumman TF-1 Trader—and, eventually, the pure-jet navy carrier-based bombers, Douglas A3D Skywarriors. Later, I would also jump the air force C-130 Hercules transport aircraft into Korea on a night jump with Capt. Bob Burhans, with 10th Special Forces from Okinawa. In addition, in the Philippines we jumped the marine H34 Sikorsky Seahorse helicopter.

The Grumman TF-1

One of our highest priorities within Test Unit 1 with respect to reconnaissance and pathfinder insertion by parachute was to expand Marine Corps capability in jumping from carrier aircraft. To be considered a carrier aircraft, a plane must be structurally designed to carry the heavy and repetitive G loads from catapult shots and the rapid stops from arresting wires transmitted through the aircraft's tail hook.

Beginning in May 1956, Capt. Joe Taylor, S.Sgt. Bob Zwiener, and I drove to NAS North Island to VR-5, the fleet transport squadron belonging to ComFLogWingPac (commander, Fleet Logistic Wing, Pacific) of ComAirPac (VR-5 later was redesignated as VR-21). We spent hours examining the Grumman TF-1 Trader. The Trader is a twin-engine, high-wing plane, the transport variation of the navy's Grumman S2F antisubmarine aircraft, appropriately called the Tracker. It was known as a COD (carrier onboard delivery) aircraft, whose primary mission was the delivery of personnel, mail, and critical parts for the carrier or its squadrons directly onboard the carrier itself. It could operate off of every size of navy carrier, from the smallest upward.

Detachments of Fleet Transport Squadron VR-5 were located pretty much every place that our navy aircraft carriers went. In the Pacific, in addition to North Island, there was a detachment at Alameda NAS as well as in Hawaii, Japan, and the Philippines. Many navy carriers had their own COD aircraft, initially the TF-1, as part of their mix of the types of aircraft they carried. If we could prove the feasibility of the TF-1, we could be assured of worldwide capability, a factor in future potential utilization.

The TF-1 had nine rear-facing passenger seats, all of which could be folded and stowed away. With two very powerful engines for its relatively small size (the Wright R-1820-82, with 1,525 horsepower each), the TF-1 could take off on land in four hundred eighty feet with a clear overrun and in seven hundred eighty feet was able to clear a fifty-foot obstacle. The TF-1 was thus very adaptable for small-field operations. (We field tested this capability later in a training exercise: the aircraft touched down, on the swing-around the team boarded, and they were off within thirty seconds of touchdown.)

Our problem was that the TF-1 had never been jumped before, and no one at Grumman had ever considered its use for the drop of parachutists or of high-priority cargo. Having crawled all over and inside of the aircraft, we knew it was the ideal aircraft for off-carrier operations.[1] For the loading of special cargo, there were two thirteen-foot aluminum I-beam rails running fore and aft through the cargo compartment. These proved ideal for bolting on an anchor-line cable, to which the parachutists hook up for static-line jumps. On the left side of the fuselage was a two-piece door—the rear portion being the passenger door, the forward permitting large cargo to be loaded when both portions were open. The passenger portion of the door was only thirty-two inches in width and only forty-nine inches in height—a size that necessitated our crouching down to make an exit.

I was initially concerned about the engine nacelle, which was just sixty-seven inches from the face of a jumper crouched in the door ready to make a positive exit. In addition, the engine nacelle extended twenty-three inches to the rear, past the after side of the passenger door. In exiting the TF-1, a parachutist literally leaped out toward the engine nacelle. As it turned out, however, the location of the exit door—about eight feet behind the gigantic three-bladed prop turning on the engine—forced such a strong slipstream through the space between the nacelle and the side of the fuselage (probably enhanced by the venturi effect), that despite the most positive exit that we would attempt, the moment we left the door and entered into the slipstream, our bodies were turned ninety degrees to the left (to the rear, toward the tail), making the TF-1 an outstanding jump aircraft. With the help of the parachute engineers, Ken Earle and Howard Fish, of NPU (Naval Parachute Unit) and the wise guidance of CWO Lew Vinson, we made the first live jumps that had ever been made of the TF-1 on 9–13 July 1956.

The pilot's operating handbook for the TF-1 was unclear on whether the aircraft could be flown with the rear (passenger) portion of the door removed. We had sent a telegram to Grumman several days before our first scheduled test jumps and had heard nothing back from them. With the aircraft ready and our test program all set, the morning of our first scheduled jump, in exasperation, we finally telephoned Grumman and at the last minute asked them directly, "Can the TF-1 be flown with the rear door off?" They hemmed and hawed and finally said, "We believe it's okay and that you should not experience any flutter, but let us know!" With those less-than-reassuring words in our ears, we turned to Lt. Cdr. Roy Taylor, the TF-1 aircraft commander from VR-5 Detachment, North Island, and asked him. He carefully examined the aircraft's structure around the door and said he felt the plane was built "like a brick out-house."

NPU's evaluation of the aircraft was very cautious. We first took up four two-hundred-pound torso dummies and one articulated dummy suited up with standard T-10 parachutes, complete with reserves, jump helmets, and standard equipment (weapons, packs, and so forth). We had slow-motion, air-to-air photography from an air force T-28 photo aircraft, taking both stills and motion pictures of the exits, the streaming of the static lines, and deployment bags. Roy Taylor, our pilot, flew first at one hundred knots and then later at one hundred twenty knots with one-third flaps, and there was no flutter or vibration noted. We flew back to El Centro, landed, and reviewed the air-to-air photography, and all hands concurred that the plane would be safe for live jumps.

After doing the test drops with the articulated dummies, we flew the TF-1 from takeoff to landing with the rear door removed. All we did was pad and tape the sharp after-edge of the door so that it would not fray or cut our static lines. The only apparent deficit in flying without the rear door noted by Lieutenant Commander Taylor was a "reduction of about ten knots airspeed at cruise power settings."[2]

Because the Grumman TF-1 Trader was a new aircraft that no one had previously used for parachuting, we jumped it in sticks of four, five, and eventually nine. On the first live jump of a four-man stick, I took the number-one position (first out of the door), to be followed by Lew Vinson, army captain Larry Neipling, and a navy test jumper. All of us had good exits. After landing from this first jump, Roy and I conference-called the plane's manufacturer, Grumman, and advised them of our test jumps. Roy assured the engineers that we had no problem with flutter or vibration. They were delighted and requested copies of all of our test reports.

Over the next five days we made a total of sixty personnel jumps, both day and night, from the TF-1. We varied the speed and again tried it first at one hundred knots and then at one hundred twenty with one-third flaps. On the later jumps we carried full combat equipment including weapons, packs, and an AN/GRC9 radio. We later developed an SOP for the jumpmaster for the TF-1. First, the jumpmaster had to unlatch and detach the last four seats from the deck of the aircraft to give himself room to operate. He would then fold them and stow them in the after head compartment. If all nine jumpers exited the aircraft and no jumpmaster were left aboard, the copilot would have to come back from the cockpit and pull in the static lines and replace the passenger door.

A Series of Firsts

On 26 July 1956, we actually tested our off-carrier parachute capability. We arranged for a TF-1 from VR-5 to depart NAS North Island and fly out to sea to recover aboard the USS *Bennington* (CVA-20). Refusing to "sit back" on this one, Lt. Col. Regan Fuller came aboard as an official crew member and Test Unit 1 observer. Four of us from Test Unit 1 made this off-carrier jump, which was the first in naval aviation history: Capt. Donald E. Koelper (later killed in Vietnam, winning the first Navy Cross of the Marine Corps in that war); PFCs Kenneth R. Bell and Matthew J. O'Neill Jr. (later killed in a jump at Camp Pendleton); and I. After our landing at El Centro, we all celebrated what we felt was a significant event and flew back to Camp Pendleton. With its 930-mile range, the TF-1 gave us the legs for greater depth in reconnaissance from off navy carriers.

In August 1956 we had the chance to make our first jumps from an all-jet aircraft. We used the Douglas F3D2 Skyknight, a twin-engine, two-place jet. Ostensibly to make a "simple" escape system and also to reduce the weight penalty of an ejection system, Douglas Aircraft Corporation designed the escape system for the F3D by using a forty-five-degree chute, angled to the rear and situated between the two jet engines, out of the bottom of the aircraft. For normal crew escape, the pilot would activate a small air-bottle charge, blowing the door off from the bottom of the fuselage. A small panel deflector would deploy on the forward side of the chute exit to break up and deflect the slipstream down from along the bottom of the fuselage. The F3D2 was redlined for jumping at speeds in excess of four hundred knots. Wind-tunnel tests had shown that above four hundred knots, the exiting parachutist would bounce along the bottom of the fuselage, potentially being injured or rendered unconscious from striking the bottom of the aircraft. Test parachutists at El Centro had found that exits could be made at jump speeds of one hundred fifty knots with no problem. To train its own NPU test parachutists, El Centro had a metal exit chute (similar in design and length to the one in the F3D) fabricated and installed in the bottom of its P2V Neptune. Most of us had the opportunity to "go down the chute" on the P2V and experience this different type of exit. For me the experience was not too different from sliding down a basement coal or sawdust chute as a youth in Seattle.

The F3D was initially designed as a carrier-borne night-fighter with the pilot sitting on the left and the radar observer (RO) in the right seat, side-by-side. In between the two seats on our standard Marine Corps F3Ds, there was a cluster of flight controls that one had to avoid in getting up from the RO's seat to position into the chute to drop out of the bottom of the F3D.

Before my first jump of the F3D, we had a cockpit checkout in which we were able to rehearse the cockpit procedures for the jumper to exit the aircraft properly. NPU had a mattress placed on the hangar floor, and we were able to practice five or six exits, dropping out of the chute onto the hangar floor. Prior to the jump, mechanics would remove the "blow away" door and lock the small slipstream deflector into a "down" position (using two small metal clamps). This preparation took about ten minutes and was therefore considered an insignificant modification for us to be able to use the F3D for exiting free-fall parachutists.

Jumping from the F3D2 required careful procedures in the cockpit. About five minutes out from the jump, the pilot would advise the crew of the time. We would then unhook from our oxygen supply (presuming a descent to jump altitude, where no oxygen was needed) and remove our navy pilot's hard helmet with its oxygen mask and headset and microphone (if it was not going to be a HALO exit). From that point on, communications were either by a loud voice (we were not on the intercom to the pilot) or by simple hand signals. We put on our jump helmets (which had formerly been football helmets belonging to the Camp Pendleton marine football team but were now painted Marine Corps dull dark green with one's name and rank on the front). Unbuckling from the shoulder harness and seat belt, we stowed them so they would not catch on our parachute harness while we were getting into the chute.

Just prior to climbing—carefully, in a crouched position—over the aircraft instrument console between the seats, we would attach our twenty-eight-foot T-7A reserve chute on the D rings on our parachute harness. We would then take a sitting position in the escape chute (located centered and directly behind the pilot's and the RO's seats). The escape chute was thirty inches wide, twenty-four inches in depth, and seven feet long, to the exit on the bottom of the fuselage between the two jet engines. There was a trap door, hinged at the top of the escape chute, that swung down to form the back of the pilot's compartment.

In getting into the chutes, we would push this door up and to the rear, locking it out of our way as we entered the escape chute. There was a small handhold, not unlike a chinning bar, at the top of the chute. On a "thumbs up" signal from the pilot—meaning "Stand by, we are thirty-seconds out from the drop"—the jumper would extend his body fully down into the chute and hang on this handhold bar while looking back over his shoulder at the pilot. When the pilot received the drop signal (if we were doing a ground-controlled drop, as we had done in our test jumps at El Centro), he would reach behind and tap the jumper on the helmet. Then one simply let go and, with a whoosh, one was down the chute.

Our initial jumps from the F3D were always at one hundred fifty knots (about one hundred eighty-five miles per hour at five thousand feet altitude) with speed brakes deployed. At first we took five-second delays, would stabilize to avoid tumbling, and then would pull at our desired altitude. Our first jumps on any new aircraft were always "clean" (that is, we were carrying no packs, weapons, or other gear). Later we would jump with full equipment, which was generally stowed in a small pack hung and tied down just below the reserve parachute.

I experienced one bad jump from the F3D2 at El Centro: it was my thirty-first jump and our first test-jump of the F3D with full equipment. I was wearing a small Marine Corps pack attached just below my reserve parachute. In the pack I carried two days of rations, a "grease gun" (the M3A1, which is a .45-caliber submachine gun), four spare clips of ammo, a PRC-6 radio, binoculars, a camera, and a canteen of water. I took a five-second delay from five thousand feet, had a good exit, had just stabilized and opened. I was jumping a standard twenty-eight-foot backpack with a T-7A standard reserve parachute. I had a "hard" opening (one in which the jumper momentarily sees little flashing stars out on the horizon—we used to refer to this type of opening as a "ball-buster"). My canopy had friction burns on one panel, although it was not blown; they were small enough that, in my judgment, I did not have to activate my reserve.

At the instant of opening I felt the loaded pack slam in against my hips. I experienced a flash of pain but thought nothing more of it, chalking it up to the hard-G opening. On this first full equipment jump, as we later realized, we did not have sufficient tie-downs on all four corners of the pack, just at the top where it was attached to the harness underneath the reserve parachute. The jump was at 1415 hours, and we had some afternoon desert ground winds that had picked up on the deck and were gusting to about twelve miles per hour. This caused modest oscillation just prior to my landing, but by climbing the risers, I was able to dampen the oscillation. I circled and landed into the wind.

At touchdown, I did my PLF and stood up and immediately felt pain in my hip. I collapsed on my canopy, popped a flare, and waited for the ambulance on the DZ. They took me to the naval parachute dispensary, where an X ray was made. I was informed that I had a "simple line fracture of the pelvis." I called Lieutenant Colonel Fuller and said, "Tell my wife, Jo, I won't be home tonight." By this time she had become fairly understanding about the odd hours that I kept, but I knew she would be upset by this turn of events. I was then taken by ambulance to the naval hospital at Camp Pendleton, where the orthopedist prescribed hospital bed rest for quick healing.

Five weeks later I was jumping again—although for the next few jumps, I did place several large pieces of foam rubber beneath my leg straps on the parachute harness as I buckled in, and I had no further problems. I had another twenty-one jumps from jets after this accident. CWO Lew Vinson at NPU, who was appointed investigating officer, came up with an "occurred within line of duty" finding on my injury.[3] Any significant injury required an investigation under the guidance of the *Marine Corps Manual*.

The lesson learned from this jump was that when a parachutist is exiting from a jet, the higher speed makes it critically important that the jumper have everything— every piece of gear, every weapon—tightly secured. The equipment has to be tied down or taped with rigger's tape to the parachutist's body so that the pack cannot "float" away from the jumper during free fall (before actual opening of the chute) rather than swinging back in, against the body. The NPU flight surgeon concluded that in all probability my injury was caused by my speed and body attitude in relation to the fairly heavy pack at the time of opening, in combination with the hard opening itself—which was estimated by the parachute engineers to be 8 to 9Gs (eight or nine times the force of gravity).

Now that we had a carrier-capable jet fighter that we could put one parachutist out of, we needed to develop our ability to insert a four-man recon team. Logically this kind of insertion would require a jump with four parachutists. We needed to experiment to see how best to make the drop from formation. Our first multiple simultaneous drop was done on 6 February 1957 by S.Sgt. Lonzo M. Barnett and me. Barnett had also qualified as a test jumper at El Centro and, as a PFC in Korea at the Pusan perimeter in August 1950, had distinguished himself in combat with his disregard of his own safety to ensure accomplishment of his unit's mission.[4]

Our aircraft were from VMF(AW)-542 (night all-weather fighter squadron) in the 1st Marine Air Wing at El Toro. Capts. Orie Corie and Chester Tucker met us at the NPU flight line, where mechanics performed the ten-minute removal of the lower door and locked the deflector panel in place. Our briefing of the marine pilots included the USAF T28 chase-plane pilot, who would shoot air-to-air photographs, as well as the ground personnel from Mount Signal DZ control, since this was to be the first simultaneous multiple-exit jump from pure-jet aircraft in formation.

After one dry run, we made a jump that came off without a hitch. Both Barnett and I were using T-10 thirty-five-foot nominal-diameter canopies (modified for free fall) and T-7A reserve parachutes. We jumped at five thousand feet and took five-second delays. The ground and the air-to-air cameras showed that our exits (by radio control from DZ control) were simultaneous and that our parachutes had opened simultaneously.

None of us knew how much lateral tumbling that we would experience (away from the center of the line of flight of the aircraft). For this first formation drop, we used a seventy-five-yard separation between aircraft. Our two-plane jump told us that there appeared to be no lateral tumbling. The next month, on 20 March 1957, we made the first four-marine recon team jump. Capt. Bill Livingston, S.Sgt. Bob Zwiener, Cpl. Gerald L. LaCoursier, and I—all from Test Unit 1—did a five-second delay at five thousand feet at El Centro.

We found that the lead pilot could coordinate the drop by radio as he flew directly over the intended DZ. He would pass the "drop" signal to the other three aircraft, and we four jumpers would exit simultaneously. As we gained more operational experience, we lowered the exit altitude to twenty-two hundred feet with a three-second delay. Later we dropped in formation at night and, after moving to 1st Force Recon, while deployed on Operation Strongback in the Philippines, we routinely dropped at two thousand feet.

We later developed approaches to the target area on the deck with the aircraft flying at one hundred feet with a pull-up to drop altitude of two thousand feet for the F3Ds. We did this same thing with the TF-1s and later with the Douglas A3D Skywarriors, with a pull-up to twelve hundred feet for the TFs and two thousand feet for the A3Ds. This worked fine and accommodated a nap-of-the-earth approach with pull-up to drop altitude to minimize radar detection.

After gaining more experience in multiple jumps, we reduced the distance between the F3Ds to wingtip alignment in a slight echelon, or standard thirty-degree division ("vee") formation. The F3D has a fifty-foot wingspan, so with no appreciable lateral tumbling, our parachutists would be approximately fifty-five to sixty feet apart on opening. Because our T-10 canopies had nominal diameters of thirty-five feet, we were all pretty close to each other on opening. We had been trained to slip to whoever opened low; this reduces the spread of the stick on the ground to acceptable tactical limits—generally four jumpers within a one-hundred-fifty-yard circle.

All of us recognized that it was very inefficient to use four aircraft to make an insertion when one could do the same job. We began to look for off-carrier jets that could carry and drop a four-man or larger recon team. We were also looking for aircraft with increased range. We first requested the Douglas A3D Skywarrior, but because of HATWING 6 (heavy attack wing) fleet commitments, we were first given the North American AJ-2 Savage, which had a range of fourteen hundred nautical miles. In December 1958, Capt. Wes "Duff" Rice, Staff Sergeant Zwiener, Sgt. Gary Marte, and I jumped the bomb bay of the AJ-2, a plane that was a carrier-based combination turboprop and jet and thus not a "pure" jet.

In the AJ-2 we would sit like a four-man bobsled team on the forward edge of the bomb bay. The only preparation was the removal of the door between the bomb bay and the pilot's compartment. We would pad the metal edges of the opening from the pilot's compartment to the bomb bay. About twenty seconds out, the pilot would pop the bomb bay doors open, we would get a tap on the helmet, and we would sequentially exit. We encountered no problems in jumping the AJ-2. Later, we jumped the A3D Skywarrior, from the bomb bay as well as down its escape chute, which was comparable to the F3D. We had found an aircraft that could exit four to six jumpers, that had a long range (twenty-one hundred nautical miles), and that operated off of all-sized carriers. The A3D and the TF-1 gave us the combinations that we needed for dropping of recon parachutists as full nine-man pathfinder teams.

We first tested the A3D at El Centro. Before making our first jump, I was sitting on the forward edge of the bomb bay with my feet on a small ledge that was below my seat but above the bomb bay doors themselves. We looked aft through the bomb bay and noted that the rear bulkhead of the bomb bay was about twelve to fourteen feet aft from my seated position at the front of the bomb bay. Many of us by now had made close to one hundred jumps, the majority of which had been free falls and a number were test jumps from jets. We were fully aware that once a jumper has exited the aircraft, his body immediately begins to slow down. The aircraft, however, is still traveling forward at one hundred fifty knots.

We were concerned about what would happen as soon as we pushed off from our bobsled seating and began to drop through the bomb bay. Would we fall clear before the rear of the bomb bay came forward and struck some part of us? We asked parachute engineer Howard Fish and NPU jumpmaster Lew Vinson at NPU for their opinions. Howard said the factors would be difficult to compute, but he believed that in all probability we would be below the after-end of the bomb bay as we passed under the tail of the A3D. Lew Vinson concurred.

Shortly thereafter we heard about Edwards Air Force Base's Maj. Chuck Yeager's use of a shortened broomstick to lock his canopy on one of his first rocket-powered flights. We found an old broom in the parachute loft and cut off the handle: we now had a broomstick about four feet long. In leading the exit on our first A3D jump, I carried this broomstick, holding it aloft in one hand as we exited. The three jumpers in trail behind me closely observed my jump to try to determine the distance between the broomstick and the after-end of the bomb bay as it continued forward. Once on the deck they assured me that I was well below the after-end of the bomb bay with my stick extended and did not even come close to touching the after-bulkhead of the bomb bay compartment. From that point on, we jumped the A3D with great success and good exits. (The following year 2d Force used this same method of on-the-deck approach and pulling up to drop altitude when Walter Cronkite filmed them for his television program "The New Recon Marine.")

All in all, it was an exciting experience. When one is sitting in the closed bomb bay and the A3D is flying low to the earth's surface, one's attention is riveted to the bomb bay doors about four feet below. Suddenly the pilot pops the doors, which are actuated hydraulically. The recon team has an instant panoramic view of blurred desert or water directly beneath the aircraft. When coming in near the surface (at about one hundred feet), one really gets the feeling of speed at one hundred fifty to two hundred knots. As the pilot pulls up to drop altitude (two thousand feet) and the team prepares to push off through the open bomb bay doors, this sense of speed vanishes. It was always an adrenaline rush to jump the A3D in such "on the deck" (nap-of-the-earth) approaches with pull-up to jump altitude.

CHAPTER SIX
Pathfinding in Test Unit 1

Writing in the 1990s about pathfinding in the Marine Corps in the 1950s and early 1960s, one must be mindful of the massive strides in navigation that have made essentially obsolete the need for pathfinders in the armed services today—in particular, the development and widespread use of the GPS (global positioning satellite) navigation system. Now almost all of the small units in the Marine Corps—helicopters and infantry units alike—are able to use the GPS to locate themselves within fifteen feet of any place on the Earth's surface, day or night, fair weather or foul. All they have to do is punch in the latitude and longitude of their prospective landing zone (LZ), and the small hand-held satellite receiver provides the marines with the compass heading, distance, ground speed, and time remaining to the intended target point (continuously updated many times a minute) from their current position to the objective.

Furthermore, pathfinding was never really required in Vietnam in the 1960s and 1970s. In all of our areas of helicopter operations there, we had no significant air threat. Our approaches could be from safer, higher altitudes, where more precise navigation was possible. At these altitudes we would be high enough to be out of the range of the 12.7-mm (approximately .50-caliber) small arms fire and, when flying on the deck, away from the RPG (rocket propelled grenade) rockets, shoulder-fired from the ground. We all learned high-spiraling approaches by helicopter to touchdown.

In Vietnam in early 1967 while I was commanding Special Landing Force (SLF) Alpha from the decks of LPH-2 (amphibious assault ship), the *Iwo Jima*, we made a series of combined helicopter assaults and over-the-beach landings in Quang Tri province along the northern coast of South Vietnam.[1] SLF Alpha consisted of a marine BLT and an HMM (medium helicopter squadron). This was the same area—La Rue Sans Joie—that the late French war correspondent Bernard Fall wrote about in his book of the same name, *The Street without Joy: The Bloody Road to Dien Bien Phu*.

As a result of the negligible air threat and the fact that we could set our approach and retirement lanes off the coast at varying altitudes, we were able to make a series of battalion-sized helicopter landings without the use of pathfinders. We used our flight control from the LPH as well as approach lanes for the helicopters of sufficient altitude that navigation by our helicopter pilots was much easier than it would have been if we had to fly long distances inland over relatively featureless terrain. We also had access to the carrier-based E-2A Hawkeyes (radar control aircraft), which could provide radar vectors, relative locations, and flight information to inbound flights of helos. Again, our marine helicopter pilots became proficient in the high-spiraling approach to our landing zones.

My discussion of the development of Marine Corps pathfinding in Test Unit 1, therefore, should be taken in the historical context of the mid–1950s and early 1960s, when the Marine Corps had to plan all of its helicopter operations anticipating vastly different operating conditions than were later encountered in Vietnam: battlefields with significant air threat, helicopter landing zones farther inland than could be controlled from the LPHs, and featureless terrain coupled with the need for landings just at dawn, making low-level helicopter navigation nearly impossible. To perform our missions during this period, therefore, we needed a viable directional capability. We had no GPS to guide us. We needed pathfinders.

The Necessity of Pathfinders

Early in World War II, both the Allies and the Axis armies had found that airborne assault units required detailed guidance to reach their proper landing zones. To provide this guidance, special units called pathfinders—specially trained personnel who are dropped from a plane into a target area for this purpose—were created. Both British and American parachute units and glider units successfully employed pathfinders to guide waves of assault troops to the target area. In the glider units, the pathfinding gliders carried beacons that successive waves of planes used as guides. In parachute units, the pathfinders used beacons, lights, radio signals, and final-guidance transmissions to guide their incoming jump aircraft.

With the advent of large-scale helicopter landings, it became apparent to some of our marine helicopter pilots as well as to some of us ground officers in the Marine Corps that we would have to develop a pathfinding capability specifically designed for helicopter landings. In April 1953, our commanding general at TTUPac in Coronado, Brig. Gen. Chesty Puller, was supportive of the research that we had done in the Amphibious Reconnaissance School contemplating use of reconnaissance personnel for pathfinding missions. In addition to insertion of recon personnel by parachute, we felt that we should concomitantly be doing something to ensure positive helicopter guidance for our marine pilots.

General Puller wrote a letter to the commandant of the Marine Corps requesting parachute and pathfinder training at Fort Benning. Chesty included the following with regard to our recommendations about pathfinding for marine helicopters:

> The Amphibious Reconnaissance School of this command has done considerable research in the potential use of parachute personnel in conjunction . . . with parachute-pathfinder reconnaissance missions in support of helicopter-borne assaults. Liaison has been effected with helicopter air group MAG(HR)-16 . . . [and] elements of the Third Marine Division. . . . Personnel of these units agreed that there were definite possibilities for development in these fields. . . . It is considered that the assignment of highly qualified reconnaissance personnel . . . would materially assist in the development of new techniques . . . in the use of pathfinder (guiding) personnel in support of helicopter-borne assaults.[2]

Within the helicopter community, there was growing concern about the ability of mass flights of helicopters to navigate accurately at low altitudes. It is extremely difficult to pick up navigational checkpoints and terrain features when flying at low altitude—a problem that is compounded when helicopters are flying in formation, having to maintain wave separation for preceding waves. In a typical flight of three helicopters, both wingmen are flying on the lead chopper, and thus their ability to navigate by any means other than following their flight leader is nil. When such a group is flying at low altitude or at night, navigation problems are further magnified.[3]

In October 1951, I witnessed a near-tragic incident over Korea with three resupply helicopters en route to the front lines of my battalion. In my rifle company (H/3/5) we were enthused about the possibility of getting hot food up from the rear to our front-line companies in marmite cans (issue hot-cold containers for carrying food in the field). We had been briefed on when and where to expect the flight of three helicopters with our hot chow. At the appointed time, up the valley came the three Sikorsky HRS-1s. They started to overfly our front lines across into Chinese territory.

I thank God that my assigned forward air controller, 1st Lt. Joe Brandon, had supplied me with .38-caliber tracer-ball ammunition, which was issued to pilots in the event of downing. As our marine helicopters flew up toward our rifle company, it became apparent that the three choppers had missed the company's air-panels marking our front lines. They were going to overfly our front lines into Chinese territory. Frantically our forward air controller began trying to turn them around by radio. I immediately pulled out my tracer-loaded .38 Smith and Wesson revolver and fired six rounds out to the front of the three helos. The tracers did the trick: the helicopters turned on a dime and flew back to the south, not to be seen again for two days. My marines were upset about missing out on the hot chow, but I was extremely glad to have been able to turn the helos back to friendly lines.

With marine pilots as well as "ground pounders" recognizing the limited navigational capability of low-flying helos, it was natural that we in Test Unit 1 would be tasked to work the problem. Implicit within the commandant's letter of instruction setting up Test Unit was our "pathfinding charter" within one of the missions: "To evolve operational concepts . . . and techniques to enable utilization of . . . airlift, for the movement to the objective area."[4]

Early on in Test Unit, direct liaison was authorized with our helicopter counterparts at El Toro and Santa Ana in the 1st Marine Air Wing. Foremost among the helicopter pilots was Lt. Col. William "Bill" Mitchell, a medium helicopter squadron commander. Bill entered into every test and evaluation with outstanding and infectious enthusiasm. After we had proven the TF-1 operationally, we began to assemble and train pathfinder teams. Each team was designed to be able to parachute in, set up, and operate one helicopter landing zone, which was to consist of one or more landing points for individual helicopters. Cross-training with the helicopter crews turned into a day and night series of trial-and-error testing. We put our pathfinder personnel into helicopters and had them fly into mountainous zones at night to give them a firsthand sense of how much the pilots would be relying on their guidance from the ground.

Communication was a problem, and 1st Lt. Donald Koelper began to assemble the necessary equipment to do the job. He used MAY radios that would network with the helicopters' radio frequencies. Having to use the MAY to communicate with the helicopters proved to be a problem in several respects, however. For one thing, in cold weather the MAY radio batteries became quite temperamental. In fact, I later learned that on foggy, cold mornings in the hills of Camp Pendleton, some of our communicators within our pathfinder teams were taking their spare MAY batteries into their sleeping bags to keep them warm and thus more reliable when needed for guidance of helicopters.

Another problem was that these MAY radios were bulky and heavy (forty-six pounds with batteries). They had to be padded and jumped in a thirty-inch-long GP (general purpose) bag carried beneath the parachutist's reserve parachute. When one was less than two hundred feet above the ground—a distance that is difficult to judge at night—one would hit the quick release, and the GP bag would drop down to the end of a fifteen-foot nylon line. The GP bag would then hit the ground, quickly followed by the jumper, who was trying not to land on top of the bag.

Don Koelper, who acquired our pathfinding gear from the 1st Marine Air Wing at Santa Ana, was able to get SE-11 signal lights as well as the Justrite, the three-colored high-intensity beam used by pilots in night landings. The Justrite had a simple visual sight on it that was intended to be aimed so that the lower edge of the bottom lens—which was red, indicating a too-low descent—sat just above any obstacle, such as trees, on the helicopter's approach route. The middle lens of the Justrite was green, and the top lens was amber. The Justrite would be set so that the pilot would always see green if he were descending on the proper glide path to landing. If he were too high, he would see an amber light, and he would know to increase his rate of descent so as not to overshoot the LZ. If the pilot saw the red light on his approach, he knew he was too low and had to decrease his descent rate and begin to immediately climb until he was back "in the green."

Because helicopter pilots always want to land into the wind (as with any fixed-wing aircraft), the pathfinder team leader—who was usually a lieutenant or staff NCO—would have his team thoroughly walk the proposed landing zone and, noting the direction of the wind, would pick the correct approach radial for landing into the wind. He would then aim the Justrite just above whatever obstacles were there.

Our pathfinders also developed a series of brightly colored nylon panels for designating sites within the zone. These panels were color-coded for the designation of the zone—for example, red panels would indicate the landing zone that had been specified as Crow. The helicopter pilot would have confidence that if he landed immediately adjacent to one of these panels, he would be on a safe site— one that had no rocks or stumps to endanger the helicopter or its tail rotor. This was one of the reasons the pilots insisted that they make a series of landings with the pathfinders in the helicopters with them—so that the pathfinders would fully understand a pilot's nighttime perspective of the landing zone and surrounding obstacles. Later we acquired some small blinking lights, similar to those used on construction sites to warn of hazards. These proved to be very workable and became an addition that our pilots counted on.

Landing helicopters at night in Camp Pendleton was always an attention-getting activity. Being "grunts," pathfinders were keenly aware of the many trees, the steep terrain, and the "clouds filled with rocks," as the pilots used to say. As a consequence of this awareness, an amazing bond of mutual trust developed between the two groups. Rank had nothing to do with it. Pilots who were majors and lieutenant colonels unquestioningly relied on pathfinders who were corporals and sergeants to get them in safely. Later, one of our 1st Force pathfinders, 1st Lt. Robert C. "Bob" Finn, crossed over into aviation, volunteered for flight training, and went on to become an outstanding helicopter pilot with a distinguished combat career in helicopters in Vietnam.

In preparation for Test Unit 1's reconnaissance and pathfinding support of AGLEX (air-ground landing exercise) 57-E scheduled for early 1957, on the night of 5 September 1956, a pathfinder team parachuted into Camp

Pendleton from a Grumman TF-1 Trader. A carrier was not available, so the team had enplaned at North Island. After their jump, they established visual and radio aids and guided four helicopters to satisfactory landings utilizing procedures and techniques worked out with Marine Air Group 36 (MAG-36). This was the first operational use of marine pathfinders.

The continued participation of pathfinders in Fleet Marine Force landing exercises and Test Unit 1 exercises and field tests brought to light certain deficiencies in our pathfinding concepts, techniques, and equipment. As a result, modifications were made and new methods were tried—many of which gradually evolved to the fully operational level and were instituted. The pilots and staff of MAG-36 at El Toro assisted in all of our pathfinding efforts in this development of usable ground pathfinding procedures in support of helicopters. Their high degree of interest, cooperation, and sound advice contributed immeasurably to the expediting and perfecting of workable pathfinding techniques.

Many of the pathfinder methods of operation were developed solely by our pathfinders themselves, however; techniques for undetected movement from their drop zones to the preselected helicopter landing sites and approach-lane control points, coordination timing for pathfinder drops with atomic or other fire support, and methods for last-minute emplacement of visual and electronic terminal guidance aids were all part of the concept. A system of communications was developed requiring that the pathfinder team be able to communicate with the incoming helicopters, using MAY ground-to-air radios; within the team itself, using organic radios PRC-6 and PRC-10s; and with higher headquarters, using the PRC-10s and later PRC-25s. Contact with the higher headquarters was always a real problem because of the usually extended distances to the carrier. We used RC-292 antennae to give us the greater ranges necessary for this leg of our communications. On occasion we were able to use carrier-based radio-relay aircraft to reach the landing force commander, a method that worked admirably.

The TF-1, which could accommodate a nine-man team, continued to be the airplane of choice for insertion of pathfinders. When the navy TF-1s were not available, the Marine Corps R4D-8 Super Skytrains belonging to Marine Air Repair Squadron 37 (MARS-37) from El Toro were used. We first began to jump this aircraft at Camp Pendleton in August 1956.

Up to this point, we had done the bulk of our advanced parachute training at NPU at El Centro. When we first jumped Camp Pendleton, we chose Chappo Flats, an area just west of the Camp Pendleton airstrip. It worked fine, except in the spring when the Santa Margarita River would begin to overflow its banks. Occasionally the first parachutist, who would be jumping to determine the proper exit point—we called this jumper the "wind dummy"—would have to slip very hard to avoid going into the shallows of the river.

In our military jumping at and around Camp Pendleton, and later at various off-base drop zones in the southern California coastal range, we had to comply with all Federal Aviation Administration (FAA) regulations with respect to the conduct of parachute activities. Central among these requirements was a forty-eight-hour advance notification to the FAA giving the time, the altitude, and the duration of our parachute activities. This information was then used by the appropriate civilian air control agency to issue NOTAMs (notices to airmen). Thus any pilots filing flight plans along the FAA's southern California coast Amber-1 airways route would be advised by the

FAA of the areas and altitudes they must maintain to avoid interfering with our parachute operations.

Prior to our making these jumps at Pendleton, we marines had always jumped on military reservations where another agency or service took care of this type of notification (NPU at El Centro, the Army Airborne School at Fort Benning, and so on). Now that we were "on our own," we picked up this responsibility—which added another dimension with regard to the preparation and the lead-time for all our parachute operations. We could not just arbitrarily say "Let's jump tomorrow" and then lay on an aircraft and jump. We would have to plan meticulously for a jump, determining what type (training or operational) of jump it would be and the type of aircraft we would need for that particular mission. And in addition to giving the FAA forty-eight hours prior notice, we had to specify the window of time we would need to carry out a particular mission.

When Test Unit 1 (and later Force Recon) was participating in a major landing exercise, we would coordinate with the aviation control element to ensure issuance of appropriate NOTAMs regarding our jumps. In addition, a parachute operations schedule (operations order) would be prepared listing all emergency telephone numbers, the location and time of the drops, the altitude, and the names of all personnel jumping, as well as the assignments of personnel who were handling drop-zone control, medical services, and parachute recovery. Copies of these parachute operations schedules were a valuable asset to me, the historical record from which I gleaned many of the details that constitute the descriptions I have given here.

On our first jump with the MARS-37 R4D-8 at Pendleton in September 1956, we were all suited up and awaiting a call from our control party at Ysidora drop zone. We had sent Sgt. Harry R. Lefthand out to the DZ with a helium balloon. He was to release the balloon from the center of the DZ and call me at the Pendleton airstrip to tell me which way the balloon had drifted. This was our method of determining the winds aloft and hence the proper offset and exit point to compensate our exit in order to place all of our jumpers on the DZ (none of the Camp Pendleton DZs were particularly large and were, in fact, minuscule by Fort Benning standards). We were all standing by the phone at the airstrip, each suited up with about sixty pounds of equipment and parachutes, sweating from the load in the Pendleton sun, waiting for Sergeant Lefthand's call.

The phone rang for me. I picked it up. "Major," I heard, "this is Lefthand. The balloon went straight up!" Then he hung up. I had not expected any extraneous conversation from Lefthand, knowing his taciturn manner from my prior experience with him in the field. But I felt his report was a bit too terse. We wanted some clarification. When I called Sergeant Lefthand back, he elaborated—but only a little. A half hour later, when we jumped, the winds apparently had changed. When Master Sergeant Pringle and I went out of the door as wind dummies directly over the center of the DZ, we both landed on a hillside, our canopies hung up in two old apple trees. As a result of this slight miscalculation, Pringle and I had to take a bit of ribbing from all the other jumpers. Neither of us was hurt, and the jumpmaster, seeing our exit and landing, adjusted accordingly. The rest of the planeload made it into the DZ itself.

As its next major exercise, Test Unit 1 participated with the 1st Marine Air-Ground Task Force in AGLEX 57-I, Operation Ski Jump, during December 1956 and January 1957. On 17 January 1957, three marines were killed on their pathfinder jumps in that operation. On 28 March 1957, three months before the disbandment of

Test Unit 1, the pathfinders jumped in HELILEX IV, a helicopter landing exercise conducted by the 3d Battalion, 1st Marines. They executed a night equipment jump into an area adjacent to the proposed helicopter LZ, moved overland, established terminal guidance aids, and successfully guided twenty-four helicopters in the assault. This was one of the last pathfinding operations before the transfer of all our jumpers and the establishment of 1st Force Recon with its multiple missions of submarine entry, parachute entry, reconnaissance, and parachute pathfinding for the Fleet Marine Force.

The Last Marine Corps Use of Pathfinders
Pathfinders were an organization designed to meet a need. Technological development of the GPS eliminated the need for their existence. The "jumping junkmen," as they came to be called (because of all the gear that they carried), passed into history within the context of force recon after their evacuation of over six hundred civilians of the Dominican Republic during the civil strife in that country in 1965. Among the first to land in Operation DomRep in April of that year were 1st Lt. Kenneth T. Taylor and his pathfinders, who set up a helicopter landing zone near Haina Port, west of Santo Domingo. After the evacuation, Taylor and his team were awarded a Meritorious Mast back aboard the LPH *Boxer*, thus ending pathfinding as we knew it in the Marine Corps.[5]

CHAPTER SEVEN
Anatomy of a Parachute Accident

Developmental work in reconnaissance and pathfinding can, as we have seen, be very dangerous on occasion. This is why all marines on jump status receive extra-hazardous-duty pay. Further, it is why only volunteers who are in excellent mental and physical condition are accepted for such duty.

I have mentioned that three marines were killed in January 1957 in the helicopter portion of Operation Ski Jump, the major amphibious landing in which Test Unit 1 participated with the 1st Marine Air-Ground Task Force at Camp Pendleton. Two distinct roles were played by the recon marines in this operation: pre-D-day parachute reconnaissance and, later, pathfinding for the upcoming helicopter assault waves.

At D-30 (thirty days prior to the scheduled landing) of this tactical exercise, the Test Unit 1 platoon—which was divided up into two reconnaissance teams—parachuted at night into two separate drop zones to conduct a recon of the planned helicopter landing zones. After their clandestine evaluation of these landing zones (much as their predecessors had done on Tinian in World War II), they reported back by radio relay to the MAGTF (marine air-ground task force) commander: they now judged one of the prospective helicopter landing zones to be unusable.

As a result of the team's report (as on Tinian thirteen years before after Merwin Silverthorn's comparable report on Yellow Beach), the landing force adjusted its plans to a better zone, which had been found by the parachute recon team. A last-minute recon was done on D-2 to confirm the continued viability of the MAGTF's plan. Current weather and intelligence information on the aggressor troops occupying the area was radioed out using MAY radios to an airborne radio relay. The parachute recon team then left the immediate area, where a simulated tactical nuclear weapon was scheduled to be set off, minutes prior to the planned pathfinder drop and follow-on helicopter landing of a battalion of marines.

The accident occurred in the dawn parachute drop of pathfinders into the easternmost (and highest) part of Camp Pendleton, some ten miles inland from the coastal beaches on a twenty-five-hundred-foot high, rocky and wooded plateau called Case Springs. As the predawn darkness softened, the light had revealed two silver-gray Grumman TF-1s at four thousand feet in an orbiting holding pattern over the Pacific Ocean some twelve miles south and seaward of Oceanside and Encinitas, off the coastal beaches. The planes were designated Vitalis 777 and 772, Vitalis being the call sign for VR-5 detachment, San Diego, while 777 and 772 were the last three digits of the bureau numbers of the aircraft. They were being piloted by our four most experienced navy TF-1 drop pilots: Lt. Cdrs. Oscar Folsom and Donald Oliver were piloting Vitalis 772; Lt. Cdrs. Roy Taylor and Lloyd Hardy were flying Vitalis 777.

Weather was clear with surface visibility of twenty-five miles and a thin overcast at eighteen thousand feet. Takeoff from NAS North Island had been routine at 0700, and by 0730, the two jumpmasters in each plane—Capt. Joe Taylor and 1st Lt. Ken Ball—had begun removing and stowing the after-seats in preparation for the TF-1s' scheduled exits at 0815. Winds on the beach were measuring six knots out of the east. Mild turbulence aloft caused two of the jumpers—Cpl. Ben Simpson in 772 and Staff Sergeant Lee in 777—to feel a bit queasy, but no one actually became airsick. Once the after-doors had been removed in flight, everyone was buoyed by the fresh air whipping into and around the cabin. All hands were eager to jump.

Ken Ball was the jumpmaster in 772. It was to be a single stick of six jumpers including Ball, who would carry the GP bag containing their MAY radio, then Sgt. Joseph Hooker, Cpl. Ben Simpson, PFC Matthew J. O'Neill Jr., Cpl. Frank Kies, and S.Sgt. Charles Vigil. They were scheduled to jump into DZ Yellow at 0815 onto the southern end of the Case Springs plateau. Capt. Joe Taylor was jumpmaster in Vitalis 777 bound for DZ Red, two miles to the north of Yellow. His jump was a bit more complicated because he would have to drop his eight jumpers in three sticks to cover the convoluted shape of their DZ.

The first stick was led by Sgt. Bob Zwiener, who was followed by M.Sgt. Neal King (carrying the GP bag) and Sgt. Conrad Turney, with S.Sgt. Bill Lee at the end. The second stick was a single jumper, Cpl. Gerald LaCoursier. Joe Taylor led the third stick, followed by S.Sgt. Neil Avery with the GP bag and the last man out, Cpl. Stan Mills. Their drop time was also 0815. Jumpers in both aircraft were loaded with full combat equipment, weapons, and ammo, plus their pathfinding gear, beacons, panels, and radios.

As the senior parachutist at Test Unit 1, I had arrived at Case Springs at 0615 and established DZ control on the ground for both Yellow and Red. Since this was a "tactical" jump, we were making the conditions as close as possible to those encountered in combat (with some concessions for parachutists safety). We had smoke grenades to signal the pilots and the jumpmasters in the door: red smoke meant "danger"; green, "Okay to jump." Most important, I carried the anemometer, which we habitually used to determine wind speeds and direction on the DZ. We had an ambulance and corpsmen for both Yellow and Red DZs, as well as a PC (three-quarter-ton utility truck) for each DZ for pickup of the parachutes following the jump. We did not have radio contact with the aircraft, using instead the visual smoke grenades for ground-to-air communication.

The simulated nuclear blast in between the two helicopter landing sites was to go off at 0810, five minutes before the scheduled drop. (This had all been worked out with radiation dissipation schedules that approximated those of an actual tactical nuclear weapon.) A fifty-five-gallon drum of napalm had been buried with explosives on the bottom. When detonated, these nuclear blast simulators threw a fairly large mushroom-shaped cloud and the typical smoke ring that orbits up from an atomic blast site. These atomic simulators were always spectacular and made good shots for the press photographers who were covering the landing. By giving evidence of the winds above the ground surface, these press photos were to play an important role during the investigation of the three deaths.

First Lt. Don Koelper had jumped his parachute-recon team two nights before the landing (D-2) and had radioed wind data via airborne radio relay on the night prior to the drop. His message was "Pathfinder wind in DZ: steady 10 [knots], gusting to 15 or 20" (since Lieutenant Koelper was a "tactical" reconnaissance person and was thus not carrying an anemometer, he had to estimate the wind speed).[1] The pilots and all jump personnel received this information prior to enplaning at North Island at about 0700.

At about 0750, while in orbit, both aircraft intercepted another weather report, essentially the same as their previous briefing: "winds steady, nine to fourteen, with occasional gusts to twenty."[2] The jumpmasters were on headsets, and when they received this information, they passed it on to all of their jumpers.[3] In a tactical jump, there are three people who can—at any time—abort the jump for safety reasons: the DZ control officer, the pilot, and the jumpmaster. They do not have to check with each other, and they each can abort the jump on their own initiative without having to answer to anyone.

We had the utmost confidence in our four pilots—Lieutenant Commanders Folsom, Oliver, Hardy, and Taylor. We had made over six hundred jumps with them. The care with which they carried out their responsibilities had been illustrated two days earlier when they had taken their aircraft out over Case Springs. From their holding orbit position, each pilot had made five to seven practice runs in. They all wanted to be thoroughly familiar with the drop points and important terrain features and with the inbound timing of their runs to their respective DZs. They did not want to make any mistakes.

In addition, two weeks before this rehearsal by the pilots themselves, all of our key parachute officers—including Capt. Joe Taylor, 1st Lt. Don Koelper, 1st Lt. Ken Ball, and me—and a number of our enlisted jumpers had all jumped the DZs that were to be used in the landing. Both S.Sgt. Dionicio Garcia and I also jumped as wind dummies on separate passes on this 3 January rehearsal and had landed in our intended zones. Winds at the time in Case Springs were ten to twelve knots.

During their orbits at their hold point southeast and

seaward of the city of Oceanside, the pilots and pathfinder jumpers observed the plumes of smoke from the stacks on the Encinitas power plant on the coast just below Oceanside. The smoke appeared to trail seaward with the appropriate velocity and direction for the winds on which all hands had been briefed. Both the pilots and the jumpmasters observed these same smoke plumes from their position out of their open doors and passed the information to their jumpmasters.[4] Having previously timed the run-ins, at about 0810 both 772 and 777 descended to thirty-five hundred feet (their intended drop altitude because of the elevation of the DZs), accelerating to two hundred ten knots and began their formation approach to Case Springs.

As DZ control officer on the ground, I had been shuttling back and forth the two miles between DZs Yellow and Red, continually taking anemometer readings. We were concerned because the wind speed was edging up toward our upper limits for a safe jump. We would abort the jumps if the wind steadied at fifteen knots (about eighteen miles per hour). At about 0730 we drove to DZ Red to locate 1st Lt. Don Koelper, who had parachuted in on D-2 with the recon element. I was concerned about the winds on the more open DZ Yellow, so I pulled Don out of the problem and made him control officer for DZ Red. He had jumped into DZ Red on our rehearsal jump, and I had jumped into Yellow.

Don protested. "But I am tactical!" he shouted, meaning he was still supposed to be there as a member of the recon team.

"Lieutenant Koelper," I replied, "I relieve you of your tactical duties. You are now drop zone control for landing zone Red."

Don gave a cheery "Aye, aye" and took over DZ Red as I departed in my jeep with my corpsmen for DZ Yellow. We raced our jeep the two miles back to the western edge of DZ Yellow. Lt. Col. Regan Fuller, our "boss" in all of our parachute developmental work, was a quarter of a mile to the east of us, on the upper (higher) end of DZ Yellow to observe our pathfinders in this major exercise.

Precisely at 0810 the atomic simulator went off, and we watched the characteristic large smoke ring drift skyward. It did not appear to be dissipating but kept its shape as it drifted west toward our position. This reassured me that the winds aloft were reasonably the same as what we were measuring on the deck with the anemometer. At two minutes to exit time for the parachutists (0813), I took one final reading—the wind was steady at nine knots with occasional gusts to fourteen knots, still within our safety limits. I had my driver, PFC Thomas Szymanski, double-check my readings. He confirmed the steady nine, gusting to fourteen.[5]

As both aircraft came in on their final approach, about one minute out, they dropped one-third flaps and slowed to one hundred knots—our usual jump speed on the TF-1. I popped a green smoke grenade to give the jumpmaster in the door a visual on the surface winds and direction as well as an observable communication to the pilots that the DZ was clear for their drop. Don Koelper did the same over on DZ Red. Vitalis 777 broke formation inbound about thirty degrees to port to line up on DZ Red. Vitalis 772 bore on their original course.

Within seconds of each other, the two pathfinder teams—a total of fourteen jumpers, six on Red, eight on Yellow—exited their respective aircraft on schedule (0815) and began their descent. Both of the jumpmasters, Lt. Ken Ball and Capt. Joe Taylor, were aware of the winds, and each of them delayed his first jumper's exit until they were very close to the eastern ends of their respective DZs, reasoning that the winds would carry them back into their intended landing sites. Their exit altitude was thirty-five hundred feet, which was twelve hundred fifty feet above the highest terrain. With four seconds for the T-10 parachutes to fully deploy, this exit would normally give a heavily laden jumper about forty-five to fifty seconds until he hit the deck.

Openings were good for all parachutists. None had any malfunctions (blown panels or line-overs). As they descended toward the rolling grassland interspersed with oak trees in the draws, all noted severe lateral movement from the wind. Later, before the board of investigation appointed to examine the situation surrounding the deaths in the jump, the eleven survivors gave consistent testimony: they all felt that somewhere between seven hundred feet and two hundred feet above the ground, they had run into very strong cross winds that were carrying them out of their intended landing sites.[6]

At about two hundred feet, the jumpers carrying GP bags—Ball, King, and Avery—unhooked them and dropped them to the ends of their lines. I was watching Ken Ball, and it was at this point that I observed his rapid lateral movement. All jumpers in both DZs later reported hard landings and difficulty standing up to collapse their chutes. Those who did make it to an upright position were immediately jerked off their feet by their billowing canopies and dragged along the ground, stunned—and, in several cases, were knocked unconscious.

From the beginning of training, every parachutist is taught the dangers of being dragged across the ground by winds. There are four basic methods of collapsing a parachute and recovering from drag. The first is by rapidly getting up on one's feet and running around in front of the canopy and falling on it. Second, parachutists are taught that if they cannot get on their feet, they can pull in on the lower risers, hand over hand, to bring the lower portion of the canopy in flat on the ground and continue to reduce the sail area of the canopy until it collapses in on itself. The third method of collapsing a canopy is by an "assist" from another jumper or someone else on the DZ: the person either falls into the canopy or uses a vehicle to drive into it. This entangles and collapses the canopy, literally taking the wind out of its "sail" effect.

None of us put much faith in the fourth method. The standard issue T-10 parachute had a "quick release" on the front of the harness. It was located on the jumper's chest, with the reserve parachute over the top of (and in the way of) the quick-release device. To get out of the parachute harness with this quick-release, you first had to unbuckle and drop one side of your reserve parachute, reach in and pull a safety clip (designed to prevent inadvertent release of the harness while you were in the air) out of the quick-release, grasp the metallic face of the quick-release, turn it ninety degrees, and then sharply pound it inward, toward your chest. If this procedure works, it releases three of the four harness straps holding you to the parachute. Although every parachutist practices this process over and over, it is very difficult to do when you are being dragged, bumping along the ground at ten to twelve knots (fifteen miles an hour). In addition, dirt and small rocks along the ground frequently foul the quick-release so that it does not work.

Lieutenant Ball and his five other pathfinders had run into severe winds aloft, which carried them along the ground into the peripheral areas that bordered DZ Yellow. Ball, as jumpmaster, was first out of the door and was thus the first to hit the DZ. He was knocked unconscious on impact and had no chance to collapse his canopy. He was dragged 287 feet (all distances of drag were later measured precisely), with his helmet, GP bag, and other equipment being torn off in the process. His skull was fractured.

The T-10 thirty-four-foot canopy, when fully inflated and dragging the parachutist, has a tendency to "roll," or rotate, as it goes along the ground. As soon as one of the many suspension lines encounters a rock or stump, the canopy rolls over it, and the wind pulls the jumper against it. Thus when one suspension line goes over a rock, the pull of the canopy drags the jumper toward that rock. If the jumper's helmet comes off during the drag, then his or her head is literally pulled into the rock or stump, and usually the person's skull is crushed. In the case of all three of our jumpers who were killed, their helmets were torn off in the drag.

Lieutenant Ball's pathfinder team communicator, Sgt. Joseph Hooker, was the second man out of the door. His drag began where he hit, a point south and east of Ball. While the parachutists were still in their descent, we in the DZ control party on the ground realized that they had run into severe winds aloft—winds that we had been completely unaware of. I was standing next to my DZ control jeep. We always kept the motor running on any vehicle on the DZ so that we could move it if a jumper appeared to be coming toward it, or if someone were hurt, we could instantly go to their aid. From seeing the jumpers' swift lateral movement, we knew they were going to be blown out of the zone.

My driver, Szymanski, was not a parachutist and was not quite aware of what was going on. Yelling at him to jump in the jeep, I tossed the anemometer to him. As he dove into the back, I spun the wheels and accelerated over the rough terrain to the nearest canopy to try to collapse it. Szymanski later testified that he was "hanging on for dear life" and noted the speedometer at thirty to thirty-five miles per hour as I drove the jeep into the canopy. That canopy later proved to be Sgt. Joseph Hooker's. Hooker was dragged 653 feet before our jeep stopped his canopy. I helped him out of his harness. He was cut around the face a bit but was more stunned than anything. I told Szymanski to get Hooker onto a helicopter and evacuate him to the hospital. I noted two canopies just below me in the trees in a small draw, below where we had been able to stop Sergeant Hooker.

The next two jumpers, Cpl. Ben Simpson and PFC Matthew J. O'Neill Jr., were dragged 1,179 and 1,056 feet, respectively. Their skulls had been crushed. Their canopies had then snagged on the limbs of oak trees, and the men were hanging in their harnesses from the trees when I got to them. The first one I reached was O'Neill. He had lost his helmet in the drag. His head was battered and bloody, and his face was blue. I did not know if he were unconscious or dead. Using my K-Bar to cut him out of his harness, I lowered him down to the ground. I felt for a pulse and found none. When someone else came up and began to check him over, I ran to the second jumper, Corporal Simpson. He was also without his helmet, and his head and face were battered and bloody. I felt for a pulse and determined that he was also dead. I cut him out of his harness and brought him to the ground. We carried O'Neill and Simpson to the top of the hill and popped a red smoke grenade to hail a chopper to take their bodies and the dying Lt. Ken Ball to the hospital. Lieutenant Ball had received a depressed skull fracture and died the next day in the Camp Pendleton hospital.

The final two men in the pathfinder stick were S.Sgt. Charles Vigil and Cpl. Frank Kies. Corporal Kies had had a slow opening and had thus dropped below the normal four-second-delay opening altitude before he got a full canopy. This delayed opening probably helped save his life. Both Vigil and Kies had been carried to the next parallel ridge to the south. Vigil was dragged six hundred fifty feet but had been able to regain his footing several times before being dragged down into a small ravine, which collapsed his canopy. Corporal Kies had been dragged six hundred ninety feet down into an adjacent ravine, where his parachute "took a turn to the left in a gully and stopped."[7] Neither Kies nor Vigil was injured in the jump. Interestingly, Vigil had seen the green smoke that I had popped just before he had jumped, and he had begun trying to compensate for the wind on the deck by attempting to slip his canopy back to the east into the wind. On DZ Yellow, two of the six-man pathfinder team, Simpson and O'Neill, were killed outright in the drag. Sergeant Hooker was hospitalized with multiple contusions; Staff Sergeant Vigil and Corporal Kies were examined, released, and returned to duty.

Having loaded Lieutenant Ball, Corporal Simpson, and Private First Class O'Neill into the first available helicopter, and knowing that Sergeant Hooker had already been evacuated, I checked on the status of Vigil and Kies and then popped another red smoke grenade to commandeer another chopper to take me to DZ Red. After this disaster on Yellow, I wanted to know how our pathfinders on Red had made out.

We landed in the commandeered chopper on the upper portion of DZ Red, where we found S.Sgt. Bill Lee and M.Sgt. Neal King. Though they had been blown out of their zone and knocked about on landing, we learned, Capt. Joe Taylor's eight-man pathfinder team on Red had fared relatively well. I saw that Bill Lee had a bloody nose and bloodshot eyes, but I held the chopper, asking the pilot to wait for the possible evacuation of others. Master Sergeant King had received multiple contusions. I found Sgt. Bob Zwiener and saw that he also had been shaken up in his drag. He was obviously in shock; his canopy had collapsed as he had gotten to the edge of a ravine. Bob, like Bill Lee, seemed a bit punchy: he kept telling me that he wanted to go back and get his equipment. I believed he had a minor concussion, and at that point, I decided that both Zwiener and Lee should be evacuated. I put Neal King on the same chopper and told him to watch the other two men. We did not want anyone going out the open door of the chopper en route back to the hospital.

I located Corporal LaCoursier in his assigned zone. He had made a hard but decent PLF and, despite all of the disaster around him, was unaware of his teammates' injuries. He had already put his pathfinder panels in place for the incoming helicopters. I was very proud of his carrying on with his mission. A good marine. I did not see Sgt. Conrad Turney but later found out that he had been knocked unconscious on landing. While Turney had been in the drag, a motor transport driver in the area, a Corporal Johnson, had collapsed his canopy. Since Turney had been knocked out, he was also evacuated to the hospital. He was later diagnosed as having sustained a broken collarbone.

Still looking for Captain Taylor, we found Cpl. Stan Mills, the last man out in the last stick. Mills had landed in some bushes but was immediately dragged into the side of a small hill. He was being taken up the hill when his canopy snagged in a tree and stopped. He was uninjured. Because of the unusual configuration of DZ Red, Joe Taylor had led the last (third) stick out of Vitalis 777. He and S.Sgt. Neil Avery had exited the plane as one and two, and both had ended up going over the edge of the large ravine sloping seaward below Case Springs. Avery carried the GP bag, and although he had made a hard landing, he had been able to get up several times during his drag. His canopy had gone over a small ravine and collapsed of its own accord. Other than being shaken up, he was not injured.

Finally we located Capt. Joe Taylor. He had just made his way up and out of the canyon to the west. Joe recounted a harrowing ride. He had jumped at twelve hundred fifty feet above the terrain, and when he had gotten down to eight hundred feet, said Taylor, "I moved out very rapidly in a southern direction from my intended landing spot, and then I went down in a canyon."[8] Some of the canyons adjacent to the small DZs at Camp Pendleton are very steep-sided. When you are being swept along down inside a canyon before touchdown, your blurred perception of the canyon walls going by you horizontally is an experience that you will never forget.

Later that same day, our Test Unit 1 CO, Col. Edward Rydalch, appointed a board of investigation headed by a lieutenant colonel, with two majors as board members. Being the senior marine parachutist involved with the jump, I was named as a "party"—a person whose conduct is being investigated. An attorney was appointed for the board, and I was given the opportunity to obtain legal counsel. I took it.

During nine full days of hearings, before a court reporter, the board took sworn testimony from thirty-two witnesses and from me as party. The board had as evidence copies of all jump orders, medical records of those killed and injured, and photos and measurements taken of the accident scene and of the bodies. In sum, a very thorough investigation was made of this tragic accident. It was not done to "hang" anyone but to find out as fully as possible what had happened and how it happened and to recommend disciplinary actions, if any were indicated. The board was also tasked to come up with any cogent recommendations on any actions, procedures, tactics, or equipment that should be modified or added to prevent a similar type of accident from occurring in the future. Every person on the jump—every parachutist, hospital corpsman, radio operator, pilot, copilot, and witness—in short, anyone who could shed any light on the facts was called, sworn, and provided testimony for the record. The proceedings were formal and conducted in closed session—that is, in order to preclude the possibility of any tainting or influence of testimony, no witness who had not yet testified was allowed to hear the testimony of others.

When called as a party, I was naturally very concerned—not frightened but worried. Was there some action that I, as senior officer on the jump, or any of our junior officers or NCOs could have taken that might have prevented this accident? I searched my mind for hours and days (and nights), trying to determine what we might have done that could have saved those lives. In the end, in anguish, I concluded there was nothing we could have done. I felt confident that we had planned and rehearsed in every way possible. Our pilots had done a superb job. There is no way we could have predicted or determined those unusual and severe winds aloft, which were so different from my ground anemometer readings.

Reinforcing my conclusion about the winds was the testimony of two chief warrant officers who were called as expert witnesses. CWO Lew Vinson, jumpmaster from NPU at El Centro, opined that it is impossible to predict with any accuracy the winds aloft—a conviction he had gained from his experience in over 655 test parachute jumps. Winds aloft are unpredictable and can place any parachutist at risk. The second witness, CWO L. G. Boyd, was a Marine Corps meteorologist (aerographer and aerologist) who advised that even if a qualified meteorologist had been standing beside me in the drop zone, there would have been no way we could have predicted the unusual winds aloft. After the receipt of all evidence and prior to the conclusion of the findings of the Board, I was dismissed as a party—that is, I was exonerated from any allegation of negligence or wrongdoing.[9]

This was of course, a great relief to us all. Looking back now, from the twenty-eight years since my retirement from the Marine Corps and my "second life" as a trial attorney, law professor, and law school dean, I believe that the process in the investigation of the parachute accident at Case Springs was as thorough and as fair as it could have been under the circumstances. None of us ever liked "green table time"—the colloquial, irreverent term used by marines and sailors to refer to an appearance before a court-martial or a board of inquiry into incidents of death or injury (the term comes, of course, from the green cloth that traditionally covers the table at which one sits when appearing before a court-martial or board of investigation).

On a positive note, however, the board of investigation concluded that we could improve the equipment that we provided our parachutists. CWO Lew Vinson had suggested that a Capewell canopy release be installed on all of our parachutes (static-line or free-fall) to permit the jumper to get out of the harness if caught in the drag. Marine Corps Test Unit 1 endorsed this recommendation in a formal statement to the commandant, dated 1 March 1957. Later the army parachute boards at Fort Benning and Fort Bragg came to the same conclusion. The army had recently had six of its jumpers killed from the drag at Fort Bragg. These two accidents, the army's and ours at Case Springs, with the nine deaths they caused, were the initiating factors that led to servicewide adoption of the requirement to modify all marine and army parachutes to include Capewell releases.

The Case Springs accident also had a salutary effect on all future Test Unit 1 and force recon parachute operations. We now tried to reason our parachute operations through with great precision and clarity. We would constantly plan, schedule and reschedule, change and correct, and always provide constructive criticism to each other to improve our parachuting safety as much as humanly possible. In our discussions eliciting suggestions, rank had no importance. We listened and sought input from all ranks. Each of us was well aware of the dangers inherent in military parachuting, but we were also aware of the necessity of using the parachute to accomplish our mission. We attempted to avoid any mistakes. Of course, we made a few mistakes in the future, but everyone again tried to learn from these errors and to improve our methods and our equipment so that we were doing everything in our power to prevent future injury or loss of life.

While we mourned the loss of our friends, we knew they would want us to carry on with our work and not allow the memory of their deaths to dampen our ardor and enthusiasm for the continued development of parachute pathfinding and parachute reconnaissance for the Marine Corps. And indeed, it never did.

CHAPTER EIGHT
Forming 1st Force Recon

In April and May of 1957, we began to wind down Test Unit 1 with our final reports on those missions tasked by the commandant of the Marine Corps. Test Unit 1 was scheduled to complete its developmental activities and to be disbanded on 30 June. This signaled the completion of Test Unit's assigned mission in the development and testing of new tactics and techniques for the nuclear age. During the final two years, we had conducted intensive research, study, and field tests and developed organizational and operational concepts in parachute reconnaissance and parachute pathfinding.

These developments were validated in two major Fleet Marine Force exercises, AGLEX 57-D and AGLEX 57-I Ski Jump, as well as the smaller HELILEX IV, a battalion-size night helicopter operation. During these operations, after rehearsals and trials of new techniques and equipment, the twenty-plus marines at Test Unit 1 made over seven hundred individual parachute jumps, primarily at El Centro, at Camp Pendleton, and in several off-base operations into the Laguna Mountains between Camp Pendleton and the Salton Sea.

We reported to the commandant that the Marine Corps now had a proven, fully operational method of insertion for deeper preassault and postassault parachute reconnaissance, which would supplement the already existing methods for amphibious reconnaissance of areas close to the landing beaches. The marines now had the capability of carrier-launching recon teams, day or night, for effecting penetration of enemy radar air defenses and postdrop retirement of the carrier aircraft.[1]

Within these capabilities were the methods for prereconnaissance briefings for our parachute pathfinder personnel, the pilots and crews of the support aircraft for pathfinding missions, and the pilots and crews of the helicopters designated to be guided in. Further, we had been able to develop the requirements, techniques, and methods of clandestine reconnaissance of helicopter landing zones and approach routes—much like the methods developed in World War II by Maj. Jim Jones and his Amphibious Reconnaissance Battalion, V Amphibious Corps, for island beaches and beach exits.

Recovery of Pathfinder Teams

Important among the elements we began to improve upon were the existing methods of postreconnaissance evasion and recovery of our recon and pathfinder teams. Ordinarily, pathfinders would be retrieved after the landing zone had been secured, and they would come back on the empty helicopters following their assault landings. The marine air wing had its own control personnel, who had radios and radio jeeps with greater signal strength than ours. In addition, they had their own control gear. After our pathfinders had provided initial terminal guidance for the assault landings, the air wing control people would take over, and our pathfinder missions were virtually completed.

Reconnaissance parachutists are frequently inserted as

early as D-30 (thirty days before a scheduled landing). We wanted to improve on the current means of recovery of the recon teams. If they were close enough to evade overland to the beach, they could be picked up by submarine or seaplane. Evading overland in enemy territory, however, greatly increases the chance of discovery— which was something that had to be avoided at all costs. The potential for disclosure of a forthcoming landing was ever-present. Because of the possibility that a deeply inserted recon team would be unable to evade back to the beach for a sea pickup, we had to train our teams for overland evasion. We continually worked on this problem, particularly after we formed 1st Force Recon.

During our training prior to the forming of 1st Force, one of the most beneficial of our evasion exercises was a September 1956 operation into the Laguna Mountains east of San Diego. This was the first reconnaissance parachute jump by Marine Corps Test Unit 1 personnel into areas away from Camp Pendleton or El Centro. We had found that too much familiarity with the terrain and training areas at Camp Pendleton degraded the recon teams' training and skills. All hands knew the Basilone Road and Case Springs at Camp Pendleton and knew the location of these sites in relation to other terrain features. We desperately needed terrain that was absolutely unfamiliar to the recon teams in order to hone our marines' orienteering and cross-country evasion skills. Fittingly, our best evasion operation was executed in the area between Camp Pendleton and El Centro. This region contained some of the most rugged and remote terrain in Southern California, from the Coastal Range inland to the Salton Sea.

On several flights on a Cessna OE-1 Bird Dog (a liaison-type aircraft, nearly identical to the army's L-19A) coming back from El Centro, we had spotted what appeared to be a suitable DZ. On our aviator's sectional charts it was listed as Cuyamaca Reservoir. There was absolutely no water in the "reservoir," and it turned out to be an ideal large, grassy area suitable as a night drop zone for the landing of parachutists and for a subsequent helicopter landing. We sought out the owner of the property, a local rancher, who told us he had no objection whatsoever to "our marine boys" parachuting into his fields. To cement community relations, we invited both him and his family to the DZ to watch our first night drops into the area.

We wanted to combine a night parachute entry into an unknown DZ and a typical recon mission. We considered having the team evade overland for pickup out of the area, across terrain that no one on the team was familiar with. We planned entry for three successive nights from Grumman TF-1s as well as two nights of jumps from marine F3D Skyknight jets. The platoon was broken down into four-man recon teams. Each team was assigned a typical pre-D-day recon mission (looking for potential helicopter landing zones and sites). Later in Vietnam, this four-man insert team was expanded to a six-man team because of casualties on missions and the higher survival rate of a greater number of recon marines. Our four-man teams felt confident that, following their mission, they could evade overland without detection. We arranged for a Martin P5M Marlin seaplane for dawn pickup of the teams at their ultimate destination, off the western shore of the Salton Sea.

This operation took an incredible amount of detailed planning with civilian agencies. In order to create maximum realism in this evasion exercise, we alerted every sheriff and law enforcement agency in the area to be on the lookout for our marines. We notified the FBI, the U.S. Border Patrol, and the U.S. Immigration and Naturalization Service, as well as all police agencies working in the area. (This was in the days before the Drug Enforcement

Agency was created and began patrolling our southern borders for drug smugglers.)

We readily admitted that we borrowed the idea for this long-range, cross-country evasion exercise from our peers in the Royal Marines, one of whose evaluative evasion exercises was depicted in the 1956 movie *The Cockleshell Heroes*, with José Ferrer and Trevor Howard. Our recon marines' route would take them across sixty miles of California desert from their drop site in the Laguna Mountains due east, through the foothills of the Chocolate Mountains, to pickup on the Salton Sea. With each of our marines carrying a .45-caliber M3A1 "grease gun" (purposely without any ammunition), we were collectively pleased that there were no reported sightings of an "armed group of men" advancing across the territory.

Each recon team's mission was to last three nights, with pickup at dawn on the morning of the fourth day. Since they were crossing the desert, water was going to be a problem. We solved it by having each marine carry two canteens, replenishing at every opportunity from streams or the sporadic desert water-storage sites for cattle. The teams slept where they could, some in ranchers' outbuildings and barns. One local sheriff had gotten a report of barking dogs, but none of the marines were spotted. We checked with this sheriff on the incident and found that the residents, whose ranch was located a few miles from the Mexican border, had presumed the dogs were barking at illegal immigrants.

Lt. Col. Regan Fuller and I rode the seaplane from NAS North Island in San Diego for the first of a series of three dawn pickups in the Salton Sea. It was pleasing for us both when our P5M splashed down for landing in the Salton Sea and two of the first teams inserted (eight marines), who were scheduled for the first day's recovery, were at their rendezvous, on time, treading water with all of their gear. Our two navy pilots could not believe that our marines had come sixty miles across the rugged desert for their recovery in just three nights. Indeed, new boots were in order for some of the teams because of the desert rocks.

After the teams arrived at NAS North Island and had hot showers and a breakfast that everyone wolfed down, our intelligence people spent several hours debriefing them and developing their 35-mm rolls of film. The teams had also carried Polaroid cameras, which gave them immediate awareness as to whether or not their photographs were capturing the assigned helicopter landing zones properly. Their pictures were excellent and were an irreplaceable adjunct to the teams' oral and written debriefings.

Jumpmaster Training

Because of our increasing number of operational jumps, those of us with background from Test Unit 1 and the more sophisticated training from the NPU at El Centro had to quickly build up a cadre of officers and staff NCOs who could assume the duties of jumpmaster. Jumpmasters were responsible for the overall conduct of a jump— from initial briefings at the company, to later briefings with the pilots and DZ control, to the rigging of the aircraft. Each aircraft was slightly different and required some special preparation. Frequently, this preparation was done by personnel from the squadron that we were jumping with.

The jumpmasters and the pilots always had to make the final inspection, working with our parachute riggers to ensure that everything was safe for the jump. On the Grumman TF-1s and Douglas R4D-8s, this required taping the sharp edges of the after side of the exit doors and checking and testing the anchor line cables. (The anchor line cable, which generally runs the length of the plane's cargo compartment, is the woven steel cable that the parachute static lines are attached to—the static lines in turn being attached to the parachute packs on the jumpers' bodies for the purpose of automatically opening each chute after the jumper has exited the plane.)

We found through experience that the marine Douglas R4D-8—which was larger, longer, and faster than its C-47/R4D predecessors—had a slightly different distance to the horizontal stabilizer. This required a four-foot static-line extension for using the T-10 parachutes. Once these extensions were fabricated by our parachute riggers, we had no further problems with the deployment bags hanging up on the forward edge of the horizontal stabilizers. The jumper always was well below the horizontal stabilizer, but before we had the extensions, deployment bags would occasionally hang up on the forward edge. On the F3Ds, the jumpmaster would have to ensure that the small deflection panels on the bottom of the aircraft, on the forward side of the escape chute, were clamped in place (a five-minute job). When this clamping was done, the pilot did not have to activate the small air bottle to extend the deflector below the fuselage.

Those of us who had already qualified as jumpmasters (Capt. Joe Taylor, Capt. Bill Livingston, Lt. Don Koelper, Lt. Dave Ramsey, M.Sgt. Neal King, several of the staff NCOs, and I) would ride on jumps with the prospective jumpmasters to check out their performance. These checkouts would usually start with a straightforward day jump from the TF-1 or R4D-8 and progress to night jumps and later the F3Ds and A3Ds, first in the daytime and later at night. It normally took about five jumps as assistant jumpmaster for a jumper to be fully qualified. One of the more important aspects of this training was the jumpmaster's judgment, on conferring on the headset with the pilots, regarding the desired run in and the altitude. In addition, the jumpmaster would determine the exit point that would best get his stick into the DZ, taking into account the winds both on the ground and aloft. Eventually, all of the staff NCOs on active jump status qualified as jumpmasters.

Occasionally during our jumpmaster checkouts, something humorous would happen. One such incident took place while we were checking out 1st Lt. John Hamber, of the parachute reconnaissance platoon, on one of his first night jumps. John, who had been a Little All-American football player at the University of the Pacific, was not only huge but also in impressive physical condition. During his college football career, John lost most of his center front teeth, and so he had a plate replacing them. Not wanting to lose his dentures when his parachute opened, he would always take his plate out of his mouth just before he exited the aircraft door.

On this particular jump, I was crouched in the after-corner of the TF-1 to observe John's actions. In the dim glow of the red night-vision lights, inbound on the final approach for Ysidora DZ, John pulled out his teeth, stuck them in the webbing of his helmet, and abruptly turned to the young marine who was making his first night jump with us. John's shouted "Stand by!" seemed almost a snarl as he looked back at his number-two man in the stick. The young marine shrank back from this apparition: Hamber's toothless face, bathed in sweat and red light, inches from his own face. He quickly recovered, however, and followed Hamber out the door.

A good-natured practical joke or two definitely made our troops better able to absorb the sometimes grueling tempo of operations. As skipper, I naturally became the brunt of several of these pranks. Once on a day jump into De Luz DZ at Camp Pendleton when we were rotating the jumpers who carried the GP bags, I had agreed to let one of the new jumpmasters put two of us out on a single pass with both of us carrying GPs. The DZ was a bit tricky; it was small and sloped, and there were cattle grazing on it, which were obstacles we had to miss. On a GP bag jump, we would attach the bag to our harness, below our reserves, usually at the last minute before we stepped out the door. I had one bag, and S.Sgt. Neal Avery, our operations chief, had the other. I was to follow him out the door in this two-man stick. Just prior to my exit, Sergeant Zwiener hooked my GP bag to my harness as usual, and I waddled to the door, not really realizing the weight I was carrying.

After exiting, I dropped like a shot. I knew instantly that my bag was filled with something very heavy. The extra weight caused me to quickly pass Avery on the way down. As I went by him, I noticed his GP bag floating out to his front. With my faster-than-normal rate of descent, I quickly tried to pick a landing spot among the grazing steers below. I pulled the quick-releases, and the very heavy GP bag dropped below me, pulling me down even faster. When carrying any GP bag, a parachutist will attempt to avoid landing on top of the bag to prevent injury. I did manage to miss the GP bag, but I hit the ground hard, my parachute boots planted and now sinking into the steer-loosened mud. The GP bag embedded itself about four inches into the same mud.

As Staff Sergeant Avery landed beside me, he was laughing, as were all the DZ control people. The riggers had loaded my GP bag with old truck batteries, which must have made its weight over a hundred pounds. Joining in their laughter, I went over to check Avery's "floating" GP bag, which was filled with wadded paper equivalent in weight to Ping-Pong balls. All hands had a good laugh later that Friday night at Happy Hour.

One of our more ingenious practical jokes was actually a double-edged affair by two staff NCOs, S.Sgts. Dionicio Garcia and Charles Vigil, that took place shortly after the company's arrival at Camp Del Mar. The initial victim was S.Sgt. Lonzo M. Barnett, an NCO who had just used his newly acquired jump pay and his reenlistment bonus to buy himself a new Pontiac from the dealer in Oceanside. He was very proud of his new acquisition and washed and polished it at every opportunity. Garcia and Vigil filled a Coke bottle with transmission fluid, and each day they would pour a small puddle of the fluid onto the ground immediately below the differential of Sergeant Barnett's new car. Barnett would come out, notice the puddle, and drive back to the dealership for repair. This happened several times, and the poor Pontiac dealer was practically torquing the bolts off the differential, trying to stop the transmission from leaking.

Finally someone took pity on Barnett and alerted him. Biding his time, he got his revenge on Staff Sergeant Vigil, who was trying to lose some weight. Barnett stealthily began to cut half an inch off Vigil's dress belt each day. The other NCOs had been alerted, and Vigil was kidded unmercifully about his having gained weight. His waistline was now hanging over his belt.

A Force Reconnaissance Battalion

Initially, Test Unit 1 had concluded that parachute recon and parachute pathfinding capabilities would exist at force level (above the marine division in command hierarchy) in the form of a force recon battalion. This battalion was to have as many force recon companies as there were division-wing MAGTFs in the particular fleet marine force, with one force recon company assigned to each division-wing team MAGTF. This recommendation was generated as a result of the experience of V Amphibious Corps's recon battalion under Maj. Jim Jones in World War II, as well as other positive organizational experiences that Lt. Col. Regan Fuller had at Camp Lejeune in the early 1950s with his formation and command of the 2d Amphibious Reconnaissance Battalion.

Recognizing the budget crunch that existed in the Marine Corps at the time (1957), Test Unit 1 now wisely recommended that the battalion-sized force recon unit be limited to full mobilization plans in the event of war. Accordingly, we at Test Unit 1 came up with our recommendations for the initial establishment and formation of a single force recon company: that the present 1st and 2d Amphib Recon Companies be reorganized and redesignated under one of the two proposed tables of organization (T/O) and tables of equipment (T/E) that Test Unit submitted to the commandant.

As an aside here: In addition to the formation of one force recon company on the West Coast, Colonel Rydalch—by personal letter to Maj. Gen. Edward Snedeker, G-3 of the Marine Corps at the time—recommended that our Test Unit 1 jumpers be split up into three groups. He recommended that I, along with four other experienced test parachutists, be assigned to the Marine Corps Development and Education Command (MCDEC) at Quantico, Virginia, to serve as a test and development team for Marine Corps parachute and reconnaissance matters. Included on the proposed list for Quantico were S.Sgts. Lonzo M. Barnett, Bill Lee, and Levi Woods, and Sgt. Bob Zwiener.

As the second group, Capt. Bill Livingston (who had been awarded the Navy Cross in the Korean War) and "Mr. Pathfinder," 1st Lt. Don Koelper, were to take M.Sgt. Neal King, S.Sgt. Dionicio Garcia, Sgts. James Larson, Gerald Lundemo, and Conrad Turney, Cpls. Weldon Allen and Herschel Amos, and PFC Kenneth Bell into 1st Amphib Recon Company at Camp Pendleton. As the final group, Capt. Joe Taylor was to take S.Sgts. Neil Avery and Charles Vigil, Sgt. Harold Hooker, Cpls. Dennis Dickinson, Gerald L. LaCoursier, Harry R. Lefthand, and Roy Gallihugh to 2d Amphib Recon Company at Camp Lejeune, North Carolina.[2] Had this recommendation been accepted, it would have dissipated the high level of collective experience that these specially trained parachute officers and enlisted men provided and would thus have delayed the orderly development of force recon within the FMF.

Indeed, in hindsight we can all heave a collective sigh of relief that the commandant decided instead to send all the personnel with this extensive parachute recon and pathfinding experience to form 1st Force Recon Company. After the first year of practical experience in the FMF, we were to split off half our jumpers and some of our divers and send them back with Capt. Joe Taylor to form 2d Force Recon at Camp Lejeune.[3] The Marine Corps recon community can thank Col. Donald "Buck" Schmuck, who was the action officer in G-3 HQMC, for his insight in keeping us together for the first year.

Tables of Organization and Equipment

In coming up with the T/O and T/E, Lt. Col. Regan Fuller tasked Capt. Joe Taylor, 1st Lt. Don Koelper, Sgt. Bob Zwiener, and me to sit down and write our collective recommendations in two versions: an ideal, or "optimum," organization and its required equipment and a slightly reduced, or "austere," version of the optimum organization. Our communications personnel helped with their recommendations regarding the gear they needed to do their jobs, as did motor transport and supply. Sergeant Zwiener served as our parachute rigger "expert" and filled out our thoughts on what we needed in the way of parachute gear.

Both Joe Taylor and I handled the amphib recon portions, having had fairly extensive submarine and rubber boat experience.

Our optimal T/O and T/E included a company headquarters and five platoons: a parachute recon platoon, a parachute pathfinder platoon, an amphibious recon platoon, a communications platoon, and a supply and service platoon. This last unit would contain the usual housekeeping functions of supply, mess, and motor transport, with the added parachute loft and maintenance personnel. The company ideally was to be manned with eighteen officers, two hundred twenty-one marines, and eight navy corpsmen. Fourteen of the officers and one hundred fourteen enlisted personnel were to be on jump status.

The recommended austerity T/O and T/E was for a company of fifteen officers and one hundred forty enlisted, broken down much the same as the optimal T/O. The communications platoon was reduced to a communications section; the pathfinder platoon was reduced from four to three pathfinder teams; the parachute reconnaissance platoon was reduced from ten four-man recon teams to five. Similarly, the amphibious reconnaissance platoon was reduced from ten four-man teams to five amphib recon teams. With minimal reductions in other sections, the austerity T/O was submitted. The T/E reductions were primarily in weapons and associated gear for the comparable reduction in personnel.[4]

When the commandant gave final approval to our provisional tables, the austerity T/O and T/E that were adopted were augmented modestly to a total of fourteen officers and 147 marines and two navy corpsmen. The amphib recon platoon and parachute recon platoons were equaled, at five four-man teams each, and the pathfinder platoon remained at three teams of one officer (a lieutenant) and ten enlisted pathfinders each.[5]

Parachutes

With the use of parachutes being an integral element of the soon-to-be-formed company, the new T/O and T/E provided only for field-level parachute maintenance. For major modifications or repair on the six hundred eighty parachutes (one hundred seventy T-10s and one hundred seventy T-7As, with a comparable number of brand-new parachutes in metal mount-out steel deployable containers for operational mount-out), provision was made for field and depot maintenance from the U.S. Air Force at its San Bernardino Air Materiel Area, Norton AFB, California.[6] After 1st Force was actually formed, this procedure for major modification and maintenance support was institutionalized, and we were supplied and maintained by the air force depot.

One of the final missions that Capt. Joe Taylor and I had while still at Test Unit 1 was to provide a Marine Corps evaluation of a proposal for the corps to purchase some unique steerable parachutes and to train marine skydivers. At the outset, we opposed the use of the term "skydiving" because we looked on what is called by that name as an improved method of delayed opening, free-fall parachuting. Basically, with training, free-falling parachutists can change direction, make turns, and increase and decrease their rate of descent by manipulating their arms and legs during the free fall, prior to the chute's deployment. Skydiving competition at the time involved the jumpers' using small-diameter, more steerable types of parachutes and carrying absolutely no equipment (only a main and reserve parachute with an altimeter and stop watch and wearing a helmet). All competitions—held in France and Russia—had been into huge drop zones of several miles across, usually at large airports.

A colorful commercial parachutist, Jacques Istell, came to the Marine Corps and began to proselytize senior marine officers on "skydiving" and the parachutes sold by his company, Parachutes, Inc. (which were actually manufactured by Pioneer Parachute). Jacques was a talented free-fall parachutist who had served as cocaptain of the United States parachute team that had recently taken part in its first world competition in Russia. Having served as a marine reserve officer in Korea, Jacques approached the MCDEC at Quantico, where he demonstrated his skydiving techniques. He was seeking a contract to train marine parachutists in the techniques of skydiving—as I remember it, he was asking for ten thousand dollars to train six of our parachutists. The Development Command suggested that he come out to MCB Camp Pendleton and talk to those of us test parachuting in Test Unit 1.

Jacques Istell began a series of presentations at Camp Pendleton to sway senior marine officers to buy his parachutes and skydiving training. Pioneer Parachute, a respected manufacturer, was to fabricate the parachutes to his specifications. Joe Taylor and I spent hours with Jacques as he used a small articulated mannequin to demonstrate his various skydiving positions. Istell was doing an entirely different type of parachuting from our Marine Corps mission-style, and we were at first a bit skeptical as to its adaptability to our very specific and demanding Marine Corps requirements.

After Captain Taylor and I had the opportunity to discuss at length with Jacques his techniques, we wrote a balanced but modestly skeptical critique of his proposal and his equipment.[7] Istell had never jumped our carrier-capable operational-type aircraft, had never made a night jump, had never jumped out of a jet, and had never jumped into the extremely small DZs that to us were routine. We were not critical of him or his equipment per se, but we were wary of his very light-weight, small-diameter parachutes, which permitted the "skydiving" parachutist to arch his back to help achieve lift and the capability to turn and maneuver. When we questioned Istell as to the size of the DZs needed for his "skydiving," he looked out of the base headquarters window at the sixty-four-hundred-foot airstrip outside and opined that it "was not quite large enough." We had been consistently jumping into DZs in terrain compartments as small as two hundred to three hundred yards square and others two hundred yards by nine hundred yards, with a high degree of accuracy, mostly at night.

In the Marine Corps, we looked on the parachute only as a means of getting us where we needed to be to perform our mission. It had to carry each of us, fully equipped for our ground mission: weapons, rations, ammo, radios, and so on. That gear, plus the forty pounds of our two parachutes, made many of us weigh over three hundred pounds at exit. In his entire jumping career, Istell had never jumped other than "clean" (with absolutely no equipment). We were thus skeptical, but we remained open-minded in our report and recommended further Marine Corps evaluation as to the adaptability of both his techniques and his equipment. Our recommendation was implemented a year later, in May 1958, when Istell was ordered to temporary active duty as a reserve officer after 1st Force had been in existence for almost a year.

Closing Down Test Unit 1

Finally we were ready to leave Test Unit 1 and amalgamate with the 1st Amphibious Reconnaissance Company—out of which, like the phoenix from the ashes, we would form "1st Force Reconnaissance Company, FMF." M.Sgt. Neal King, our senior NCO in the recon platoon, brought the bulk of the enlisted personnel when they transferred into the company in May. The four parachute-qualified officers—Joe Taylor, Bill Livingston, Don Koelper, and I—would have to wait nearly a month while we finished writing all of the wrap-up reports on Project 6H, the commandant's tasking of recon and pathfinding to Test Unit 1.

Our sixty-plus-page final report was a summary of everything we had accomplished in the past two years in the area of parachute reconnaissance and parachute pathfinding. Little had been done at Test Unit I toward the advancement of techniques and upgrades for amphibious reconnaissance. Test Unit was, as I have mentioned, the means to test and evaluate new methods of insertion and extraction. Amphib recon was an area that had already re-ceived a lot of attention for a number of years. The up-grade and furtherance of new methods of entry by water would come later in both 1st and 2d Force.

Capt. Joe Taylor, 1st Lt. Don Koelper, and I spent our last three weeks at Test Unit 1 with S.Sgt. Bill Lee churn-ing out our "final" report. All along we had been writing and sending a series of periodic reports on virtually every new tactic, new technique, and new airplane, as well as every operation and every accident. As a consequence, our final report was not so much writing something new as it was summarizing and putting it in a cogent and un-derstandable form for the commandant—and for the fu-ture division commanders and staffs who would use force recon in the field.[8]

Four days later, on 18 June 1957, we reported to the 1st Marine Division, then to Headquarters Battalion. In taking command of the 1st Amphibious Reconnaissance

Company, I relieved the charismatic Captain Michael Spark, who was later killed in action in Vietnam and was awarded the Navy Cross. Because he and I had known each other since Korea, it was an easy turnover. Mike was a chain smoker, and his fingers were stained from constantly holding a cigarette as it burned down to a stub. He had a habit of gesticulating to emphasize a point, and my fond memory of him is his punctuating the air with a lit cigarette while stressing some idea or another. Mike had one bad habit. When he was distracted by something, he would put his burning cigarette down on a window sill or other wooden surface. As a consequence, our "new" office was replete with cigarette burns on every available flat surface.

Six months earlier, the 1st Amphibious Reconnaissance Company had returned from an operation in the Panama Canal Zone aboard a submarine, the USS *Perch*. While in Panama, Mike had managed to set the military commander of the Panama Canal Zone on edge. He had gone prowling around the canal, the pump houses, and the penstocks that run the locks. After his "recon," he had concluded on his own that our Panama Canal was vulnerable to sabotage. When Mike reported this finding, the military commander did not believe him.

To prove his point, Mike, together with a few of his recon marines, went around during the next several days surreptitiously placing fake (wooden block) "explosive" charges on key pieces of machinery—the various penstocks, pumping stations, and other critical operation features of the locks. He then told the military commander of the Canal Zone what he had done. The commander was extremely displeased, however. Mike did not get any commendation for his clandestine efforts, but the United States did benefit from his expertise: the Canal's security officer was subsequently reassigned. Beyond that, I have every reason to believe that the Panama Canal was indeed made more secure as a result of Mike Spark's initiative.

The amphib recon company under Mike Spark had a number of outstanding recon marines. Several of the NCOs that I remember because of their particular abilities are T.Sgts. Bobby J. Patterson (an innovative and outstanding diver), Robert L. Guttierrez, and Milton E. Runnells (both also outstanding swimmers and divers), and Sgts. Jimmy Howard (later awarded the Medal of Honor in Vietnam) and Johanne Haferkamp.

We were fortunate in getting 1st Lt. Ernie DeFazio, who had been with Capt. Kenny Houghton in 1st Marine Division recon in Korea as a gunnery sergeant. Ernie, having been commissioned after Korea, had just returned from marine barracks duty in Adak, Alaska, and he recommended a young Naval Academy graduate, Lt. Bill McKinstry. Bill was inbound from Adak to the 1st Marine Division, and with a few telephone calls, we were able to have him diverted directly to us at 1st Force. Together, DeFazio, McKinstry, Patterson, Guttierrez, and Runnells would be the bedrock stalwarts of our new amphib recon platoon and would do much in our expansion of submarine techniques. Ernie was so at home in the water that the troops used to nickname him "the Seal."

In late May and early June we brought in the final few jumpers from Test Unit 1 and were joined by several more who had been to jump school but were serving in the 1st Marine Division Recon Company. Included within this group from the division was Gy.Sgt. John R. Massaro, who was the epitome of a recon NCO and was always steady under pressure. John later fittingly became the sergeant major of the Marine Corps.

The New Company Is Born

On 19 June 1957, we received orders from FMFPac via the 1st Marine Division; the colors for 1st Amphibious Recon Company were quietly folded, and the new guidon of 1st Force Recon Company took its place. We were unlike any other unit with the designation "company" that was either organic to or attached to the 1st Marine Division. We were in the Fleet Marine Force, and we were ready to prove ourselves.

Our new unit was blessed with an understanding and progressive-thinking Headquarters Battalion commander in Lt. Col. Lew Treleven. At the rank of major, I was company commander, and Joe Taylor, a captain, was the executive officer. Bill Livingston, also with the rank of captain, was the operations officer, and 1st Lt. Don Koelper was his assistant S-3. Our communications officer was 1st Lt. Phil Arman. Our supply officer, Lt. Anthony D'Arco, was soon relieved by Capt. Bill Block, who proved to be a real hard charger. Bill had been with us for only a short time when he requested orders to jump school. His completion of jump school made him an even more outstanding and effective supply officer. He now knew about parachutes from having used them himself, and he always went the extra mile to ensure that we were fully equipped in all areas. Every one of us thought most highly of Bill Block.

As an organization, 1st Force Recon was much like a small, independent battalion. Our special equipment—parachutes—was markedly different from that of the other units of Headquarters Battalion. All of our recon gear—the inflatable boats and scuba gear—was very expensive and required unique training and facilities and special care in its use and maintenance.

In our first several months in the FMF, we added a

number of officers and enlisted personnel to the company—and the majority of them were not yet parachute or scuba qualified. We used as many marines as possible from the 1st Amphib Recon Company, and we gained a number from the 1st Marine Division's recon company. Yet we still had to expand manyfold.

The first priority in our selection process was the candidate's infantry or communication MOSs (military occupational specialties). Equal to the MOS requirement was physical fitness and endurance. We would task an NCO to take the candidates, officers and enlisted alike, through a very grueling fitness test. Our evaluations were always rank-neutral; no preference of any kind was ever given to anyone. We were looking for the "best of the best," and I do believe our NCOs took an almost perverse delight in conducting the tests.

Pull-ups were the starting point: all candidates had to do this exercise until they dropped off the bars from exhaustion. A great number of wanna-bes were eliminated here. Next were sit-ups—three or four times more than what the marine standard physical fitness test required. After this warm-up, the candidates were given a three- to five-mile run, and they were required to chant all the way. This latter requirement may seem to be overdoing it a bit, but the U.S. Army Airborne had long ago proven that chanting while running is a far more demanding type of exercise than simply running—and creates, therefore, a far more meaningful test of physical stamina. Over time, it also builds up one's wind and endurance. These runs removed another tier of prospective applicants.

Finally, the open-water distance swim of one mile pared the numbers down to a relative few. Then, after their open-water swim, we had those remaining candidates run again. A few would actually lose consciousness from the exhaustion because they were trying too hard.

And these were usually included among the ones we selected. A marine who wanted to be in recon so badly that he would push until he passed out—that was the kind of person we were looking for. We knew we could develop the endurance, fitness, and style of those dedicated few.

In the swimming test, style was not high on our list of criteria. From my experience in teaching combat swimming in World War II with the marines who had made the Tinian reconnaissance, what we needed to be looking for was endurance. The ability to stay afloat for half an hour with full equipment was far more important than technique. After enduring this series of physical evaluations, we then turned to the mental: a panel interview.

The interview was intense but not as severe as the Admiral Rickover style of interviews for nuclear submarine officers that our submarine officers from the *Perch* told us they had been subjected to. We did not use the light shining in the face or the chair with the short front legs to put the interviewee in as uncomfortable a position as possible, a la Rickover. Instead, our interviewees faced a panel of six to eight officers and NCOs who bombarded them with questions on every imaginable subject—both to see how they would react under pressure from peers and seniors and to learn more about them as individuals, their backgrounds and personalities.

Our selection rate for new members of 1st Force was probably comparable to that of other unique organizations. About 8 percent of all enlisted candidates who applied were selected. The numbers were even smaller for the officers, probably on the order of 3 to 5 percent.[9] We did expect, however, to exceed the T/O limits for the number of marines in the unit because we were aware that in ten months, Capt. Joe Taylor would take half of our jumpers to Camp Lejeune and replicate the formation of 2d Force Recon Company.

Housing for us was something of an issue. The amphib recon company had been located inland in the central part of Camp Pendleton, not too far from division headquarters. But there was little room in those barracks for our expansion in numbers and for our diverse requirements such as facilities for parachute packing and so forth. The division G-4 and the base housing assignment officer were able to locate superb facilities for us down on the Camp Pendleton waterfront at Camp Del Mar, near the boat basin and LVT facility. For our amphibious reconnaissance platoon, with both its rubber boat operations and scuba training and exercises, this was a more suitable location than ten miles inland at "mainside." Here, they were able to set up a dive locker and appropriate storage for the inflatable boats.

To support our parachute activity, there was a large warehouse that was quickly adapted into a parachute loft. We requisitioned long mess tables, built taller legs for them, and bolted them together, and Sgt. Bob Zwiener quickly had them waxed to a fare-thee-well. Parachute packing tables are usually about thirty feet long and are almost chest height for ease of packing by the riggers. Zwiener acquired our necessary sewing machines, and we were in the parachute packing and repair business and our riggers began "whipping silk."

Our communications officer, 1st Lt. Phil Arman, soon had a number of antennae up and, for all of our radios, had the field maintenance shop going. Motor transport (MT) was located immediately nearby within Camp Del Mar, and we were able to run our own maintenance shop and set up our own MT dispatch.

These latter elements were extremely important to us because parachute and submarine operations required a great deal of transport. Drop-zone control and ambulances had to be emplaced. Jumpers had to be take to the airfield. After the jumps, parachutes and gear had to be picked up at our variously distanced drop zones. And our amphib recon personnel frequented diverse beach locations and had to be taken to the submarines in San Diego. But finally, now, we had our own barracks and it made an overall pleasant arrangement. In a short time we were off and running.

Within 1st Force Recon we had three major operational elements: parachute reconnaissance, amphibious reconnaissance, and pathfinders. Capt. Ernie DeFazio and 1st Lt. Bill McKinstry had the amphibious reconnaissance platoon in good order. The parachute reconnaissance platoon was commanded initially by 1st Lt. Don Norris, with Lts. Bill Lowery and John Hamber. Our pathfinder platoon was commanded by 1st Lt. David Ramsey, assisted by Lts. Cy Gonzales, Bob Finn, and Harry Barnes (Barnes is currently a circuit court judge in a state in the mid-South).

As I mentioned previously, the majority of the senior marine officers with whom we in 1st Force Recon had to deal were understanding of our mission and our special requirements. This is not to say that these senior officers made life easy for us. On the contrary, we had to prove ourselves every inch of the way. More than once we would hear comments that we were "a bunch of hot shots," or words to that effect. We quickly learned to develop thicker skins—to ignore the detractors and go about our assignments, doing them better than the detractors thought possible.

Our two commanding generals—Maj. Gen. Dave Shoup (who was to be our commanding general on Operation Strongback in the Philippines and was later made commandant of the Marine Corps) and Maj. Gen. Edward Snedeker—were both strongly supportive of force reconnaissance. They understood the interplay and differ-

ence in roles between their organic division reconnaissance battalion and our much smaller but more depth-
capable force reconnaissance company. The G-3 of the
1st Division, Col. Russ Honsowitz, was a strong supporter of force recon and would instantly weigh in against
any negativism.

The fact that we were getting jump pay was an understandable irritant to the infantry grunts, who felt that they
too were in a dangerous profession (which they were).
They could see little reason why we should wear jump
boots and shiny jump wings and get fifty-five dollars per
month as enlisted personnel and one hundred ten dollars
per month as officers. Later, when we went aboard submarine, the pay was higher than jump pay—a situation
that caused some problems early on in the company between the amphibs, who were performing the dangerous
missions of submarine diving with no routine extra pay,
and the parachutists, who were on jump pay.

Our difficulties with regard to pay were resolved
through the strong positive leadership of Lieutenants De-
Fazio and McKinstry and Gy.Sgts. Robert "Guts" Guttierrez, Bobby Joe Patterson, and Milton E. Runnells.
They made every effort to get the amphibs aboard submarine as much as possible to rectify the pay differential. As
a result, our marines were always eager to report aboard
submarine for an operation because of the pay. For any of
them who had been on jump pay, the jump pay would
cease and the submarine pay would replace it for that interval of service—an accounting juggle that gave our dis-
bursing officer fits. We were aware of a few fights
breaking out in the bars of Oceanside and San Diego over
jump pay, jump wings, and jump boots. Fortunately, as
CO, I was never officially made aware of any such con-
frontations; our staff NCOs handled these matters in their
own way.

Camp Del Mar, on the beach of the Pacific Ocean, was some twelve miles from Division Headquarters. However, Del Mar had its own branch post exchange (PX) and a staff of civilian girls who quickly took to our younger jumpers. The PX began to stock Corcoran jump boots (the favorite of most of our parachutists) and jump wings and a few diving watches for our divers. (This was before diving became the popular civilian sport that it is today; most places that sold wrist watches did not carry quality diving watches, which were specially constructed to withstand one hundred to two hundred meters depth-equivalent of atmospheric pressure.)

The Del Mar Officers' Club provided us with certain benefits that Camp Del Mar could not fully equal, however. Some persons of a more puritanical nature may wonder why I would appear to be touting the advantages of a Marine Corps Happy Hour. But I must say, through direct experience, that Friday night Happy Hours at the Officers' Club, with subtle control and leadership, were one of the best ways to sort things out within a unit at the end of a week. There was no formality to them, just a group of marine officers (and, in their clubs, the NCOs and the enlisted) sitting and having a beer or soft drink with a healthy exchange of ideas and humor. They were helpful for all of us as individuals and as a unit. If someone had something on his chest, the Happy Hour was an informal means by which we could get it hashed out with a minimum of fuss and resolve a potential problem. I am reminded here of my earlier days as a lieutenant and then as a captain reading the "Base Plate McGurk" series in the *Marine Corps Gazette* in the 1940s, which provided items and words of wisdom on leadership in resolving common problems in Marine Corps units.[10]

Our Friday night Happy Hours did not last late, for many of us were married and our families did not see us much anyhow. On occasion we would call home, and our wives would get baby-sitters and join us for dinner at the Officers' Club. Our NCOs at the Staff Club and our personnel at the Enlisted Club did basically the same thing. We had feedback on many positive ideas from these sessions that helped us along in the continued development of 1st Force Recon.

One of the most positive side effects of these Happy Hours was the mixing of the diverse elements within the company—the jumpers mixing with the divers and the pathfinders, while the exec, the S-2, the S-3, the communications officer, and the supply officer were all putting in their oars. Barriers were quickly broken down, and we began to work as a team.

CHAPTER NINE
Submarines and Beyond

While parachutes have been a central focus thus far in this story of the formation of 1st Force Recon Company, it is important to recognize that recon marines were working with submarines and rubber boats and using surf swimming for a number of years before the start of World War II.

In his comprehensive treatise, *The Developments of Amphibious Tactics in the U.S. Navy*, Lt. Gen. Holland M. "Howling Mad" Smith describes fleet landing exercises that were carried out from 1934 to 1941. In these operations, destroyers were used as personnel transports for the first time. The positive experience of landing two rifle companies of marines from destroyers during Fleet Landing Exercise 4 in January of 1938 led to the conversion of several of the old World War I four-stacker destroyers to troop transports and to the birth of what were then called high-speed destroyer transports, or APDs. Later APDs were constructed from destroyer escort keels up, replacing the previously converted World War I four-stackers.

The marines first used rubber boats in a pre-H-hour reconnaissance on Culebra, Puerto Rico, in 1938. These craft were incorporated into the navy's landing operations doctrine in Fleet Training Publication 167, which specifies the use of rubber boats for landing recon patrols and agents on an enemy beach.[1] The after-action report of Company F, 5th Marines, of 5 March 1938 describes their recon patrol's landing from the submarine S47 after dark and their subsequent activities.[2]

Test Unit 1 gave the Marine Corps the opportunity to expand beyond these amphibious methods of reconnaissance entry and exit. As soon as we were formed as 1st Force Recon in the Fleet Marine Force, Test Unit's emphasis on parachuting was diminished, and the focus was partially directed back to amphibious reconnaissance. Within the original 1st Amphib Recon Company was a nucleus of well-trained and highly qualified divers. Capt. Mike Spark and the bulk of his officers were reassigned within the 1st Marine Division, having completed their FMF tours.

I did not want to be in command of a unit composed of two diverse types, parachutists and divers, where neither was talking to the other. Of course we all recognized the two different methods of entry, and we appreciated the difference between parachuting and diving as two distinct types of training. As time went along, however, it became apparent that the type of marine you would ask to jump out of a jet airplane at night into an unknown terrain was the same caliber of marine—with the same strength, training, and attitude toward the mission—that you would ask to swim from a submerged submarine at night into unknown waters. Both tasks required volunteers who could fully utilize their highly specialized training when faced with the kind of life-threatening situations that lay in the background of most of our operations.

We found that the screening for our swimmers and divers drew much the same type of marine volunteer as the parachutist screenings did. Later when we began to cross-train the divers as parachutists and, with more diffi-

culty, parachutists as divers, we found that not all parachutists were adaptable to diving, particularly night diving and diving in claustrophobic situations such as in the
very tight escape trunks on the fleet diesel submarines.

When we finally formed 1st Force Recon, we were
given the task of applying the tactics, techniques, and
equipment honed in Test Unit 1 to the practical support of
the Fleet Marine Force in its assigned missions. When I
look back on the history of our corps, I am always
amazed at how foresighted our predecessor leaders were
in their activities. Indeed, Lt. Gen. "Howling Mad" Smith
described the period in the Fleet Marine Force between
1934 and 1941 as "one of application, test and experimentation in the development of amphibious tactics. The
doctrine which had been developed in the preceding fifteen years was put to practical test by the organization for
which it had been promulgated, and its efficacy was
demonstrated."[3]

I look on our missions during the first two years of 1st
Force in much the same context as the tasks given our
pre-World War II marines as General Smith described
them. We in 1st Force Reconnaissance Company were
given a similar but more narrow mission by the commandant: to further prove the Test Unit 1 doctrines, tactics, and equipment in order to refine and better support
the FMF.

It is appropriate within this context to look at the state
of the art of amphibious reconnaissance in June 1957,
when we formed 1st Force. At that moment, there were
five primary modes of insertion of recon teams via the
water: submarines, APDs, seaplanes, inflatable boats, and
swimmers, with and without scuba gear.[4]

The submarine that we usually used was the *Perch*;
later, 2d Force Recon used its East Coast counterpart, the
Sealion (APSS-315). We also would use fleet diesel sub-

marines (SSs) when the transport submarines (APSSs) were not available (the *Bream*, the *Queenfish*, the *Redfish*, the *Ronquil*, and others). The majority of techniques for submarine operations were equally applicable to both classes of submarines.

The *Perch*—311.5 feet in length (a little more than the length of a football field) and displacing approximately 1,545 tons on the surface, with 2,424 tons while submerged—was initially built by the Electric Boat Company in Groton, Connecticut. She was commissioned in 1943. After active war patrols in 1944 and 1945, the *Perch* was decommissioned. She was then recommissioned in 1948, when she was converted from a fleet-type submarine to a troop carrier at Mare Island Naval Shipyard.[5]

Two of the *Perch*'s four diesel engines were removed to provide troop and cargo space for embarked recon marines and UDT. All ten torpedo tubes were removed to create more space in the forward and after torpedo rooms—as they are still called by many marines, despite the fact that the official terminology now substitutes the word "space" for "room" (old, familiar shipboard vocabulary dies hard). These changes permitted space for one hundred ten troops and their equipment, though I must say that if that many people were aboard, the vessel would be overcrowded.

Both the *Perch* and the *Sealion* were equipped with snorkels to permit use of diesel engines while running submerged, as were their fleet diesel boat counterparts. The only armament left aboard the *Perch* and the *Sealion* were two 40-mm and two .50-caliber machine guns (the 5.38-inch deck guns having been removed). The fleet submarines retained their 5.38-inch deck guns as well as the 40-mm and the .50-caliber guns.

For a time, the *Perch*—and later the *Sealion*—had mounted on its afterdeck, aft of the conning tower, a unique thirty-six-foot-long (sixteen feet in diameter) cylindrical tank called a hangar. This tank was designed to carry an LVT with a jeep and a pack howitzer inside of it.[6] Some of the submarine crews and a few marines were initially skeptical about the watertight integrity of the seal on this large cylindrical door on the after-end of the cylinder. If the seal ever cracked, the cylinder could fill with water. The location of the hangar and its seal, above the center of gravity—the marines reasoned in their estimations, calculations, and informal discussions—could cause the *Perch* to have stability problems, either submerged or on surfacing, because of the weight of the sea water in the flooded hangar in relation to the metacentric height of the area.

At the outbreak of the Korean War in July 1950, the *Perch* had immediately been sent to Korea for war patrols with assorted army special activities units, navy UDT, and marine amphibious reconnaissance personnel, as well as the 41st Commando of Great Britain's Royal Marines. En route from Pearl Harbor, the *Perch* made nineteen dives, and in the words of her official "Report of First War Patrol," "the numerous drills and dives had convinced the crew that the *Perch* was not the left-handed, dangerous freak that she was once thought to be. Experience showed that the ship dives faster than a normal submarine (forty seconds), and can take and recover from large [dive] angles easily."[7]

I did not have the opportunity to operate aboard the *Perch* when she had an amphibious tractor aboard. I did, however, operate aboard with UDT during the period from 1952 to 1954, when she had a small, inboard-engine powerboat that was called the *Skimmer*, or the *Suzuki*, meaning "perch" in Japanese. This craft was used, on occasion, to tow our rubber boats. When we had the hangar aboard, we could store all of our rubber boats inflated within it. The *Perch* would surface, and we would open the hangar door and launch the boats. She would then flood down by the stern to where the *Skimmer* could come out on its own trailer on wheeled tracks. It would float free, much like launching a civilian boat from a boat trailer at a boat launch. She would then ballast up; the hangar door would be closed and dogged down and the submarine would submerge. The *Skimmer* would then tow us in closer to the beach, and we would paddle from that drop point.

Later the large hangars were removed from the *Perch* and the *Sealion*, and they resumed the general silhouettes of their World War II diesel boat heritage. Although I cannot pinpoint the specific dates they were removed, Capt. Joe Taylor, who commanded the recon of Iwo Jima done from the *Perch* in June 1955, confirmed that the hangar was still aboard during some of Test Unit 1's operations in 1956. It had been removed, however, by the time the new executive officer, Lt. Paul Keenan, reported aboard in April 1957. According to the *Dictionary of American Naval Fighting Ships*, the *Sealion*'s hangar was removed during overhaul sometime between October 1956 and her deployment to the 6th Fleet in the Mediterranean in August 1957.[8]

Cold Weather Operations

The vast amount of our submarine and rubber boat operations took place in moderate climes. Four months after 1st Force Recon was formed, however, our amphibious reconnaissance marines got the chance to hone their techniques under very cold, wet-weather and subarctic conditions. We were scheduled to operate aboard the *Perch* in RECONEX 58D at Kodiak island (phase 1) and later at Adak island, Alaska (phase 2), during the period from October through November 1957. This operation was designated as a COWLEX (cold-weather landing exercise). First Lts. Ernest L. DeFazio and William E. McKinstry of the amphibious reconnaissance platoon plus eighteen enlisted men—among them, T.Sgts. Robert L. Guttierrez and Milton E. Runnells—made the Kodiak and Adak operation.[9]

In view of the fact that UDT and marine divers were aboard, the commander of SubRon 3 (Submarine Squadron 3) and the commander of SubFlot 1 (Submarine Flotilla 1) deemed it desirable to have a diving medical officer (DMO) accompany the *Perch* on these operations. A young navy doctor, a lieutenant DMO, thus accompanied us. In addition, we had an intelligence officer from the 1st Marine Division's Intelligence Section, Chief Warrant Officer Woods (who had been commissioned as CWO out of Test Unit 1). Gunner Woods was an expert in bringing together the raw intelligence from a recon patrol and putting it into readily usable and understandable information.

Instead of sailing aboard the *Perch* from San Diego, DeFazio, McKinstry, and Woods, along with the eighteen enlisted, flew by marine aircraft from MCAS El Toro to NAS Kodiak to rendezvous with her upon her arrival. Making this flight had two positive advantages for the marines. First, because they were not subject to the enforced inactivity (and the boredom) that is the norm for recon personnel aboard a fleet submarine en route to a target area, they were in better physical and mental condition when they arrived at Kodiak. Second, they were able to spend the seven days before the submarine arrived acclimating to the arctic climate and carrying out a four-day survival training exercise. All major patrol gear (inflatable boats, scuba, individual diving equipment, and so on) had been stowed aboard the *Perch* prior to her departure. The troops brought all of their individual equipment, weapons, cold-weather gear, and so forth with them by air.

Conditioning hikes of up to twelve miles each day reinforced the marines' excellent physical condition. A four-day survival exercise at Isthmus Bay, Kodiak, tested our marines' survival skills and their cold-weather gear—primarily, the wet-weather parka and pants and the arctic overshoes. These waterproof overshoes—worn over the combat boots—proved adequate for the temperatures we encountered at Kodiak. Consideration was given to use of the Thermo, a one-piece molded boot made by a company in Holland, which will protect down to zero Fahrenheit. But the arctic overshoe won out in our marines' opinion as being the better for Kodiak and their scheduled operations. All agreed that the Thermo boot would have been better had the weather been colder (many of us marines had gotten used to these in North Korea during 1950–52).

Marine camouflage utilities with long underwear, cushion-sole socks, and gloves completed the standard outer uniform. Natural shelters were constructed using Sitka spruce and blue spruce. Heavy rains dampened everything that was not in waterproof containers. The wind chill from the forty-two-degree temperature made the exercise miserable but instructive. No ponchos or shelter halves were used, but the inflatable mattresses were deflated during the day and provided protection from the incessant "horizontal" heavy rain that entered the shelters because of the strong winds.

Only one day's ration was issued to each marine for the entire four days—with instructions to supplement from indigenous foods, plants, and animals. Foraging and fishing were done during the daylight hours. Clams and salmon proved tasty and easy to catch. Only one recognizable palatable green was found—a local plant called "scurvy weed," which no one really tried. Wildlife regulations precluded the taking of any of the plentiful waterfowl. Administratively, a Winchester Model 70 rifle with .220 silvertip ammo was taken as a precaution against possible undue interest by Kodiak bears, known to be in the survival area. Technical (Gunnery) Sergeant Guttierrez was the designated "bear shooter." This precaution carried over into the actual rubber boat landing later as well.

Before commencement of the tactical portions of the Kodiak landings, the skipper of the naval air station requested that force recon do some administrative shallow-water dives off the seaplane ramps to search for jettisoned ordnance. By this time, 1st Lieutenant DeFazio had gone forward to coordinate the Adak exercise. First Lt. Bill McKinstry and Gunnery Sergeants Guttierrez and Runnells dove on 10 and 11 October without finding any jettisoned ordnance. For this extremely cold water, all of the divers wore our new black neoprene wet suits underneath a rubber Pirelli dry suit. Wearing two exposure suits required additional weighting to give them the necessary negative buoyancy. Lieutenant McKinstry had a tear in one knee of his dry suit, and the extremely cold water caused his leg to become numb within half an hour, forcing the termination of his dive.

The tactical mission of Force Recon's amphibious reconnaissance was to conduct a beach and inland reconnaissance for the later scheduled landing of 2d Battalion, 7th Marines, BLT. Specific recon missions were assigned for the location of beach exits, and trafficability for tracked vehicles (amphibious tractors and tanks) along the inland Chiniak Road to the BLT objective, Hill 827. D-day for the BLT was 23 October 1957.

At 2100 hours on the evening of D-5, the *Perch* launched a six-man team (one officer, Lieutenant McKinstry, and five enlisted—Runnells, Patterson, Aitken, Oziah, and MacKenzie) from a nine-man inflatable boat (IB), powered by a ten-horsepower outboard motor. The IB with Lieutenant DeFazio at the conn with a "drop party" approached to within seven hundred yards of the beach, where the motor was cut. The team paddled in, and Lieutenant McKinstry's tactical recon party was dropped off on the beach after traversing the light surf. The ten-knot offshore wind and steady rain prevented any noise of the motor from alerting the "aggressors" (the personnel of Naval Station Kodiak).

It was planned for the recon team to return the IB to the submarine because of the lack of adequate harbor sites (hiding spots) on the beach. The *Perch* had recently installed an eductor system for very rapid deflation of the IBs. The device sucked the air out of the boat in short order. The five-man team made it back to the *Perch* and recovered aboard, while the recon team commenced its reconnaissance of the beach and inland. Lieutenant McKinstry's patrol was to be recovered on the night of D-3, having three nights and two days to accomplish their mission. (Two of our nylon IBs had been lost overboard from the submarine during her diving operations in the vicinity of Sitken Sound when hatches on the topside stowage areas became undogged because of high seas. This loss was our only real casualty during the operation.)

In addition to Lieutenant McKinstry's tactical recon exercise, an administratively landed recon party composed of Lieutenant DeFazio and the remaining thirteen enlisted men was landed by rubber boats, again using outboards at the BLT's Pasagahak Beach, at dawn of D-4. They were scheduled to recover aboard the *Perch* by 1600 the same day. Because of increasingly severe winds (twenty knots) and increasingly dangerous sea conditions (six- to eight-foot swells), the chances of a safe recovery of rubber boats at the scheduled 1600 diminished. The skipper of the *Perch*, Lt. Cdr. Frank T. King, decided to cut the patrol's administrative mission short, and the marines were recovered back aboard at 1145 the same day.

Although the persistent rainy weather became the main factor to contend with, McKinstry's tactical patrol had in the meantime accomplished the bulk of its assigned missions. These included fording a number of streams and walking in knee-deep marsh and streams to do the required bridge recons and to scout for tank bypasses along Chiniak Road. (Thermo boots were not usable by the marines patrolling in and out of full-flowing streams, or in the water and marsh adjacent to the bridges along the recon route, because these boots lost their effectiveness if they were fully immersed.) At 2000 on the second night of their mission, McKinstry contacted the *Perch* by radio, requesting an earlier recovery because of the illness of two of the six-man patrol. They were suffering from severe racking coughs and respiratory problems and the increasing symptoms of "immersion foot," a painful condition resembling frostbite that results from exposure to cold and wet. Despite the tactical nature of the mission, the safety of the recon marines was paramount.

The patrol had sent periodic abbreviated-transmission tactical reports by radio to the *Perch*, which was lying three thousand yards off the beach. After these reports were forwarded to the landing force, McKinstry and Lieutenant Commander King conferred by radio and jointly determined that the mission had been accomplished with the patrol's having been able to remain undetected by the aggressors. The medical danger to the patrol from hypothermia and immersion foot was a primary factor in their decision to recover the patrol one night early. Lieutenant Commander King also decided that the twenty-knot wind and the eight-foot swells now sweeping the submarine's decks did not augur for a safe recovery of the six-man patrol. It would have been too dangerous for both his rubber-boat recovery crew and the marines trying to scramble up over the side in the exposed, open waters.

The mission was tactically terminated at this point, and the patrol was administratively returned on the night of D-4 to the *Perch* at her mooring alongside Naval Station Kodiak. Although the remaining officer and three men were cold and wet after twenty hours in wet clothing with the minus zero wind-chill factor—several of the marines were suffering from hypothermia—they considered themselves fully capable of carrying on the mission "until D-day if necessary." As happens in peacetime training operations, however, the safety of the troops was the overriding concern. Four sick marines were hospitalized at Naval Hospital Kodiak during this first portion of the exercise. Although all of the submarine crew had received flu shots, neither the force recon marines aboard the *Perch* nor Ens. John Grobe's UDT team on the USS *Weiss* (APD-135) had been given them. It was after this particular reconnaissance exercise that flu shots became a positive recommendation for all future arctic and subarctic recon and UDT operations.[10]

The *Perch* departed Kodiak at dawn on the morning of 22 October, arriving four days later at dawn off Adak on the morning of 26 October. She made a submerged approach toward Kulak Bay, site of one of her proposed launch sites. Weather conditions were typical of the williwaw—the sudden, violent squall that blows down from the mountains to the sea in near-polar latitudes. The winds were twenty to twenty-five knots, and the swells were ten to fifteen feet. Visibility was less than one mile. As the heavy weather from the north continued, the proposed landing in Kulak Bay was made impossible.

Moving to a more sheltered area near Sand Bay, Adak, the *Perch* remained overnight and then returned to Kulak Bay the next morning. Because the bad weather conditions had still not abated, it was decided that, in the interests of safety of the personnel, the recon of Adak would be done by an administrative landing. To ensure that one of the main purposes of the exercise—testing the military security of the island of Adak—would not be completely lost, the *Perch* sent a message to the commanding officer of NAS Adak, recommending that the exercise continue but that rubber boat landings not be attempted in the severe conditions. The CO concurred, and the *Perch* moored alongside fuel pier 7 in Sweepare Cove at the Adak naval base. From here, initially, two force recon teams and one UDT team were landed surreptitiously at 2000. The combined security-testing and recon of the air station and the fuel farm was to continue until the teams were captured or returned the following night at 2100.

Both Lieutenant DeFazio and Lieutenant McKinstry were disqualified from participation in the Adak operation because they had previously been stationed there. Seven other marines were administratively disqualified from the Adak phase of the RECONEX because of medical problems or other reasons. Thus eight marines (two four-man patrols) and the UDT team (one officer and two enlisted) participated initially. At the request of the commander of NAS Adak, another three-man marine patrol was later administratively landed, bringing total participation to eleven enlisted marines in the operation. The CO of Adak wanted a large team because he was determined to have his security force put to a real test, fully exercised in their ability to deal with infiltrators.

Periodically during the one-day, two-night operation, patrol reports were radioed out from the three marine recon teams. In the course of the exercise, one four-man marine patrol, one UDT team member, and one marine from a second four-man patrol were captured. All others returned undetected. Two prisoners—members of the navy and marine security force for NAS Adak—were taken; one was released, and one was returned with the patrol on its night administrative pickup.

Although the marines gained important experience in their attempt at the clandestine reconnaissance of a heavily patrolled "enemy" naval air station, force recon personnel noted in their postoperation critique that the entire Adak security force, in addition to wives and children, had been alerted that "infiltrators were to be expected" during a three-day period. That information was used to put the entire "augmented" security force on full alert—a circumstance that was considered to be wholly unrealistic. A more true-to-life scenario would have been created if the base commander had been alerted that infiltration was due to occur within a period of twenty to thirty days. This imprecise time for the landing would have forced base security to employ realistic and maintainable security forces rather than remaining on an unrealistic full alert.

Following the conclusion of the tactical portion of the exercise, NAS Adak requested that our force recon divers search for two missing bodies, as well as the code books, from a navy P2V7 bomber that, on 10 October 1957, had landed long in foul weather and gone off the seaward end of the airstrip into about a thirty-foot depth of ocean. Lieutenant McKinstry and his divers—Guttierez and Runnells—again obliged and, using a YTB (large harbor tug) as a tender, were able to recover the classified material.

A tragic aspect of this accident of Patrol Squadron VP-19 was the fact that several of the crew had apparently opened their survival, or "Poopy," suits anticipating their arrival back on the runway. When the P2V shot off the end of the runway into the ocean, the men were unable to resecure their survival suits quickly enough to keep them from filling with water. As a result, their exit from the sunken aircraft was slowed considerably. Two of them made it to shore. Another four were recovered by a YTB—three of them survived, and the fourth died of hypothermia before they could get him ashore. The two men whose bodies our divers were looking for were never recovered, and both were officially listed as "lost at sea."[11]

Force recon personnel returned by air to MCAS El Toro and returned to the company at Camp Del Mar. These subarctic operations proved an eye-opener, and we brought home to all hands the lessons that were learned. Putting the cold-weather experience behind them, the amphib recon platoon and others of us in the company who were dive-qualified and submarine-qualified began expanding our capabilities in those areas.

Wet and Dry Launches

"Dive! Dive!" The Klaxon blares, and the boat takes a downward angle at the bow, the bow planes knifing below the bow wave. The water quickly covers the foredeck as we begin to submerge. The skipper and quartermaster and his bridge watch have just come down into the conning tower and secured the hatch. The conning tower, the high main structure amidships on U.S. Naval Fleet submarines, is the place from which the submarine is conned (steered) while it is traveling on the surface. (On the nuclear submarine boats and the newer attack-class submarines, the comparable high midships structure is referred to as the sail.)

On occasion, to save time and to permit the submarine to submerge more rapidly to avoid radar detection while on the surface, we would do what is called a wet-deck launch—that is, we would launch our rubber boats from the fantail of the submarine as the vessel submerged from beneath them. In training our marines for these wet-deck launches, we would first practice them several times during daylight so that everyone, including the submarine crews, felt comfortable with the procedure. We then would do the night launches, which were always a little bit more dicey.

For a wet-deck launch, we would bring our rubber boats out from the "doghouse" (the free-flooding storage area located at deck level on the after-end of the conning tower), and the submarine deck crew would quickly hook up air hoses to inflate them. We would then immediately load our gear in and position the boats on the fantail. The skipper would first command "Lookouts, below!" and then "Clear the bridge!" All hands, in other words, were to go below, with the skipper being the last, to ensure that no one was left topside as the vessel submerged. As the last person on the bridge dropped down and secured the bridge hatch, the klaxon horn blared and the 31MC (general announcing system) sounded "Dive! Dive!" The submarine would gradually sink away from underneath us as we waited in our rubber boats.

When a submarine is submerging, a series of valves pop open from the top of the diving ballast tanks. When we were doing this kind of submerged launch, it was always a bit of an attention-getting experience to have these water jets shooting compressed air and water four to six feet in the air, all around your rubber boat as the submarine dropped from beneath you. This was accompanied by a series of very sharp "pwoosh" sounds, much like a number of air hoses being simultaneously disconnected from their compressed-air fittings. With this many valves all opening at about the same time, it was always noisy and startling at night to the recon marines who were making their first few submerged launches.

At the stern of the submarine sits an eight-foot steel pole, or stanchion, called the jackstaff. It is used to fly the national colors while the ship is under way on the surface. At night, when the submarine is running with lights on the surface, the light on the jackstaff may serve as the submarine's stern light, and in port it may be used as the stern anchor light. During wet-deck launches, it is extremely important that the jackstaff be unshipped (unhinged and cleated horizontally to the deck, out of the way) because it can be a serious hazard to those on the fantail in the rubber boats.

The reality of this potentially lethal situation was made clear to me in 1952 when I was the OIC of the Amphib Recon School at Coronado, which was conducting a joint submarine operation with UDT. As soon as the submarine (not the *Perch*) began to submerge and move away beneath us, it was also moving forward, as was the erect jackstaff, with some speed. Thus the minute we had water sufficient to float our rubber boats, we had to start paddling away in order to avoid the advancing jackstaff. If the jackstaff had struck the rubber boat, not only would it in all likelihood have injured the coxswain, who sits in the rear, but it would very possibly have dumped all of the recon marines or UDT and their gear into the water—which could prove deadly because of the submarine's propellers, turning just below and to the rear of the jackstaff. The submarine's wake can drag a body into the propellers—an occurrence that is not conducive to retiring on thirty years' service and one of the reasons that marines serving aboard submarines get submarine pay. As a result of this first experience on a wet-deck launch with the jackstaff still up, we began to take precautions from then on, and we also had a few words with the chief of the boat.

Another technique we practiced was the dry-deck

launch, in which the rubber boats were lowered down the side of the submarine, and, using a hand line, we walked down the side of the submarine to get to the boats. The submarine crew would then lower our weapons and gear down to us. This whole process was always a bit tricky because the green algae and slime on the submarine's sloping hull close to the waterline created a very slippery surface. And compounding our loading and unloading problems over the side, the rubber boats were generally heaving up and down with any state of sea swell running.

One other technique that we practiced—one that had been tried in the mid-1950s by both marine recon and navy UDT—was to have the submarine tow the rubber boats by attaching a line around the periscope. Once the boats were launched by whatever method, we would run a towing line between them. The submarine by this time would have submerged and swung around in a circle with only the top several feet of its periscope showing on approach. There was always a small feather wave or periscope wake about a foot high that came off the back of the periscope. One could usually spot the periscope about fifty yards out; at night that distance was somewhat less, but good phosphorescence—the light the marine plants and animals chemically generate—helped.

The sub skipper would guide in on our lead rubber boat, using his periscope to conn the submarine toward us on a collision course. In the submarine, it sometimes became difficult for the diving officer to "keep his bubble" (an even or level trim) on the submarine in the vertical plane at very slow speeds—two to three knots for periscope tows. We always found that we had to paddle about ten or fifteen yards one way or another at the last minute as the periscope approached so that we could grab it as it went by. One of us would position himself in the bow of the rubber boat, with the other marines hanging onto the belt of the "grabber" (to keep the grabber from being sucked out of the rubber boat by the mass of the submerged submarine moving beneath us). The grabber would momentarily throw his arm around the periscope until he could pass our towline around it. After he removed his arm, we would let out the top rope until our rubber boat was about twenty-plus feet behind the periscope.

Every time we placed our arms around the periscope, it was always slick, slippery, and covered with grease—it reminded me of trying to climb a greased pole back in my NROTC midshipman hazing days. We shifted our weight toward the back of the rubber boat and were off on the tow. A rubber boat has a tendency to yaw (swing from side to side) when towed in anything other than a flat calm. Any chop makes it difficult to hang onto and more difficult to steer.

Many of us concluded that the periscope tow was an option that none of us wanted to use operationally unless we were forced to do so by the mission's conditions. When you examine the vulnerability of the submarine running just beneath the surface, with a possible radar target—our rubber boats—on the surface, it just did not make good sense. Making the rendezvous and initial hookup with an arm around the periscope was always dicey at night, even though the phosphorescence in the Pacific Ocean would usually provide us with fair ability to see the approaching submerged submarine's periscope.

Later developments in periscope tows were logical and dissipated many of our prior concerns. Two rubber boats launched would be secured together about seventy-five feet apart. The respective rubber boats would paddle in opposite directions to get a taut line stretched between them. The submarine would then submerge to about keel depth (fifty-nine feet for the fleet diesel boats), circle around, and "split" the two boats on the surface. This would cause the two boats to come together in tow behind the periscope. Ideally the submarine skipper would try to favor his conn toward one boat to keep the two boats from bumping into each other in the tow. The other boat would then be in trail behind the boat that the skipper had conned toward. The submarine would tow the boats to a given point (determined by the depth vis-à-vis the submarine, such as the ten- to twelve-fathom line).

As the alternative to periscope tows, we preferred for the submarine to approach our beach to a distance of about one thousand to two thousand yards, depending on the depth configuration of the undersea topography. Then the sub would surface and make either a wet-deck or a dry-deck launch, and we would paddle in from there, heaving-to just off the surf zone. Swimmers would then go in for a preliminary look from the surf zone, and if it were okay, we would land—all of this always done at night.

Scuba Divers
With the introduction of scuba diving into our recon inventory in the early 1950s, we acquired another means of entry without requiring the submarine to surface. Both the *Perch* and the *Sealion* had retractable sound and sonar heads that made it possible for the submarine to bottom (that is, to rest on the ocean floor) if the offshore bottom topography were suitable. For normal operations, sonar and sound heads project below the bottom steel hull of the submarine, and thus they would have to be retracted for this particular procedure. Most of the other diesel boats did not have the capability of retracting their sound and sonar heads—although some, if not all, were later retrofitted. When we bottomed the submarine, desirably on mud or sand rather than rocks, we usually tried to have

the submarine skipper put us in about sixty feet of water, keel depth. This put about thirty to thirty-five feet of water over the deck when we were resting on the bottom, depending on the sea swell.

In the forward torpedo room of a submarine, there is a trunk designed for escape from the vessel if it were sunk. Both UDT and marine recon began to use the forward escape trunk using scuba gear as a means of lock-in (entry) and lock-out (exit) when the submarines were submerged. The forward escape trunk can best be described as a cylindrical compartment that reminded one of a six-foot-tall tin can. At the top of the escape trunk was a small (twenty-five inches in diameter) round hatch. Never used for scuba exit, this hatch was instead the primary exit for crew being rescued from a submarine in difficulty.

During an actual submarine rescue, a highly visible yellow-colored float would be released with an ascending-descending line that would rise to the surface of the ocean. The rescue float had a light and a telephone for rescuers to make contact with the distressed submarine. Having arrived on the scene, a submarine rescue vessel (called an ASR) would position itself overhead to the submarine and then either send divers down the line from the float to the escape trunk or lower a diving rescue bell. The ASR would attach to the top of the submarine and open the upper hatch to help rescue the crew from the forward or after torpedo room. (Today there are deep submergence rescue vehicles [DSRVs] that are designed for this purpose.)

The overhead (upper surfaces) of the torpedo room was actually the lower deck of the escape trunk (as if at the bottom of our six-foot tin can). The bottom of the escape trunk was a rectangular dogged hatch measuring twenty-one by twenty-seven inches. There was a collapsible metal ladder that led down to the main deck of the torpedo room. When the escape trunk was not in use, this ladder would be folded and stowed away since it was right in the middle of the companionway in the forward torpedo room. Duplicate controls similar to those in the escape trunk were located immediately adjacent to the lower hatch entry. During operations of the escape trunk, these duplicate controls and the 31MC communications gear in the forward torpedo room were manned by the ship's first lieutenant or his designate, either a junior officer or a senior petty officer.

For our swimming lock-outs, in the center of the forward escape trunk at waist-level (when we were standing in the trunk), on the after side (facing toward the stern and toward the forward edge of the conning tower) of the trunk was a large, circular dogged hatch that was thirty inches in diameter. It was large enough for a single swimmer, even wearing scuba gear, to come in and go out of. The escape trunk itself was slightly over six feet in height (seventy-six inches) and was forty-four inches in diameter.

Wearing their face masks, scuba tanks, and small UDT-type inflatable Mae West life jackets (which are small and flat when not inflated) and carrying their swim fins, only two swimmers could operate with relative ease and safety in the forward escape trunk. Four swimmers without scuba would really crowd the trunk.

The recon team would enter the forward escape trunk via the ladder and go through the lower hatch (on the floor of the escape trunk) with their scuba and patrol gear. Once everyone was up and inside the forward escape trunk, we would carefully drop the lower hatch down into place and dog it down. All submarine hatches have dogs, or metal levers, spaced around the edge of the hatch, which are rotated until they lock against the edge of the hatch. They thus secure the hatch to its watertight seals—something that is critically important in a submarine, as is the watertight integrity of its pressure hull.

Once the team has entered the trunk and dogged the lower hatch, all commands are cleared and repeated by use of the 31MC intercom with the diving officer or his designee, who is located in the forward torpedo room. In the event of failure of the 31MC, we had an alternate signal system: tapping, using our K-Bar knives, on the hatch. But in all of the submarine operations that we did, the 31MC never failed.

There are two pressure gauges and corresponding control valves with circular handles in front of the team leader at eye-height. One gauge indicates the outside seawater pressure shown in pounds per square inch (psi), transposed from the water depth. As the U.S. Navy decompression tables demonstrate, for each thirty-three feet of sea-water depth, there is an increase of one atmosphere of pressure (14.7 psi). Thus, if you are at one hundred feet, there are three atmospheres of water-depth pressure plus the normal 14.7 pounds of surface air pressure, or a total of four atmospheres of pressure, in which case the sea-water pressure gauge would read approximately 59 to 60 psi. The left gauge read the water depth in psi; the right gauge showed the air pressure psi in the escape trunk.

A diver would advise the diving officer by 31MC, "I am opening sea flood." He would respond, "Opening sea flood, aye." Our commands from the trunk were always repeated to ensure complete communication and no misunderstanding; we would wait for the repeat of our commands before we actually did what we had said we were going to do. As soon as the diver received an acknowledgment, he would open the sea-flood valve, which permitted sea water to flow into the escape trunk. By use of the air-vent valve, we would rapidly flood the escape trunk with sea water from the open sea outside to just above the top edge of the side exit hatch. We would bleed in compressed air to help unseat the side hatch off its seal so that we could open it. These procedures filled the trunk to just below our chins.

This was one of the main reasons that all divers underwent submarine physicals, part of which was an evaluation by a psychiatrist to ensure that no one was bothered by claustrophobia. We used the term "clausty"—for example, "Corporal Smith was a bit clausty." We did not need anyone to get clausty in the escape trunk on our type of mission.

We would then equalize the two gauges so that they both read the same pressure in psi, by bleeding in just enough air from the air vent. We had to continually equalize our ears as we were filling the trunk (in the same way that one has to do when descending in a dive in open water): when we were in the forward torpedo room and when we first entered the forward escape trunk, our ears would close to the normal atmospheric pressure of 14.7 psi in the torpedo room, and we would have to equalize them to a pressure of approximately 45 psi if the submarine were close to sixty feet at keel depth. The team leader in the trunk was constantly checking his teammates to ensure that everyone was equalizing and staying "ahead of the pressure." We wanted to ensure that no one was having difficulty with his ears. We did not need one of our team members to be incapacitated by a ruptured eardrum.

This equalization in the escape trunk meant that there was no longer any differential of pressure on the side hatch. It had equal sea-water pressure on both sides. Once that was done, it could be undogged and the side hatch swung open to the sea. Actually, we came out of the side hatch about six feet beneath the upper (weather) deck surface of the submarine. There was a small ladder—a set of metal stairs—leading to the upper deck of the submarine. The two-man scuba team closed and dogged the side hatch if there were no operator left in the escape trunk. After this was done, we swam onto the beach on our mission.

Scuba-trained recon marines use pressure-proof wrist compasses for swimming a compass course to the assigned beach. Our wrist compasses and depth gauges were luminescent since it is generally during the hours of darkness that one makes such a swim to an enemy beach. We wore depth gauges because, on scuba, we were inhaling compressed breathing air.[12] We had to be constantly aware of our depth and our diving time at such a depth.

We wore face masks and UDT-type (very large, ribbed) swim fins. And we always wore Mae West life jackets, which are made of a treated gray nylon fabric. Mae Wests have two relief valves that, in the "open" position, permit air to escape when over 2 psi; if the valves are closed, the Mae West works like a standard life jacket. For most missions we also wore skintight, standard black neoprene exposure suits with hoods that were full-flooding—which means that the body heats the water seepage that gets between the suit and the skin, and the tepid water is what keeps you fairly warm, except in very cold water or on long swims. Our first exposure suits in 1st Force Recon were made of neoprene, three-sixteenths of an inch thick. Some of us later bought our own thicker, one-quarter-inch suits, which kept us a bit warmer.

And, of course, we wore diving watches. Generally, it was a Hamilton, which had a pressure-screw cap with a chain for retaining the screw cap to the stem of the watch, a depth gauge, and a tank-pressure gauge so that we would know how much air remained in our bottles. The watches helped us keep up with our "bottom time"—that is, the time we could remain at a particular depth without having to decompress or, in other words, ascend to breathe at a more shallow depth so that our bodies could allow the compressed breathing air to be normally absorbed and dissipated in our bloodstreams. We did not want to exceed the standards recommended in the navy decompression tables.

Recon divers are exposed to all of the same diving diseases as anyone using scuba or hard-hat gear is. These include anoxia, air embolism, decompression sickness (caisson disease, or "the bends"), oxygen toxicity, carbon dioxide toxicity, nitrogen narcosis (called "rapture of the deep"—a state of euphoria, like being drunk underwater), and barotrauma, or "squeeze" (ear, thoracic, or intestinal). There are technical treatises on diving that fully explain these conditions—for example, the U.S. Navy's *Diving Manual* and the material put out by the National Association of Underwater Instructors (NAUI) and by the Professional Association of Diving Instructors (PADI).

Excessive underwater time at depth causes the nitrogen in the diver's compressed air (78 percent of all breathing air is nitrogen) to dissolve into the bloodstream under whatever pressure—that is, at whatever depth—he or she is diving. Through many years of experience, the navy's diving school has determined divers' bottom time. These times and depths are all put down in standard navy decompression tables, which are currently used in most civilian scuba training courses. Failure to follow the navy's tables, or diving at greater depths for a longer time than the blood can absorb, will cause a diver to suffer from a case of "the bends," or caisson disease.

Though all of our marine recon missions were at fairly shallow depths, we always followed the navy decompression tables. We watched the bottom time most closely, however, for our administrative safety divers when we were doing lock-outs and, later, buoyant ascents from a submerged submarine. The divers would be making repetitive descents, and the situation was most critical when the submarine would bottom anywhere from sixty to one hundred feet below the surface.

One of the rarer diving diseases we had to be aware of was oxygen toxicity, or oxygen poisoning. As an alternative to scuba, UDT would on occasion use the oxygen rebreather, which is a self-contained air-purification system that uses pure oxygen. No bubbles show from a closed-circuit rebreather.[13] When divers are doing shallow-water work, it is important that no air bubbles show on the surface. For clandestine swimming, the standard scuba regulator has the disadvantage of creating a telltale stream of bubbles arising to the surface—a trail that an enemy may use to track an underwater swimmer's course and activities. The oxygen rebreathers were specifically designed for, and limited to use in, shallow water. Rebreathers have to stay at a depth of twenty-five feet or less (slightly less than one atmosphere of pressure, which would be thirty-three feet, or two atmospheres absolute pressure).

On the early oxygen rebreathers, if divers using rebreathers strayed below twenty-five feet on their dives, they became susceptible to oxygen toxicity. They would lose consciousness and drown. While I was OIC of the Recon School at Coronado, two UDT officers on a clandestine night training dive in San Diego harbor apparently went below twenty-five feet and died as a result of oxygen toxicity. At the time that 1st Force Recon was conducting these operations, the Marine Corps did not officially use the oxygen rebreathers; however, I was aware that, on an evaluation basis, Gunnery Sergeants

Runnells and Guttierez did "try" the rebreathers and one of UDT's underwater sleds.

Finding the Submarine

One of the continuing problems that amphib recon marines have is getting back aboard the submarine once their mission on the beach is completed. During World War II the submarine would surface, and the deck crew would assist the marines back up the sides of the vessel and quickly deflate and stow the rubber boats. The submarine would then submerge as quickly as possible. The surface was regarded as a place of extreme vulnerability.

For as long as we were doing amphibious reconnaissance we were always looking for better and more reliable ways of getting back to the submarine. In the Amphib Recon School, we had worked closely with the Navy Underwater Sound Laboratory at Point Loma. Their underwater sound engineers bent over backwards trying to help us solve this continuing problem. We tried a number of devices to help the swimmer locate the submarine. One early device was a small directional antenna worn on the head, like a baseball hat without the front bill. It was supposed to pick up the signal from the submarine via the AN/PQC-1 underwater sound telephone system so that the swimmer could home in on the submerged submarine. The head device had the appearance of "Beany," an early 1950s cartoon character on television, and that was the nickname we gave it. The Beany proved too omnidirectional, however, and our swimmers were ingesting too much sea water, and getting sick, while keeping their heads "up" on the surface swims, trying to locate the submerged submarine. We quickly abandoned the Beany.

Next, 1st First Force and later 2d Force Recon began

to experiment with having the submarine track our sound signals—made by our striking two K-Bar knives together or banging the knife on a scuba tank—by use of their organic JT sonar. Sound travels about three times faster in water (3,240 feet per second) than in the air (1,090 feet per second). In our submarine diving, we tried to take advantage of this fact. We found that submarine sonar personnel could, with some limitations, home in on the sounds and that the sub skipper could conn on a collision course for rendezvous and subsequent recovery. We would swim on a known course, for a known (timed) distance from a general point of departure. Thus the submarine, subject to the vagaries of tides and currents, would know our approximate location and the approximate time it needed to be in the rendezvous area.

The ocean is a thermally stratified body of water—that is, the water exists in layers that become increasingly colder with increasing depth. These layers, called thermocline, have fairly distinct borders, and sound-transmission properties will differ from one layer to another. Providing that we were in the same thermal layer of sea water, the JT sonar operators were able to pick up our knife-striking sounds up about two thousand yards. Sonar receivers on the newer type of submarine were capable of receiving this same type signal up to four thousand yards. The submarine remains completely submerged. The periscope need only be used for safety purposes (to avoid collision with fishing boats and the like).

We also used the underwater sound telephone with mixed success. This AN/PQC-1 provided limited two-way communications. We could talk swimmer-to-swimmer and swimmer-to-submerged-submarine. Although 1st Force Recon never officially used the swimmer-to-swimmer mode, I recall that Gunnery Sergeants Runnells and Gut-

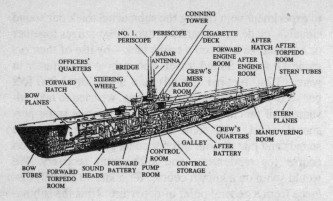

Schematic of interior of *Gato* class, WWII fleet diesel submarine. *Perch* and *Sealion* as well as other fleet boats used by Force Recon were of this general class. Both *Perch* and *Sealion* were modified by removal of both forward and after torpedo tubes. The non-APSS submarines used by recon (e.g., *Bream, Queenfish, Redfish,* and *Ronquil*) still had their torpedo tubes during recon operations.

From Rear Adm. Richard H. O'Kane's book, Wahoo: The Patrols of America's Most Famous WWII Submarine (1987). *Reprinted with permission of Presidio Press, Novato, California.*

tierrez did try it. And 2d Force, when it was formed, did do some testing of the AN/PQC-1s. Better results were obtained by a combination of the JT sonar or other type of tracking sonar with the sonar operator attempting to refine accurate bearings and ranges using the swimmer's transmissions.

A more efficient method that was developed later was an AM infrared image-forming receiver, carried by the recon team in a waterproof plastic container. It was used to home in on the infrared transmitter that was on the masthead of the submerged submarine. While this device worked well in calm seas and at fairly short ranges, it pointed to a need for longer range and more all-weather recovery methods.[14]

Development of new tactics and techniques is always an evolutionary process. The work done in Test Unit 1, and later in 1st and 2d Force Recon, in submarine diving and swimming and in periscope tows provided the Marine Corps, as well as the U.S. Navy's UDTs and SEALs, with a number of new methods for the emplacement of recon personnel. Finally freed from the dictates of the past and from the World War II technology of using rubber boats, United States armed forces collectively could now conduct seaward reconnaissance entry utilizing a broad spectrum of alternative means.

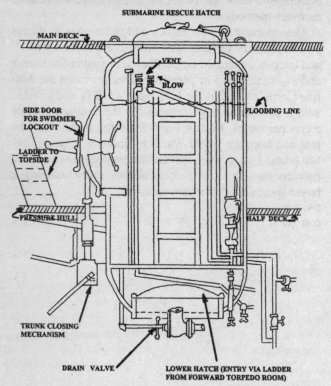

Schematic of escape trunk in forward torpedo room

Adapted by author from "2d ForR SOP [2d Force Standard Operating Procedure] for Submarine Operations."

CHAPTER TEN
Buoyant Ascents

Although the development of scuba gear opened up a new method of reconnaissance entry by underwater swimming, the limitations of scuba diving for marine recon soon became apparent. The standard seventy-two-cubic-foot Marine Corps air bottles contained about 2,250 pounds of compressed breathing air—which amounted to between forty-five minutes and an hour of swimming for the average marine recon diver on a mission. Some of our divers could make their bottles last longer, but the typical four-man team was pragmatically limited to the air supply of the marine recon team member who used the most air.

The usage of air by any diver greatly depends on the type of diving being done, the depth and temperature of the water where the diver is operating, and the experience of the individual diver. If diving on a sunny day without a "mission," almost anyone can make his or her air last longer. But if you add darkness and the task of coming out of a submarine, then the air intake of any diver is measurably increased.

I remember an incident when I was doing a thousand-yard underwater-compass practice swim in lower San Diego Bay at the UDT scuba school. I was swimming with a UDT officer as my diving partner. For safety, we were tethered together by a fifteen-foot quarter-inch line. We took turns doing the "lead" (the swimmer in front and usually several feet lower) swimming. The course was designed to have us surface on the Coronado Strand adjacent to our target, a parked truck. We were swimming in a slightly elevated echelon "formation," much like aircraft flying in formation. I was up and slightly to his right rear.

I had ample opportunity to observe his use of air by the size of his breathing bubbles. They appeared to be about fifteen to eighteen inches across. We were swimming at a depth of only about sixteen feet, in the murky water that is typical of the lower San Diego Bay. Our compass course eventually took us over a fairly large stingray lying, presumably asleep, on the mud bottom. This stingray was probably over four feet across, from wingtip to wingtip, and had a tail about six feet long. At that moment, my partner's air intake doubled. The next series of bubbles arising from his scuba regulator were 200 percent larger than they had been—almost two feet across.

Clearly, when any diver runs into a situation that is either unexpected or causes him or her apprehension, the diver's air intake (and the drain on the air bottle) is increased tremendously. Although my UDT officer swim-partner had pulled out his dive knife and appeared as if he were going to try to impale the stingray on the bottom, I pulled on our buddy line and motioned with a "No!" shaking of my head. We did not need to be skewered by the very sharp and infectious stinger in the creature's tail. We both agreed to bypass the stingray and continue on our compass swim. At that moment, I made a half-turn back toward the surface and observed my own inhalation bubbles arising from my regulator. They were the same size as my UDT partner's. I have witnessed the same phenomenon when diving at night aboard a submarine. Even though divers may be very experienced, when they are in an unusual situation—and we found that night diving compounds the effect of anything unusual—their normal usage of breathing air will increase dramatically.

In addition to the issue of air supply and the telltale stream of bubbles on the surface that is created by the standard scuba breathing regulator, which I have previously discussed, there are other disadvantages to the use of scuba by an amphibious recon patrol. For example, the divers' equipment: they must either hide their scuba gear, air bottles, regulators, Mae Wests, face masks, and swim fins on the enemy beach or sink and secure them in the water with rocks. It is patently unfeasible for divers to bring equipment along with them on the land mission.

A New Idea

Earlier I recounted the development of parachuting as a way other than the rubber boat to make clandestine entries off carriers. Along a similar line of thinking, those of us who were swimmer-qualified and submarine-swimmer-qualified in 1st Force Recon began to examine some alternatives to the use of scuba. We were aware of a technique of using buoyant ascents to escape from sunken submarines. To my knowledge, it was the method developed by the German navy—there were a number of recorded instances where German submariners had swum up from their sunken boats by use of buoyant ascents, some from over four hundred feet. We immediately tried to get all the information that was available on these buoyant ascents.

Buoyant ascents were not being used by the U.S. Navy Submarine Service as one of its escape techniques. Within our navy, the history of submarine escape, like that of amphibious doctrine, was relatively recent, dating back only to the late 1920s. While serving in a submarine safety test unit, Cdr. Charles Momsen developed a submarine escape device that became known as the Momsen lung. Adopted in the early 1930s, the lung was used until the start of the Cold War.[1]

It was not until the early 1960s that navy submariner Lt. Harris E. Steinke developed a replacement for the Momsen lung. The "Steinke hood," as it became known, consists of a Mae West life jacket (not unlike our UDT life jackets) that has a plastic hood with a transparent face piece and a standard compressed breathing-air fitting at the bottom front. Prior to ascent, the jacket is filled with the compressed air, which the hood uses as its air source. The jacket has two release vents that are opened for free ascent with the hood and, once the wearer is on the surface, closed so that the jacket retains its buoyancy and acts as a life vest.[2]

The Momsen lung and the Steinke hood were the state of the art in 1958 when we began to research the idea of using the buoyant ascent. I drove down from Camp Pendleton to San Diego and went aboard the USS *Nereus* (AS-17). She was moored out in the stream in the sunny harbor with her nest of fleet submarines alongside. The *Nereus* was the submarine tender for SubRon 3 and Sub-Flot 1. I sought out the navy doctor who was the DMO for the attached submarines. He was a commander, and I outlined our plans to him, describing how we wanted to test and evaluate the use of buoyant ascents from a submerged submarine for the entry and exit of reconnaissance swimmers.

DMOs are navy physicians who have gone through navy diving school and additional specialized training. Most of them wear the gold submarine dolphins, indicating that in addition to being navy doctors, they have also qualified aboard submarines. They are fully knowledge-

Col. (Lt. Gen.) Lewis B. ("Chesty") Puller USMC, who supported our ideas leading to the formation of 1st Force Recon. *Official U.S. Marine Corps photo*

Night launch (dry-deck) over the side into rubber boats. *Official U.S. Navy photo*

First operational parachute jump from Grunman TF-1 Trader off-carrier aircraft at Test Unit 1, Camp Pendleton, Calif., 1957. Author is jumper in air, followed by Master Sergeant Pringle. *Official U.S. Marine Corps photo*

On 11 April 1958, after receiving permission from CNO, 1st Force Recon jumped four pilots from VR-21 who, after flying 1st Force for so many drops, had "wanted to try it!" TF-1 "Vitalis 772" in background. Left to right: Capt. Don Koelper, Capt. Joseph Z. Taylor, Lt. Paul Rupert USN, Lt. Cdr. George Loggans USN, and author. (Not in photo: Lt. Cdrs. Lloyd Hardin and Don Oliver, who also jumped this date.) *Official U.S. Marine Corps photo*

First off-carrier parachute jump in naval aviation history, 26 July 1956. Cat shot (launched by catapult) from USS Bennington (CVA-20), recovery at Naval Parachute Unit, El Centro, Calif. Left to right: Lt. Col. Regan Fuller, PFC Matthew J. O'Neill Jr. (later killed in parachute accident at Camp Pendleton), author, Capt. Don Koelper (KIA Vietnam, Navy Cross), PFC Kenneth R. Bell, pilot Lt. Cdr. Roy Taylor USN, parachute rigger S.Sgt. Bob Zweiner. *Official Marine Corps photo*

Author on first Marine Corps reconnaissance jet aircraft jump, 8 August 1956. Navy (Douglas) F3D-2 Skyknight aircraft from Naval Parachute Unit, El Centro, Calif. *Official U.S. Navy photo*

First parachute jump from bomb bay of navy (North American) AJ-2 carrier-based prop jet bomber, 3 December 1958. Naval Parachute Unit, El Centro, Calif. Parachutists from left to right: S.Sgt. Bob Zweiner, Sgt. Gary Marte, Capt. Duff Rice, and the author. *Official U.S. Navy photo*

Parachutist exiting navy F3D-2 Skyknight at Naval Parachute Unit, El Centro, Calif., 1957. *Official U.S. Navy photo*

First simultaneous jet parachute jump from four F3Ds. VMF(N)-542 at Naval Parachute Unit, El Centro, Calif. Note deployed "speed brakes" (jumpers 1 and 2) to slow exit from jet at 150 knots (172.5 mph). *Official U.S. Marine Corps photo*

Navy Douglas A3D carrier-based bomber used to drop four-to six-man parachute recon team using bomb bay exit. *Courtesy of Boeing (Douglas) Aircraft archives*

First live-buoyant ascents from U.S. submarine, 25 August 1958, off Coronado Strand, Coronado, Calif. Photo of author positioning just outside forward escape trunk opening in foredeck, preparing to "Blow and Go!" *Official U.S. Navy photo*

Gy.Sgt. Levi W. Woods in first live pickup using Fulton Skyhook extraction system, Quantico, Va., 12 August 1958. Aircraft used was specially configured navy P2V Neptune with yoke forward of propellers to snatch pick-up line held aloft by balloon. *Official U.S. Marine Corps photo courtesy of Robert W. Fulton III, inventor of the Skyhook*

able navy divers in every respect. Our DMOs did not just tap our chests and listen to our hearts and lungs—they had been there, and they knew firsthand the dangers of submarine operations and diving. They were knowledgeable on squeeze, nitrogen narcosis, the bends, air embolisms, oxygen toxicity, and carbon dioxide toxicity. For most training, persons taking submarine physicals are put in a recompression chamber (usually aboard a submarine tender) and run down to an equivalent pressure for one hundred twenty feet. The DMOs knew the navy decompression tables inside-out, and they would be in the pressure chamber with us that first time.

We had absolute confidence in our DMOs. We considered them "one of us," and we followed their advice and recommendations very carefully. I have lived and worked with both navy and marine pilots, and I know that we divers had with our DMOs that same sort of confidence, trust, and camaraderie that one sees between naval aviators and their flight surgeons.[3] Marines always have had the highest respect and esteem for navy doctors, corpsmen, and chaplains who serve with us. Their bravery and dedication to taking care of "their" marines are legendary. All combat-seasoned marines have seen their corpsmen's and navy doctors' dedication and expertise in combat, and our DMOs were simply a follow-on of that same close type of relationship between our navy "docs" (doctors and corpsmen) that we had previously experienced in infantry units in combat.

In 1st Force Recon we reasoned that if we could use buoyant ascents for insertion of amphibious reconnaissance swimmers, we would not have the limitations created by the use of scuba gear for an underwater swim to an enemy beach. If we could exit our submarine using buoyant ascent, we would then make a surface swim— and use netting on our heads to break up the outline of our heads in the water, if that seemed necessary. Moreover, such a team of surface swimmers would not be limited to one spot for both the ingress and the egress. We could swim into one part of a beach and have the flexibility of leaving from another. We would not have the burden of the scuba bottles and regulators. Each diver would carry only swim fins, a face mask, and a Mae West in addition to the gear needed to do the land portion of the reconnaissance—weapons and ammo, camouflage utilities, and other normal land patrol gear.

Our DMO proved to be an enthusiastic supporter of our idea for this new method of entry. Together, he and I sat down and framed a test diving plan for buoyant ascents from the submarine *Perch*. I next approached the new commanding officer and the executive officer of the *Perch*, Lt. Cdr. Elmer "Mac" McKeever and his executive officer, Lt. Paul Keenan. They both agreed that—with proper preliminary training of our marines in buoyant ascent and with approval of SubPac (Submarine Forces, Pacific) and other necessary higher headquarters—the *Perch* could be our test bed. Mac McKeever and Paul Keenan were a "can do" team, and any caution they expressed was always for our safety and for the safety of the boat, the approach that any good submariners would expect.

In May, Mac McKeever and I submitted nearly identical requests to our respective higher commands for permission to run the buoyant ascent tests. The *Perch*'s request went to ComSubPac (the commander of the navy's submarine forces in the Pacific) via his immediate commanders, ComSubFlot 1 and ComSubRon 3. My request, as commanding officer of 1st Force Recon, went to the commanding general of 1st Marine Division, Maj. Gen. Edward Snedeker. In turn, he effected liaison with the respective submarine commands to show his positive

support of our proposed tests to develop this new method
of entry.

Testing Buoyant Ascents

Our plans were to conduct live buoyant ascent tests from
the *Perch*, initially submerged at one hundred feet or less
off the Coronado Strand and later in one of the submarine
operating areas off the California coast. The Coronado
Strand was an ideal location for these tests. It was close to
the outer harbor of San Diego. To reach the site, the *Perch*
would get under way from the nest of subs tied alongside
its tender and then turn south as it passed by the harbor
entrance at NAS North Island, opposite Point Loma. We
would be over our bottoming area in about one hour.

The sea floor off the Coronado Strand was sandy and
flat, ideal for bottoming our submarine. We planned to
start out bottomed off the Strand and initially make ascents from the forward escape trunk. Later we planned on
underway ascents and ultimately underway recoveries
back into the escape trunk out in the open sea, away from
the Coronado Strand.

Our DMO suggested that we have a recompression
chamber handy overhead (that is, moored over the submarine) in the event that one of our marines ran into any
unforeseen problems. We planned to use a submarine rescue vessel, the USS *Chanticleer* (ASR-7), overhead for
this safety feature on our first buoyant ascents.

In my experience, before any military testing process
on any new tactic or technique is begun, all levels of command who have any responsibility in the matter carefully
review what is planned and how the procedure is to be executed. Only then will approval for the test be granted.
And so it was with our planned buoyant ascents. Our
DMO insisted that all personnel involved undergo imme-

diate submarine physicals to ensure our currency and that
we then go through refresher training at the submarine escape tower at Pearl Harbor.

I had selected the two most experienced amphib recon
officers who were my best divers: Capt. Ernie DeFazio
and 1st Lt. Bill McKinstry. I let Ernie and Bill, in turn,
choose their best divers. They selected eight: T.Sgts.
Robert Guttierrez and Milton Runnells, S.Sgt. John Freitas, Sgts. Ken Aitken, Walter Johnson, and Bob Knorring, and Cpls. Jim Broderick and Stanley Hejna.
Initially, we were to join five recon divers from Lt. Col.
Bill Chipp's 1st Marine Division recon battalion. For
whatever reason, however, that arrangement was delayed,
so only Captain DeFazio, Lieutenant McKinstry, our
eight enlisted marines, and I continued to prepare for the
first live buoyant ascents from a United States submarine.

Our DMO set our requalification submarine physicals
for the following week, and all of us came through them
with good reports. With our DMO in the chamber with
us, we did a recompression chamber bounce dive down to
the customary one hundred twenty feet and back up to the
surface with all required decompression stops as set forth
by the navy's *Diving Manual*. This was done to ensure
that none of us had any problems with our ears or had difficulty clearing our eustachian tubes. And as I have mentioned, claustrophobia was one condition that we did not
want to see in any of our swimmers. Few of our enlisted
were aware that the young doctor (a lieutenant junior
grade) who was assisting the DMO on our physicals was
what we affectionately referred to as a "talking doctor"—
that is, a psychiatrist. All of us had been swimming in
tight situations before, and everyone passed this portion
of the sub physical without any problem.

Approval for our proposed tests finally came through
from SubPac and SubFlot 1, with SubRon 3 writing the

appropriate letter of instruction. On 21 June 1958, eleven of us traveled by naval aircraft to Pearl Harbor, where we reported in to the OIC of the submarine escape tower at the naval submarine base for a six-day period of instruction in buoyant ascents.

Learning to "Blow and Go"

We checked into Lockwood Hall (named for Vice Admiral Lockwood, who was commander of the Pacific Submarine Fleet during World War II) and prepared for our initiation into buoyant ascents. We had been thoroughly briefed by our DMO before departure from California, so we pretty much knew what we were going to be doing.

The submarine escape tower was a one-hundred-ten-feet-deep circular metal tank that stood above a building containing air compressors and support equipment. The tower itself, about twenty-five feet in diameter, was filled with sea water. At its bottom was an escape trunk—identical to that in the forward torpedo room of a fleet diesel submarine. The tower was equipped with an overhead hatch, and there was a circular side hatch on the trunk. In addition, there were pressure locks at twenty and fifty feet for safe havens if a diver got into trouble.[4]

Early on Monday morning we reported to the chief petty officer, who was a senior diving instructor at the Pearl Harbor submarine escape tower. We were dressed in our swimsuits, fins, masks, and Mae West life jackets. The chief gave us a quick briefing before we started our instruction. Somehow we sensed that the chief and his staff of instructors had some doubts about marines' swimming ability.

Before we got into the water, during his indoctrination on the features of the tower, the chief—who exuded a "salty" personality—had one of his senior instructors get into the center of the tank. The chief then tossed a standard white-colored navy mess-hall dinner plate (about ten inches in diameter) into the water. Fascinated, we all leaned over the edge of the tank and watched the plate sink, spinning to settle as a white speck at the bottom of the blue-green water. The first-class diver—treading water in the center of the tower and wearing only swim fins and a face mask—hyperventilated for a moment and then, with an easy push over into what we called a "duck dive," swam down to the bottom of the tank and recovered the plate. He then came back up to the surface and handed the plate to us.

We marines had just witnessed a free dive—that is, without any scuba gear or any other form of breathing apparatus—down to one hundred ten feet. Each of us was thoroughly impressed with this demonstration of what we believed to be an unusual swimming ability. We all glanced at each other a bit apprehensively—and privately we wondered if each of us could meet the demands of this highly specialized area of training. We spent the first day familiarizing ourselves with the escape tower, its dangers and its safety features. All the while we were under the watchful tutelage of perhaps the finest group of diving instructors assembled anywhere within the world. Submarine escape tower instructors were all highly qualified navy divers. All were graduates of the navy diving school, then located in Washington, D.C., and the majority of them wore submarine dolphins, indicative of qualification aboard a submarine at sea.

The instructors had a small diving bell and platform, which we used to descend—first to fifteen feet, then to twenty-five feet and, as the day progressed, deeper and deeper. As the bell was lowered, we would be breathing compressed breathing air from inside the bell and equalizing our ears as we descended. When we had reached the selected depth, we orally inflated our Mae Wests, set them in the escape position, and ducked out and under to the outside edge of the diving bell. We held on securely to the outer edge of the diving bell while we exhaled every bit of air in our lungs. Using our fins and masks, we would then ascend to the surface. The positive air pressure in our Mae Wests was pulling us up, the air expanding as we ascended. The two relief valves on our vests, set to open at two pounds of overpressure, permitted the excess and expanding air to be expelled and thus kept the vests from exploding. The whole process was classic "blow and go."

As I have discussed earlier, the pressure of the atmosphere at sea level is 14.7 psi. Sea water, being much denser than air, exerts a pressure of one atmosphere at a depth of thirty-three feet. Every additional thirty-three feet of sea water adds another atmosphere of pressure. Thus, at thirty-three feet, our lungs and every square inch of our bodies are subjected to two atmospheres of pressure, or 29.4 psi. The term "absolute pressure" includes both the atmospheric pressure caused by the depth of water and the one additional atmosphere of pressure that is pressing down on the surface of the water from above.

As a diver descends with a breathing air source (from scuba gear or from compressed breathing air, as in a diving bell), his or her lungs are taking in the exact amount of air needed for normal respiration. The demand regulator on the diver's air source (either from a scuba tank or at a lesser pressure from the diving bell air source) provides exactly the appropriate amount of air pressure for the lungs to remain full and comfortably normal at each particular depth (this is why it is called a "demand regulator"—one's body "demands" enough air to feel comfortable at whatever depth one is diving). Thus at thirty-three feet, the lungs are filled with 29.4 pounds psi of air.

The greatest danger to a diver who is breathing compressed air and making a buoyant ascent is embolism—in which the lungs "blow up" because the air pressure in the lungs exceeds the capacity of the lung tissue to hold the air. A bubble of air immediately exits the lungs into the pulmonary venous system. The air is carried into the heart and then into the arterial systemic circulation, resulting in an air embolus (blockage) into the coronary, cerebral, or other system arteries. The brain is most frequently affected since the diver is usually always in an upright position during an ascent. When the embolus reaches the brain, it generally causes instant death. Deaths have been recorded from air embolisms that have occurred in ascents of as little as seven feet. The bottom line of our marine buoyant ascents, therefore, was training, training, training. Each of us knew that at one hundred ten feet, we would have close to sixty pounds per square inch in our lungs. To avoid an embolism, one must continually and forcefully exhale in ascending. To not exhale in a buoyant ascent could mean instant death.[5]

Pearl Harbor was hot in late June. The submarine escape tower was painted a light yellow-tan to reduce heat retention. We found, however, that the tower's color did not do the job as advertised. The Hawaiian sun's continual beaming on the steel sides had heated the sea water inside the tank to over eighty-five degrees, and it did not cool down at night.

Having been swimming in this hot water since eight in the morning, all of us were feeling tired and were looking forward to securing the training for the day. Our senior instructor lined us up at the top edge of the tower and turned to us and announced, "Let's see how you marines do on 'skinning it in' at the fifty-foot lock." Most of us had been free diving for abalone and langusta, using only face masks and fins, but our dives had always been to about twenty feet or less. None of the eleven of us marine recon divers had ever "skinned-it-in" to fifty feet before.

The chief was looking at me as he said this, since I was the senior marine. Taking my cue from our earlier demonstration by the first-class diving instructor, I put my mask and fins on. I jumped into the top of the tank, quickly checked the location of the fifty-foot lock below, hyperventilated briefly, and pushed over in a duck dive.[6] Before I knew it, I was slipping into the fifty-foot lock. Our large ribbed, black UDT swim fins gave real thrust power when you kicked them with force. Whether it was my adrenaline or my urge to show the chief diving instructor that we could indeed swim, I surfaced inside the lock with plenty of air. In short order came Capt. Ernie DeFazio (we nicknamed him "the Seal"), followed by 1st Lt. Bill McKinstry. One after the other, all eleven of us made it into the fifty-foot lock. We were pleased and knew that we had performed up to what the senior chief had expected of us. He gave us a rather salty and laconic "well done" and secured us for the day.

The next four days went just as quickly, with more lessons on pressure and perfecting our techniques for buoyant ascent. I must mention that there were always safety divers stationed at varying levels throughout the tower, depending on the depth of our ascents. There were, affixed to the inner walls of the escape tower, a number of underwater lights and other sharp devices of various kinds that could easily open a skull if a diver deflected toward one of the tank walls. The safety divers had scuba or regulators on air hoses so that they could move quickly from the side of the tank to protect the diver from going into one of the underwater lights or to intercept a diver who was ascending without exhaling all of his air. If the safety divers saw any diver in a buoyant ascent who did not appear to be exhaling vigorously, they would shoot from the side and, with their arms extended, use their fists to strike the diver in the upper stomach and mid-chest to

force air from his lungs. Fortunately, all of us had learned
our lessons well, and we continuously blew as we ascended. None of my divers needed a fist to the stomach to
remind them to exhale. For me, the easiest way to exhale
continuously was to do an underwater version of a yell as
I ascended. That ensured a continuous large stream of
bubbles coming out of my mouth as I shot to the surface.

Finally, our ultimate "blow and go" was from the bottom of the escape tower, a depth of one hundred ten feet.
We ran the drill the same way we did aboard actual submarines. For safety, in order for the instructors to be able
to evaluate each diver individually, only one of us would
ascend at a time. As the senior, I was first to go. By now,
there was no longer the strong rush of adrenaline that I
had noted during my first buoyant ascents. We had all become more proficient, and although not completely re-
laxed, we were more comfortable than we had been. We
each climbed into the escape trunk with one of the instructors, who was handling the flood and vent valves and
would close the side hatch once we were out. As soon as
the water level flooded to just above the top of the side
hatch, we charged our Mae Wests, opened the side hatch,
ducked out, and held onto the side of the deck coaming.
Under the watchful eyes of a scuba-equipped diving instructor, stationed just outside of the hatch, we would
forcefully exhale all air, let go, and kick once or twice,
and we were shooting to the surface.

I found that I was most comfortable with my hands
clasped together over my head, in front of my face mask,
thumbs locked together and fingers spread out. This made
a mini "diving plane" out of my hands. By flexing at the
wrists, I was able to steer so as to keep going straight up
the center of the tower, pointing toward the round blue
circle of light that was the water's surface at the top of the
tower. There was no natural light in the escape tower.

Once a diver was down about twenty-five feet, his visibility diminished. To counter this darkness, strong underwater lights had been strategically placed around the edges of the tower at varying depths.

As I ascended, my Mae West was expanding rapidly as the pressure reduced and the volume increased. My ascending was so rapid that I shot out at the center of the water's surface in about seven seconds from the time I left the bottom of the tank. The upper part of my body, almost to my knees, rose straight up out of the water. The fact that, at six-foot-three, I exited the water about four feet above the surface shows an acceleration in rate of ascent of approximately ten miles per hour. Most of us were traveling so fast in our ascents that we had a cavitation bubble forming outside and below our face masks, streaming bubbles with our exhaling air. Our two relief valves, anatomically located over our chests, were also producing two steady streams of escaping air bubbles from the Mae Wests.

Each of us made several of these deep buoyant ascents, and the chief instructor passed us off as "fully qualified for open-water buoyant ascents." We flew back to Camp Pendleton the next day.[7]

The First Buoyant Ascents from a U.S. Submarine

Stowing our diving gear aboard the *Perch*, we bedded our enlisted down in the forward torpedo room, while Ernie DeFazio, Bill McKinstry, and I shared the minuscule officer cabins that are pro forma on the fleet (diesel) submarines. It was 24 August 1958, and we finally had all elements pulled together. We had the *Perch* with our DMO aboard, and we had the *Chanticleer* moored in our selected test diving area, just off the Coronado Strand. A safety boat with safety scuba divers was to be stationed at the surfacing point, adjacent to the moored *Chanticleer* for the live tests. Then at last we received final approval from both navy and marine commanders up the line in the chain of command.

On 25 August, skipper Lt. Cdr. Mac McKeever bottomed the *Perch* in a little over fifty-five feet of water on a sand floor, just off the Coronado Strand. This position gave us about twenty-eight to thirty-four feet of depth over the forward escape trunk for the first day and night buoyant ascents. Starting the day ascents at about 1430 hours, the eleven of us finished at 1923, having made twenty-eight buoyant ascents with scuba reentries without any problems. Following dinner, at about 2030 we commenced our first night buoyant ascents; we completed them two hours later, having made fourteen night buoyant ascents and scuba reentries. These first day and night buoyant ascents we made "clean"—that is, without any recon gear.

The next day, under essentially the same conditions and depth, we again made twenty-eight buoyant day ascents, but this time we went heavy with our recon gear. We had full packs—waterproof bags made from surplus gunnel tubes from our rubber boats—containing our uniforms, boots, weapons, ammo, rations, and equipment. Wearing a black exposure suit, fins, mask, and Mae Wests, each of us would ease the pack out of the trunk and then ease himself out, holding onto the pack until he was ready to ascend. Our packs had positive buoyancy—that is, when we released them, they would shoot to the surface. We would then exhale, let go, and ascend to the surface, where we would recover and tie ourselves to our packs. With only a slight amount of leakage, all our gear came through dry.

For scuba reentry, we had a floating nest of several inflated Mae Wests on the surface. These were tied to a descending line secured to the submarine foredeck (near the ladder descending down the six steps into the escape trunk). When ready to reenter the submarine, we would deflate our Mae Wests, swim down the descending line, and lock back into the escape trunk, towing our packs. Because each returning diver took only about thirty seconds to get to the escape trunk, a team was able to "make-do" with one small (thirty-eight-cubic-foot) lock-in scuba bottle, scrounged from our naval aviator friends. The scuba-equipped recovery swimmer, stationed on the surface, would accompany the returning recon swimmer with the lock-in bottle down to the escape trunk, recover the bottle, and take it back to the surface for entry of the next recon swimmer.

After recovery of all of our buoyant ascent swimmers, the *Perch* surfaced, and we were soon under way for the submarine operating areas near the Los Coronados Islands, in Mexican territorial waters, southwest of the Coronado Strand. Arriving in the Sierra-Sierra submarine operating area, Skipper McKeever broached the *Perch* with her keel depth at forty-eight to fifty feet, making water depth over the forward escape trunk about twenty-nine to thirty feet. We began the daylight open-sea buoyant ascents about mid-morning, and by early afternoon, we had completed fourteen ascents with the now-routine scuba reentries. We waited until dark and ran a similar pattern of fourteen night buoyant ascents with scuba reentries.

Our final tests were to be made while the submarine was under way in the open sea. Mac put the *Perch* at dead slow (about two knots submerged speed) with a keel depth of fifty-five feet. Contingent on the ocean swell, this put about thirty feet over the forward escape trunk. We rigged a half-inch nylon rope from the escape trunk aft and upward at about a thirty-degree angle, securing it to the forward edge of the conning tower. This line was to be used later in an attempt at an underway recovery when

I was going to try to reenter the submarine. For our underway ascents, Mac put the *Perch* in a right full-rudder turn to starboard. The inside starboard screw was stopped with the port screw, making turns for one-third ahead. This made her submerged speed about one and a half to two knots. The stopped inboard screw was for safety: if any of the buoyant ascent swimmers had any difficulties, the stern of the submarine would pass under them with no turns on that propeller.

The speed of our buoyant ascents picked up as we gained experience, and in one hour we had completed all fourteen daytime buoyant ascents from the submerged submarine while under way. Each swimmer made his ascent to the starboard side of the turn. No problems were encountered.

We had a recovery rubber boat on the surface for the swimmers, and then the submarine surfaced and recovered all of the divers from the rubber boat except me. I wanted to try an underway recovery using the small lock-in bottle rig. Mac took the submarine down and circled around with just her periscope showing its small feather wake. To give him as large a target as possible for his view of me through the periscope, I held my hand as high in the air over my head as I could. This was the first time anyone had ever tried reentry into a moving submerged submarine. I was going to have to "guesstimate" when to start my dive to intersect with the recovery line running down from the conning tower.

As the submarine got closer, I dove, using the small scuba bottle, and more or less held myself on an intersecting collision-course with the bow of the *Perch*. Although I was later to do this same maneuver many more times from other fleet submarines (the *Queenfish*, *Ronquil*, and *Bream*), this very first time was a real adrenaline rush. In Hollywood's submarine films, you see the submarine underwater, approaching submerged with its dive planes out and getting bigger as it nears the camera. My experience was like déjà vu from the movie scenes I had seen: I almost felt as if I were the cameraman, and to have this football-field-sized submarine coming directly toward me was awesome.

I swam an angled intersection course down to the deck to catch the previously rigged line, a few feet above the deck. As soon as I grabbed the line, I turned my head to the rear of the submarine to keep my face mask from being ripped off by the speed of the water and my own movements. I have seen a diver lose a face mask even at two knots. And while it is not a life-threatening situation if a trained diver loses a mask underwater, there are undesirable consequences: one's vision is reduced, and one is forced to breathe only from the regulator mouthpiece and not through one's nose.

The *Perch* had an operator in the escape trunk waiting for me. As soon as I swam in, we closed the side hatch and blew the escape trunk down. I reentered the *Perch* for a pleasant lunch and the run back to San Diego on the surface. The DMO had a small bottle of medicinal brandy for each of us "for the cold" of the water. This was one of the very few times that we could legally have a drink aboard a submarine—the consumption of alcohol aboard U.S. Navy vessels was prohibited in an order issued by Secretary of the Navy Josephus Daniels on 1 June 1914. However, our DMO had himself experienced water-induced hypothermia, and his prescription for the condition was brandy.

At the conclusion of these six types of tests, which were conducted in accordance with a letter of instruction from SubRon 3, Mac McKeever and I sat down in his tiny cabin in the *Perch* and drafted a report entitled "Employment of Buoyant Ascent Techniques by Amphibious Reconnaissance Personnel," which we sent to SubRon 3, to my commanding general at 1st Marine Division, to Com-SubPac, and to the commandant of the Marine Corps. We put one cautionary recommendation in our report concerning underway recovery: "No difficulty was experienced in rendezvous and SCUBA re-entry, however tactical employment of such underway SCUBA re-entry for a full four-man reconnaissance team is considered technically infeasible."[8] Later, as we gained more experience in buoyant ascents, we were able to change this recommendation and to develop very usable recovery methods that permitted underway recovery without scuba.

For me personally, one of the most important things that happened during this later phase of our work occurred when we were conducting an underway recovery at night off the California coast. As I swam at the water's surface, the *Perch* approached. Although the night was dark, the ocean was extremely phosphorescent this particular time, and I could discern every feature of the submarine's hull. As I knifed down to grab the recovery line to the forward escape trunk, her diving planes appeared enormous, completely dwarfing me. When I think of all our submarines and night operations, that vision of the *Perch* almost surrealistically outlined, inbound toward me, is the one that comes to my mind first.

Within several months of our first buoyant ascents, both 1st Force and 2d Force Recon had further developed methods for underway recovery where we would "skin it in" and not have to rely on the lock-in bottles. One caution that we learned to exercise on free dive entries was that if a swimmer missed in our swimming down to catch the recovery line strung from the foredeck, near the escape trunk up to the conning tower, he had to keep swimming completely across the path of the inbound submarine in order to get out of the way of the oncoming tower and periscopes. The situation was quite similar to what happened when we were doing wet-deck launches and had the jackstaff coming toward us at two knots submerged speed: the conning tower and periscopes approached our position on a collision course then, too.

CHAPTER ELEVEN
Shaking Down

After our establishment as an operating unit within the Fleet Marine Force, we in 1st Force Recon were continually making a series of introspective self-evaluations of our organization as well as our equipment (T/O and T/E). At the outset we had two different platoons: the amphibious reconnaissance platoon and the parachute reconnaissance platoon. As time passed and we gained more experience in actual operations, it became apparent that we could begin to cross-train the amphib swimmers as parachutists and the parachutists as swimmers, as I have discussed earlier. The four-man reconnaissance teams in both the amphib recon and the parachute recon platoons were identical, with comparable weapons (submachine guns and .45-caliber pistols), equipment, and method of operation once in the objective area. The main difference between the two was the method of entry.

Approval by the commandant of Test Unit 1's recommended T/O and T/E for the "austerity" force reconnaissance company, as opposed to the "optimum" company, mandated that we be capable of conducting three simultaneous tactical missions for the FMF: (1) the amphib recon of up to five BLT landing beaches prior to a planned landing, and up to five coast-watcher or other inland operations following the landing; (2) the parachute recon of two helicopter LZs, plus their approach and retirement lanes, prior to a planned landing, and after the landing, recon by parachute or helicopter of critical areas of intelligence interest out to a distance of one hundred miles beyond the areas covered by a marine division's own organic recon battalion(s); and (3) parachute or other pathfinder support to assault waves for three landing zones (we did not have any pathfinder reserve that could be available for short-notice follow-on helicopter landings).[1]

The austerity T/O did not include any personnel to fulfill the administrative requirements for qualified DZ control and safety parties for peacetime training operations. As a consequence, our tactical capability was effectively reduced by the equivalent of one LZ pathfinder team. When we first organized as a company in June of 1957, our pathfinder platoon under 1st Lt. David Ramsey was composed of three teams, each having one officer and ten enlisted marines. Each team would normally jump with approximately one thousand pounds of gear, which averaged about ninety pounds per marine. Our T-10 static-line parachutes with our T-7A reserve parachutes weighed something over forty pounds. The bulk of the individual load was made up of the marine's equipment (for example, a helmet, web gear, a pack, rations, an individual weapon such as the M3A1 .45-caliber submachine gun, and ammo). In addition was the team member's portion of the actual guidance pathfinder gear. Jumping with all of this equipment taped and lashed to all parts of their bodies soon gained the pathfinders the sobriquet of the "rag jumpers" or "jumping junkmen."

Each pathfinder team carried twenty, three-dimensional marker panels (in the form of tetrahedrons, which could be seen as a pyramidal-shaped panel from any direction), twelve SE-11 night marker lights for the landing zones, the Justrite landing lights, and the largest item, the MAY radios for ground-to-air communications. In addition to their individual weapons, the pathfinder team carried in one bipod-mounted machine gun (a .30-caliber M1919A1) for initial hasty landing-zone defense. Finally, there were standard air-ground marker panels for displaying the wind direction, together with PRC-6 and PRC-10 radios and an ample supply of colored smoke grenades.

When using the Grumman TF-1 Trader, which had a total of nine seats, we could jump only a nine-man team from each aircraft and were forced to leave two members of the eleven-man pathfinder team behind. Experience with these smaller TF-1 teams proved, however, that they were fully capable of carrying out their expanded mission. The two "extra" jumpers were effectively utilized as replacements, and counted within the group of extras were also the marines whom we had in the pipeline for various specialized schools—jump school, pathfinder school, SERE school, and so on. If we had to insert a team into each of two widely dispersed landing zones, we needed either two navy TF-1s or one marine Douglas R4D-8 Super Skytrain. When we could not get the Traders, we used the R4D-8, two of which were organic to the air repair squadron of the marine air wing.

Having formed in June, we came up to full strength within two months, and in September 1957 we participated in Operation Stonewall. Somewhat reminiscent of our prior long escape and evasion exercise to the Salton Sea, this was an insertion on succeeding nights of both parachute recon teams and pathfinder teams some fifty-five miles from Camp Pendleton. In this operation, both types of teams were dropped into DZs that were ten to twenty miles from their objectives. The recon teams then moved overland to their individual objectives, flood-

control dams. The recon teams were ordered to photo-
graph the dams and to obtain water samples. Division recon battalion "aggressors" had been placed to "guard"
each dam. The majority of the recon teams accomplished
their mission without detection, although one team was
captured by the aggressor partisans.

Once the parachute recon teams had accomplished
their mission, they evaded overland to an abandoned
airstrip along the Mexican border, which looked much
like the dirt strips frequently used by today's drug smugglers. To provide the maximum of training on these pickups, we usually retrieved only one recon team at a time.
The second team would call in for its pickup within a
prescheduled period. Radio coordination with a Grumman TF-1 orbiting out of sight quickly brought the aircraft in on the small strip. The TF-1 then touched down,
as the team waited at the upwind end of the airstrip. Without stopping, when the TF-1 hit the ground, it would do a
rapid one-eighty, turning in almost its wheelbase, and
start to accelerate as the team literally leaped aboard. The
total time from touchdown to takeoff with flaps and
plenty of power was under thirty seconds.

Our navy carrier pilots were as enthused as our recon
teams were about this execution of yet another method of
recovering inserted recon teams. Carrier pilots are accus-
tomed to making precision approaches, and their approach techniques for landing on aircraft carriers adapted
readily to the small dirt strips. The navy pilots felt that
with this experience, they could land on any straight
stretch of road (without telephone poles or fences alongside) and recover a team, if that were ever necessary. We
put this new capability in our books as a possibility for future pickups under operational conditions.

In contrast, on Operation Stonewall the pathfinders
went in on alternate nights with the mission of establish-

ing night helicopter landing zones. As soon as the zones were set up, the teams were notified by radio that the impending helicopter landing had been canceled. They were told to bury their gear and evade overland the thirty-five miles back to Camp Pendleton. We again alerted all law enforcement agencies and placed aggressor patrols along expected evasion routes. None of the pathfinders were spotted, however, and all made it back in good shape.[2]

Losing Half of Our Jumpers

Knowing that the executive officer of 1st Force, Capt. Joe Taylor, and half of our jumpers would be leaving us to form 2d Force Recon Company at Camp Lejeune, North Carolina, we began to prepare for this transfer and for our obvious need to rebuild our manpower. Joe and I jointly decided that, in order to give him more flexibility in planning for the reorganization of both companies, we would fleet up Capt. Bill Livingston as the new acting executive officer. Joe moved laterally across the hall to an office just off the exec's, labeled "Special Projects."

In addition to Captain Taylor's planning for the departure of his troops for Camp Lejeune in April 1958, and the required rebuilding of 1st Force to fill the gap, we were anticipating two events. One was the deployment of the entire 1st Force Recon Company overseas to Japan and the Philippines for participation in the marine division/marine air wing operation called "Strongback." The second event was the evaluation of Jacques Istell's proposal that his "Sky Diver" blank-gore parachute be used in our operational missions, which we had in turn recommended to the commanding general of Fleet Marine Force, Pacific.

Prior to Istell's arrival, Captain Taylor, Gunnery Sergeants Avery and Woods, Staff Sergeant Zwiener, and Sergeant Turney—all qualified test jumpers—went to El

Centro to jump other steerable parachutes to gain some experience that would provide a baseline for the later evaluation of the blank gore. At El Centro they jumped both the air force's steerable E-1, which was used by paramedics when jumping into small DZs at aircraft crashes, and the "Tojo," the NPU-developed steerable that had a standard T-10 canopy with a large (eighty-two by fifty-two inch) opening at the back. Because it used slip risers, the Tojo was a far more maneuverable parachute than the standard T-10 canopy. It gained its nickname from the fact that when its canopy opened, it looked like the World War II propaganda image of the smiling, toothy Japanese general Tojo.

In late January 1958, U.S. Marine Reserve Captain Jacques Istell arrived at the Camp Pendleton airstrip, flying his own civilian Cessna 182. (This ruffled the feathers of some of the marine aviators running the Marine Corps air facility at Camp Pendleton.) We welcomed Jacques at the company and provided all possible support for a valid test of his techniques for stabilized free fall as well as the Pioneer blank-gore parachutes that he was convinced the Marine Corps should buy. The company's assigned mission was precise: to make "(1) a comparison of the blank-gore parachutes and the standard T-10 34 foot canopy parachutes that Force Recon had modified for free fall, and (2) an investigation of the effects of imposition of operational conditions on the techniques of stabilized free fall as practiced by civilian 'sky divers.' "[3]

The Marine Corps's Landing Force Development Center (LFDC) ordered "their marine at Fort Benning" (serving with the U.S. Infantry Board, charged with the development of all airborne tactics and techniques) to Camp Pendleton to monitor our tests on behalf of LFDC. Arriving to work with us, therefore, was Lt. Col. Gerald P. Averill, a parachutist with considerable test experience.

Not one to stand by and watch, Gerry Averill immersed himself in our tests in a very positive way. He provided us with guidance on how the army was approaching many of these same problems. Later when Gy.Sgt. Neal Avery broke his foot on one of the jumps, Lieutenant Colonel Averill stepped in and replaced the injured Avery for the remainder of the test jumps.

Jacques Istell and Joe Taylor came up with a mutually agreeable and sensible plan to perform the necessary operational evaluations. Half of the jumps were to be conducted at the Naval Parachute Facility (NPF) at El Centro. This would take advantage of the excellent desert drop zones and the strong technical and clinically analytical facilities at the Department of Defense's Joint Parachute Test Facility at El Centro. The remainder of the jumps would be done at Camp Pendleton into the operationally small-sized drop zones normally employed by force recon. No detailed technical or engineering testing of Istell's "Sky Diver" parachutes could be done in this short period, however—a fact that would lead to later problems with this particular model.

The weather at Camp Pendleton in January can be unpredictable. High winds and overcast in the latter part of that month in 1958 forced almost half of the scheduled jumps—and all of the night jumps—to be canceled. Yet despite this setback, a total of thirty-nine parachute jumps were done, with twenty-five using the blank-gore parachutes.[4] The jumps were made into the small, unprepared drop zones that we had used in both Test Unit 1 and 1st Force.

Test-bed aircraft were our usual group—R4Ds, TF-1s, and F3Ds (Joe Taylor put Istell out on Istell's first jump from an operational military jet)—and on one jump they used Captain Istell's Cessna. Exit speeds varied from a low of eighty knots (from the Cessna) to over one hundred knots (from the R4D and the TF-1) to one hundred fifty knots (from the F3Ds). Captain Istell ably demonstrated his stabilized free fall. All six of the marine jumpers had been trained in Istell's techniques. We described this type of jumping as "stabilized free fall."

Delays in opening on these test jumps ran the gamut from ten seconds (at thirty-five hundred feet) to sixty seconds (from twelve thousand five hundred feet). The standard T-10 parachute maintained the slowest rate of descent of all parachutes tested, sixteen feet per second. Comparative evaluation was done of the air force's twenty-eight-foot flat canopy (the standard military pilot emergency parachute) and the E-1. The twenty-eight flat had the disadvantages of a high rate of descent (twenty-one feet per second) and fairly severe oscillation (which can be disastrous as one approaches the ground). It was quickly rejected for use by reconnaissance or pathfinder personnel because of these limitations.

The air force's E-1 steerable parachute, using derry slots in the rear of the canopy for steering, was tried and rejected for its higher rate of descent (sixteen to twenty-one feet per second) and its tendency, similar to the standard twenty-eight-foot flat canopy, to severely oscillate during descent. The T-10s that had been modified for free fall were sluggish in steering capability when compared to the E-1 or the twenty-eight flat, but they proved to have a much slower and safer rate of descent, considering all the gear our jumpers normally had to go in with. Jumping the Tojo modified T-10 in comparison to an unmodified T-10 was like driving a "power steering" parachute in comparison to the difficult-to-maneuver standard T-10 canopy.

The Pioneer Parachute Company's "Sky Diver" model

tested was a twenty-eight-foot canopy. It had a much denser nylon fabric (its reduced porosity was about one-third less than our standard American-issue parachutes). In the rear of the canopy (behind the jumper) was a center gore, open from just above the skirt to about forty-five inches below the apex. The harness was equipped with two Capewell harness releases (as had been recommended following Test Unit 1's accident at Case Springs). These permitted immediate collapse of the canopy upon landing.

Tests of the "Sky Diver" and the other parachutes against which it was evaluated were conducted with a weighted three-hundred-foot line hung below the jumper, which the test would deploy after his chute had opened. With the use of a stopwatch, the rate of descent—the number of seconds from the time of the weight's hitting the deck and the jumper's landing—could be measured rather precisely for each different model of parachute and equipment load. Strikingly, Istell's smaller (twenty-eight-foot diameter) blank-gore parachute with its denser canopy fabric had a rate of descent very comparable to that of the T-10 modified for free fall and the Tojo. All three—the "Sky Diver" blank gore, our free-fall T-10, and the Tojo—were markedly slower in their rate of descent than either the E-1 or the twenty-eight flat.

Glide tests were made to see the distance from the chute's point of opening to the jumper's point of touchdown that could be traversed by slipping. The T-10 was used as the mark standard, and the blank gore and the Tojo were compared to it. The aircraft held a crosswind track, upwind of the target. Three jumpers went out in very quick sequence so that they all started from about the same exit point at five thousand feet. Each of the jumpers attempted to slip toward the same target downwind. From the touchdown spot of the T-10, both the Tojo and the blank gore glided one-half mile and six-tenths of a mile, respectively, farther toward the ground target than the standard free-fall T-10.

Using several jumps to cancel out minor differences, we found that the blank gore moderately surpassed the Tojo and greatly surpassed the standard T-10 in gliding distance from point of opening to touchdown.[5] The rate of turn for all the parachutes was timed. The blank gore's three-hundred-sixty-degree turns were done in three and a half seconds versus the Tojo's ten to twelve seconds. The E-1 could do a three-sixty turn in eight seconds. Without question, the blank gore won out on handling ease and maneuverability. It was clearly a parachute that could be used to go into very small drop zones. But since virtually all of our recon jumps were made at night and in limited visibility, some of us felt that this maneuverability would not be a great advantage.

Force Recon's requirement to jump with diverse types of heavy equipment loads dictated that our evaluation of the relative stability of the different parachutes be most keenly observed. To these marine parachutists, stability meant a reduced tendency to oscillate, particularly close to the ground. If a jumper landed when he was just at the upper swing of an oscillation, the ground impact was always much greater and more injurious because of the "whipping down" effect. In our evaluation, we factored in not only the rate of descent of the parachute but also its swinging side-impact in coming down from an oscillation. The blank gore was not as stable as the free-fall T-10 or the T-10 Tojo, but it was far more stable than the E-1 or the twenty-eight-foot flat. Opening forces (measured in G forces) were far less for the blank gore than for either the T-10 or the Tojo.

It took less time to repack the blank gore than the T-10 or the Tojo. For our type of jumping, however, this was not considered a major factor, one way or the other. Once we used a parachute to get to our objective, there was no urgency in repacking it for another immediate follow-on jump, as there is, for example, in a skydiving competition.

After two weeks of intensive evaluation and testing, Capt. Joe Taylor and his fellow jumpers concluded that the blank gore (Pioneer Parachute's model "Sky Diver") was superior to the T-10 in both handling and maneuverability. It measured about the same as the T-10 in rate of descent and stability and was found superior to all parachutes tested with respect to premeditated free fall at the speeds in which it was tested during this relatively short period. As a result of these tests, 1st Force Recon recommended acquisition of twelve "Sky Diver" parachutes, six with twenty-eight-foot canopies and six with thirty-two-foot canopies—although Joe Taylor had recommended further operational testing under field conditions to determine what size canopy was best for force recon use.[6]

During the twenty months of my command of 1st Force, however, we never received any of the Pioneer blank-gore parachutes. Later, after I left the company, the Marine Corps ordered sixty of these parachutes, instead of our recommended twelve. Some time later, fifteen of them were sent to 1st Force and fifteen to 2d Force. Istell was still busy, now proposing the adoption of his blank gores by the army for its Special Forces. Before coming to the Marine Corps in January 1958, Istell—operating as president and CEO of Parachutes, Inc. and assisted by former army paratrooper Lew Sanborn—had contracted with the army's quartermaster general for the training of six army Special Forces parachutists at the 77th Special Forces Group at Fort Bragg, North Carolina.[7]

Our friend "Three-Finger Louie"—army major Lucien E. Conein, from our Fort Bragg experience—was the project officer and one of the test jumpers. After we had completed our parachute testing and evaluation, Lou sent us a copy of his report of 15 December 1957, which outlined an almost identical testing by the army's Special Forces with results very comparable to ours. We reciprocated and sent him a copy of our report.

Following its April 1958 formation from our West Coast unit, 2d Force Recon began a close and profitable association on parachuting with the Special Forces units at Fort Bragg. While at Fort Bragg, Maj. P. X. Kelley was alerted to problems that air force chief warrant officer "Chuck" Laine had experienced in testing the same type of Pioneer parachutes that the Marine Corps had just purchased. This communication was indicative of the small fraternity of test parachutists then existent in each of the armed services. Capt. Joe Taylor, Sgt. Bob Zwiener, and I had all gotten to know Chuck Laine previously—we all had been test jumping together with him at El Centro. Although based at Wright-Patterson AFB, Chuck used to come to El Centro to the air force's 6511th Aero Test Squadron for various jump tests. We knew Chuck to be a jumper of expertise comparable to our navy mentor at El Centro, CWO Lew Vinson and his successor, CWO Lew Patinetti.

P. X. Kelley personally went to Wright-Patterson AFB to learn firsthand what problems the air force had incurred in testing the "Sky Diver" blank-gore parachute. The air force test jumps had been made from a C-119 "Flying Boxcar" (similar to our marine Fairchild R4Q twin-boomed transport aircraft). On two of their drops of dummy's using the blank gore, the high-pressure area in the canopies of two parachutes had "exploded," making them dangerous and useless to the Marine Corps. CWO Chuck Laine had both still photos and motion pictures of these blank gores blowing apart under operational conditions. As a result of P. X.'s findings, 2d Force was alarmed and immediately contacted the Landing Force Development Center, alerting them to the problem. At that point, it was discovered that the Marine Corps had failed, for whatever reason, to have an engineering test done on the blank gores.[8]

Four of the blank-gore canopies were immediately sent from each force recon company to the Naval Parachute Test Center at El Centro for detailed evaluation. Engineering tests determined that there were inadequacies in either the design or the fabrication. The remainder of the eight parachutes (the harnesses and deployment sleeves) were requested by NPU for further testing. The result was that the "Sky Diver" was found unacceptable for Marine Corps use.

I have never found out exactly what caused the canopies on the blankgore parachutes to fail for the air force, which was why the Marine Corps canceled its order for the chutes. As a test parachutist, however, I would have to reason that it was a combination of two factors. First, the porosity on the "Sky Diver" blank gore (one-third denser than our standard parachutes) caused a greater resistance in the high-stress areas of the canopy, which are subjected to the most severe, instantaneous pressure on opening. Second, the chute was developed specifically for sport parachuting, where the opening speeds are much lower and dictate less stringent standards of workmanship than military parachuting does. One thing that we could say about our standard T-10 parachute and later the Tojo with slip risers: they were both engineered and manufactured according to extremely rugged standards. They were built like a Mack Truck. I have jumped the T-10s on occasion and gotten high-speed (8Gs) openings and not blown a single panel.

When we first started using the T-10 canopy for free

fall at Test Unit 1, we took considerable pains to have our experiences and our modifications documented thoroughly by the parachute engineers at the Naval Parachute Facility at El Centro. The NPF prepared engineering drawings with discrete specifications so our riggers could fabricate the safest possible free-fall parachute rig. When we disbanded Test Unit 1 and formed 1st Force, we took these same drawings and specifications with us. And a year later, in April 1958, when Capt. Joe Taylor and his riggers went to Camp Lejeune, we made certain that they took copies of the drawings and the specs with them. It was important that there always be a constant interchange on technical and safety data among both force recon companies, NPF at El Centro, and the Landing Force Development Center at Quantico. We knew we were in a dangerous business, and we took every possible precaution to alert all hands to any problems that arose.

Parachute Fatalities in Force Recon

Following my departure from 1st Force Recon Company on 15 January 1959, parachute operations continued at a high tempo. There were two fatalities, one on a static-line jump in 1st Force and the other a free-fall accident in 2d Force. Despite the fact that both of these fatalities occurred after I had left 1st Force, I believe that they merit examination here.

On 16 November 1960, a pathfinder team was making a night jump into Las Pulgas DZ in the middle of Camp Pendleton. The stick exited in good form. But when the team leader attempted to gather up and account for all the jumpers after their landings, L.Cpl. Noble S. Alford, the team's communicator, was missing. At dawn an intensive search was conducted in the hills surrounding the DZ. No trace of Alford could be found. Maj. Robert

Hunt, the CO of 1st Force, was confident that if there had been a parachute malfunction, they would find his body in the rocks surrounding Pulgas. After thoroughly searching the hills without success, Capt. Robert N. Burhans sent divers into Pulgas Lake, a two-acre lake some half-mile south of the DZ. There they found Lance Corporal Alford's body. He had drowned, apparently not expecting a water landing. He had tangled in his suspension lines and gone under his canopy—which, when immersed, will drag a parachutist down.

The subsequent investigation reconstructed what had happened. Lance Corporal Alford did not weigh very much. Other jumpers in his team remembered that when they exited in a stick, Alford would always "hang" and drift, landing long after all the other jumpers were on the ground. As a result of his light weight, Alford was always loaded "heavy," with bulky pathfinder equipment, to equalize the pathfinder team's rate of descent by increasing his downward speed. Despite this loading, the winds aloft obviously carried Alford the half-mile south, to where he entered Lake Pulgas on that dark night.[9] For me this accident rekindled memories of our tragic experience at Case Springs and the problems that unpredictable winds aloft can cause.

Three years later, on 16 January 1963, the free-fall accident in 2d Force occurred. Capt. Peter J. Johansen was killed when his modified T-10 canopy failed to deploy. He had executed a free fall out of the Grumman Trader—which, by this time, had undergone a navy aircraft designator change from the TF-1 to C-1A. Following a ten-second delay from thirty-five hundred feet, he pulled his main chute, and it had fouled. By the time he pulled his reserve, he was down to one hundred fifty feet. It failed to deploy fully, and he went in.

This was a rig vastly different from those that we had been jumping in 1st Force. Captain Johansen was making his sixtieth jump and his tenth free fall. He had a shortened GP bag rigged below his reserve parachute (there is no indication that this had anything to do with the malfunction). His 2d Force specially modified free-fall T-10 had its canopy packed *inside* a deployment bag, which permitted the suspension lines to pull out before the canopy. In theory (as with the Istell "Sky Diver"), this modification would allow a slower opening, with less shock.

Yet this particular deployment system had never been tested at El Centro or at any other qualified parachute test facility (e.g., Fort Bragg, Wright-Patterson AFB, or Soldier Systems Command [SSCO], the parachute evaluation section of the U.S. Army Quartermaster Research and Engineering Command at Natick, Massachusetts). It was strictly a locally manufactured rig, whose approval had been local—by the 2d Force Recon. After the accident, both Captain Johansen's main and reserve parachutes were sent to SSCO at Natick for detailed analysis and examination by army parachute engineers. They determined that the parachute had indeed malfunctioned as a result of a marginally effective coil-spring pilot chute, which wound around the suspension lines and prevented the full deployment of the main canopy.[10] The tragic accident of Captain Johansen caused an immediate cessation of all free-fall parachuting within the Marine Corps until the adoption of the HALO (high altitude low opening) parachute designed for the U.S. Air Force.

By the spring of 1963, which was prior to this accident, Maj. P.X. Kelley had left 2d Force Recon and become the ground surveillance/reconnaissance officer at

Quantico in the LFDC. He was most instrumental in the Marine Corps's subsequently getting the HALO rig approved for our recon jumpers. Marines in the force recon companies of today are using similar and even more advanced HALO parachute rigs.[11]

CHAPTER TWELVE
Deployment Overseas

A major amphibious landing exercise, Operation Strongback (PHIBLEX 58M), was held during February and March of 1958, with the Marine Corps and the U.S. Navy operating jointly with the Philippine Armed Forces. The area of operation was to be on the island of Luzon, in the central Philippines, some one hundred miles north of Manila, inland from Dingalan Bay on the east coast. The Coronel River valley and the Sierra Madre Mountains formed a large, broken, hilly jungle area north and east of the main Luzon plain. Lt. Gen. Vernon E. McGee, CG FMFPac, wanted force recon, among other units, tested in the crucible of a major amphibious landing into a heavily jungled area typical of Southeast Asia.

We were to pathfind and simultaneously perform both amphibious and parachute reconnaissance for the largest helicopter landing in Marine Corps history. Two BLTs were to land from two aircraft carriers (one was simulated, since sufficient LPH-type helicopter carriers were not as yet available). One of the BLTs was to land from aboard an escort aircraft carrier (CVE), the USS *Thetis Bay* (CVHA-1), and the other from a simulated carrier, the USS *Bitulok*, which was actually a dirt and pierced-steel matting strip some fifty miles north of NAS Cubi Point on Subic Bay in southwestern Luzon.

Our participation in Strongback entailed the deployment of virtually the entire 1st Force Recon Company six thousand miles overseas to Japan and the Philippines. We left Capt. Joe Taylor and four staff NCOs behind for the commandant's mandated evaluation of Jacques Istell's parachutes.

This deployment proved an excellent prototype for later deployments overseas, such as Vietnam. As a major exercise, it validated virtually all of the concepts of deep reconnaissance and pathfinding within the Fleet Marine Force. Maj. Gen. David Shoup, who had been our division commander when we were first forming, was designated as the commanding general of I Marine Expeditionary Force (MEF). The force consisted of the 3d Marine Division, the 1st Marine Air Wing, with supporting elements from force troops, the Philippine Army Regimental Combat Team (RCT2), the Philippine Navy-Marine Corps battalion in the MEF. Task Force 72 of the Seventh Fleet under Vice Adm. Wallace M. Beakley was the major naval element consisting of the amphibious task force (ATF) under Rear Adm. F. C. Htelter and a carrier task force (four carriers) and their supporting elements.[1]

The bulk of 1st Force Recon embarked in mid-January 1958 with the helicopter squadron on the helicopter carrier *Thetis Bay* en route to Japan. I took my S-3 operations officer, 1st Lt. Don Koelper, and together we flew ahead by navy aircraft to the final amphibious planning meetings with the commander of the Seventh Fleet aboard the flagship, the cruiser USS *Rochester* (CA-124), in Yokosuka, Japan. We were to join up with the company when it arrived in Japan aboard the *Thetis Bay* following its Pacific crossing.

The parachute reconnaissance platoon and our small headquarters were to be retained at MEF level for operational coordination of deep pre-D-day reconnaissance.

Our amphibious reconnaissance platoon was to be attached to the advance force of amphibious ships. It was to operate with the Philippine Marine Corps recon unit aboard the *Cavallaro* (APD-128), conducting the beach recons of the Dingalan Bay complex. The pathfinder platoon was attached to Marine Air Group (MAG)-16. This was the first time that our pathfinders were attached directly to the major aviation unit. Interestingly, when 2d Force was formed, Captains Joe Taylor and P. X. Kelley made the same sort of attachment of their pathfinders to the marine helicopter group at Camp Lejeune.[2]

With the leadership of both Lieutenant General MeGee, CG FMFPac, and Vice Admiral Beakley, the commander of the Seventh Fleet, behind us, we were easily able to gain approval for the tasking of two Grumman TF-1 aircraft and a single Douglas R4D Skytrain for support of the 3d Marine Air Wing's organic F3D Douglas Skyknight squadron, VMF(AW)-513. The marine F3Ds were for pre-D-day parachute reconnaissance. Later we took advantage of a navy A3D Douglas Skywarrior detachment from Heavy Attack Squadron (HATRON) 2, which we jumped, on an experimental basis, out of NAS Cubi Point at Subic Bay, for dropping parachute recon personnel.

Parachute Reconnaissance

The pre-D-day parachute reconnaissance provided for five four-man teams, four of which were to be inserted on the nights of D-6 and D-5 (six and five nights prior to the main landings) by TF-1 Traders flying from NAS Cubi Point. The fifth team was to drop from a four-plane formation of F3Ds, again to be launched from Cubi because of the operational commitments of the carriers.

The marine night fighter squadron that we were to be operating with in the Philippines—VMF(N)-513, whose logo was "The Flying Nightmares"—was normally based at NAF Atsugi (north of Tokyo). They had had no prior experience in dropping our parachutists. After completing our final planning meetings in Yokosuka with General Shoup's staff and with staff members from the Seventh Fleet, 1st Lt. John Hamber of the recon platoon and I drove up to Atsugi to assist VMF(AW)-513 in preparing for the F3D drops.

We briefed the pilots that afternoon and scheduled a live drop for the two of us at dawn the next morning. However, when we awakened and looked outside, the weather appeared only short of a typhoon. We as well as the squadron had only one day in our respective schedules to give the squadron the actual experience of dropping parachutists. We checked the weather again. Amazingly, the wind was reading only ten to twelve knots on the ground. There was, however, a solid overcast at two thousand feet in all directions. Wishing to make every effort to provide VMF(AW)-513's pilots with hands-on experience, we pressed on.

We jumped with the tails of our aircraft just below the solid cloud deck; John and I went out at two thousand feet in a two-plane simultaneous "jump and pull" (five-second delay) exit. We went out exactly over the midpoint of NAF Atsugi's ten-thousand-foot strip. Unfortunately, we had no information on the winds aloft. Within less than a minute after John and I opened, we were over the end of the runway—a fact indicating that the winds aloft were somewhere in excess of fifty knots. We could feel bad vibes about this jump as we were rapidly descending toward a Japanese school yard. I yelled over to John to try to land in the trees so we would not end up being dragged. I began to visualize myself hanging from the roof of a Japanese shrine, a la paratroopers in the 82d Airborne's predawn jump into Sainte-Mère-Eglise, in Normandy, during World War II.

The T-10 free-fall rigs that we were jumping had big thirty-four-foot canopies and only a modest steering capability. In the twenty-knot winds down near the ground, all I could do was generally steer for a group of evergreen trees that I had spotted. I shot over the school yard— which at that moment was filled with hundreds of little Japanese schoolboys—at about fifty feet. They were running in every direction when they saw me. I suddenly felt like a large predatory chicken hawk sailing over a chicken yard. I wanted to avoid landing among them, very probably injuring them and myself. At the last moment I was able, more or less, to steer between two of the larger evergreens that were among those ringing what appeared to be a military compound. My canopy caught over the tops of both trees, and I swung down to about ten feet above the ground.

I hung in my harness, swinging back and forth. Soon a very excited small, bespectacled Japanese man came running up to me, advising me that he was "doctor" and asking in halting English where my plane had gone down and promising me that he would get me a ladder. I assured him that everything was okay and, about that time, popped my quick release, paused, and dropped to the ground, none the worse for the wear. I immediately ran over to try to locate the rice paddy that I had seen John Hamber headed for. I was worried, surmising that he might have gone into the side of one of the three-story wooden barracks buildings close by, at the edge of NAF Atsugi.

John Hamber will never agree with me on this, but what saved him from serious injury was the "night soil" in the paddy that he had jumped into. It immediately

coated both him and his canopy dragging along the
ground. He was able to pull his canopy in from the bottom of the skirt and collapse it. Unfortunately, the night
soil that saved him also turned John into one of the most
evil-smelling parachutists that anyone has ever come
across. It gave new meaning to the phrase "He jumped
into shit."[3]

We immediately got John to a hot shower and our aviator friends from VMF(AW)-513 gave him a complete
new set of utilities. Sergeant Ford, our parachute rigger,
had to wash John's parachute thoroughly, and by using a
ladder and doing another half hour of tree climbing, Ford
was able to retrieve my parachute from its two ensnaring,
savior evergreens.

The rehearsal was successful, and later that night, back
in Yokosuka, John and I were joined by the company and
we all celebrated the event. We had a toast of hot saki at
the Kura Funi (black ship), a small waterfront bistro fa-
vored by naval aviators, UDT, and force recon. The company departed the next morning on the *Thetis Bay*, with
the amphib recon platoon on the *Cavallaro*, bound for
Subic Bay. Don Koelper (my acting S-3) and I flew down
as an advance party to arrange for quarters and operating
areas for us at NAS Cubi Point.

With the exception of the amphib recon platoon, who
were busy rehearsing their rubber boat landings with their
Philippine counterparts on the *Cavallaro*, the rest of the
company operated for the next two weeks out of quarters
and an aircraft hangar at the naval air station. We used the
time to practice landing in jungle clearings in an area
south and west of Cubi Point, on lower Subic Bay. This
was our first experience in jungle parachute landings, and
we learned very quickly. We used the navy's TF-1s and
the marine air group's helicopters to make some of these
rehearsal jumps. When the company was not busy with

planning or doing rehearsal jumps, we encouraged the men to get out into the jungle and familiarize themselves with jungle operations.

The terrain around Subic Bay is a dense, triple-canopy jungle—one that has a top layer of growth that extends to heights of ninety to one hundred ten feet, a middle layer of plants that rise to about sixty feet, and a bottom layer that reach up about twenty feet. Although I later operated in jungle environments in Vietnam, British North Borneo, and Malaya, this was the first time for force recon to have the opportunity to operate in such a classic jungle environment.

A young doctor at the naval hospital, Lt. Nick Bondurant, over a San Miguel beer at the Cubi Officers' Club, invited several of us to go wild boar hunting with him in the jungle, up near the navy communications station, several miles north of the main base area of Subic Bay. One hunts wild boar at night using a headlight and shotguns with slug ammunition. Nick promised us that we would get up into Negrito country, the territory of the dwarfish tribe of indigenous people of the Negroid race whom the Filipinos call "the little people." They lived off taro roots, jungle plants, monkeys and other small animals, and fish from the streams.

As a navy "doc," Nick had volunteered, on occasion, to treat some of the Negrito natives. I was somewhat surprised when he asked me to bring along a backpack and a case of C rations. These were a "gift" for the Negritos, and in the afternoon heat on the jungle track, I began to have second thoughts about Dr. Bondurant's largesse. Moving out by truck to north of the Subic Bay base, we dropped off our vehicles just prior to dusk. Traveling on foot for perhaps two miles along an over-grown jungle track, we entered a clearing where we could see several fires, the eerie lights of cooking being done at the Negrito camp.

The Negritos were indeed very small in stature, especially in comparison to my six-foot-three frame; the adults standing at full height reached only to my chest. Both sexes were dressed in loincloths, with nothing on their chests, and most of the children were naked. We were momentarily stunned at a sight when we looked over at a fire with a turning spit made from a green stick. This "barbecue" was being tended by a wizened, matronly gray-haired Negrito woman. Roasting slowly on the spit was what, at first, appeared to be a small human form. It was in a fetal position with its arms crossed, and it had all the physical attributes of a small child. Thoughts of cannibalism came into my mind. But on closer inspection, we discovered that the child was actually a small monkey. Just a regular evening's dinner.

The Negritos used hunting arrows tipped with what appeared to have previously been eightpenny nails. The tips had been pounded, flattened, and sharpened in two different styles. One was very narrow and pointed; used for penetration killing, it was needed, for example, when one was shooting a monkey out of a tree. The second type of arrow tip had two small, hooklike barbs (not unlike a two-sided fishhook); it was used to shoot fish in the jungle streams and pools from a position on the banks. Having expressed interest in the Negritos' weapons and way of life, I was graciously presented with a hunting bow and examples of both types of hunting arrows. (The chief, I believe, had noted who had brought in the case of C rations.) Although we heard wild boar rooting through the jungle close to our track, we did not see one or get a single shot at one.

In the Philippines, we initially used helicopters for some of our jungle proficiency jumps around Subic Bay. In jumping from a helicopter, you do not have the hundred-knot forward speed that helps your parachute to deploy quickly. Much like the balloon jumps that the RAF uses in training its parachutists, helicopter jumps give you a slower opening—about five to six seconds. Normally from a fixed-wing aircraft at about one hundred knots airspeed, you count to four and you should have an open canopy in a standard static-line jump.

On this jump, shortly after I got a full canopy over me, I descended to about three hundred feet over the grassy Luzon plain near Bitulok. I looked down and saw, immediately below me, one of the largest water buffaloes I had ever beheld. The spread on his horns had to have been close to four or five feet. And in addition to his size, he looked mean as hell. Quickly climbing my parachute's suspension lines, almost to the canopy edge, I tried to slip away from him. As I successfully did so, my navy diver's watch was torn off my wrist by the connector links on my parachute and plummeted to the ground. I landed, missing the water buffalo, and rolled up my chute. I then began to look—and to ask everyone else there to look—for my diving watch. I knew about where it landed. To lose a diving watch in peacetime meant a ton of paperwork to satisfy the supply officer.

By this time, our jump helicopter had landed and shut down, and so the pilot came over to find out what we were all bent over looking for. He glanced down and almost immediately spotted its shiny case. Amazingly it was still running and had only a small hole punched into the crystal. We shook out the broken glass, and I wore it with a piece of Scotch tape over the hole until I could get it replaced in Yokosuka on my way back to the States. I did not dive with it, of course, in the interim. After this incident, most of us never again jumped with a standard wristwatch held to the wrist by two pins alone. From that point forward we used a nylon band running underneath the watch itself so that if one of the pins were sheared, the watch was still held on by the other pin. Some of our jumpers used to wrap rigger's tape over their watches.

On one of the TF-1 rehearsal jumps out of Cubi Point, we had an incident involving a tail hook—the device on a plane that is used to arrest the aircraft's forward motion within a very short distance after it has landed on an aircraft carrier. After exit, Cpl. Charles E. Henry's parachute, as it was deploying, hung up on the Grumman's tail hook. Corporal Henry was towed briefly around Cubi Point by the TF-1 and somehow managed to shake his canopy off. The canopy then made a full deployment with no apparent damage, other than a bit of grease on the top. He landed without incident.

Sergeant Ford, our rigger, Corporal Henry, and I went down to the aircraft after it landed. Working together with our pilots, we came up with a simple but practical idea to keep this difficulty from ever occurring again. We picked up two brown grocery bags from the navy commissary and, doubling them, covered over the tail hook, taping the bags in place with rigger's tape. This may have looked a bit strange, but it made the tail hook into a streamlined object that could no longer catch a canopy. In the event that the aircraft had to use its tail hook to make an arrested landing, the bags would not interfere with the device's functioning. After this incident, as part of our riggers' and jumpmasters' preparation of the aircraft for parachute operations, in addition to our padding and taping the sharp after-edge of the exit door, we would tape two paper bags (one inside the other for strength) over the tail hook. That ended the problem. Frequently, the simplest solution proves to be the best one.

Related to Corporal Henry's incident, two years later (after I left the company), in April 1962, another parachutist got hung-up while jumping the TF-1 in the Philippines. L.Cpl. Dennis Boyle was jumping eighth in a stick of nine jumpers onto the DZ south and west of Cubi Point, at the edge of the jungle. This was a proficiency jump following the company's support of Operation Tulungan in a 3d Marine Division/3d Marine Air Wing landing exercise conducted on the island of Mindoro in March of that year.

Corporal Boyle was following out Cpl. John Broadnax in the stick. Broadnax, for whatever reason, had dropped almost vertically after his exit. Boyle, coming behind him, made a rapid, positive exit. As it was ascending from his exit, Corporal Broadnax's static line somehow wrapped around Boyle's right leg below the knee and kept him attached to the aircraft. Both Boyle's risers and his suspension lines were partially deployed, with his canopy still inside of its deployment bag. He was being unceremoniously towed behind the Grumman, upside down. Although we had earlier anticipated that a jumper who is hung up behind a TF-1 might spin, Boyle did not.

Corporal Boyle made every attempt to free his leg from the entangling static line, but it was to no avail. All of us parachuting in 1st Force Recon carried knives either stowed in the bungees on top of our reserve parachutes or strapped to our legs. Boyle got to his knife and tried to reach around and cut his static line so that he could use his reserve parachute. The one-hundred-knot slipstream prevented him from being able to reach back far enough to cut himself loose. Restowing his knife, he signaled the ninth remaining jumper, 1st Lt. Jack Phillips, the jumpmaster, that he was prepared to be cut loose from the aircraft. Our signal for this situation was to place a hand on top of one's helmet.

By this time Boyle had been towed beneath the TF-1, upside down, for over four minutes. Lieutenant Phillips pulled his knife and barely touched the fouled static line: because it had been under such unusual tension, it parted "like butter." This permitted Corporal Boyle to fall clear, and his canopy deployed normally from the deployment bag. He now had an open canopy and a badly injured leg. Unable to steer and reeling from the pain of his right knee and calf, he descended into secondary growth, landing almost sixty feet up in the tops of the jungle canopy. He hung limply in his parachute harness, some thirty-feet above the jungle floor.

Looking below himself, he spotted another marine on the ground, apparently searching for him. Boyle yelled, "Hey, Marine!" The marine below him was very startled, gasping, "We thought you were dead!" Knowing that he would have to have medical attention once he was on the ground, Boyle popped his reserve parachute, hit his quick release, and slid down the chute. With pain, he dropped the last ten feet or so to the ground—an impact that did not help his leg a bit. At that moment, two other force recon men who were searching for him, Sgt. Mike Lamb and Corporal Woodburn, came up to him, picked him up, and carried him out to a jeep. Taken to the dispensary at Cubi Point, Boyle learned that his leg, although not broken, had suffered torn ligaments. It was several months before he was again jumping.[4]

Analysis of this accident determined that the prior jumper had made a less-than-positive exit, which caused his static line to ascend up to a trail position. Boyle's very positive exit was delayed momentarily by his left arm's becoming entangled in his own static line. His exit placed his legs over the prior static line as it was ascending to a normal trail position behind the aircraft, causing the entanglement. Other than Corporal Henry's brief tail-hook hang up, Lance Corporal Boyle's incident was the first significant problem with the TF-1 in over three thousand parachute jumps from that aircraft.[5]

Capt. Ernie DeFazio and Capt. Bill McKinstry (Bill

had been promoted prior to this operation) were working with the reconnaissance element of the Philippine Marine Corps aboard the *Cavallaro* operating off Dingalan Bay, some one hundred miles north of Manila, off the east coast of Luzon. Unfortunately, the advance force had not received portions of the MEF operation plan. Despite the entreaties of both DeFazio and McKinstry, they were landed and recovered during daylight hours. The lack of availability of a fleet-type submarine had caused this rather unrealistic use of the *Cavallaro*.

Their patrols landed on Baler Bay, to the right (north) flank of the main landing area at Dingalan Bay. The amphib recon personnel, accompanied by some of the Philippine recon marines, made a three-day route-recon through the area and came back out for pickup. The recon platoon of the Philippine Marine Corps, with whom they were operating, was commanded by Lt. Rudolfo Punsalang, who later, as a commodore, was to become the commandant of the Philippine Marine Corps. (Officers of the Philippine Marine Corps carried naval ranks rather than our comparable United States Marine Corps rank designations.)

General Shoup's critique was complimentary of the amphib recon's performance but critical of the umpire agency that had failed to properly disseminate the constructive information that they were to have picked up on their beach trek. This would have somewhat mitigated the unrealistic nature of the use of the amphibious reconnaissance personnel. The most positive aspect of their deployment and participation in this operation was the cross-training with the Philippine marines and the chance to make their three-day route patrol.[6]

Four nights before the scheduled main landing, a flight of five F3Ds launched from Cubi to make a night drop of a four-man team onto the central Luzon plain, some one hundred miles north of Subic Bay. VMF(AW)-513 had rigged five F3Ds in the event that one was, in aviator's parlance, "down" for any reason. Because we had five aircraft "up," I was able to accompany the recon team on this night jump to "show the flag." And instead of a four-plane drop, we made it a five-plane formation drop, which went without a hitch. On landing, the recon team leader accounted for all his jumpers and took off on his mission.

Then, out of the darkness I heard a voice that, by its tone, I knew instinctively belonged to a very senior officer. It was calling my name. I rolled up my chute and went toward "the voice." It was Brig. Gen. R. K. Rottet, the assistant commander of the 1st Marine Air Wing, who was the operation's maneuver director. He had wanted to see his jets drop us, and he had come out from his headquarters this night by sedan to observe us firsthand. He passed me a canteen cup that, despite the pitch-black darkness, I rapidly determined to be half-full of Scotch. He then made the memorable remark that anyone who would jump out of one of his perfectly good jets needed a drink. I obliged, of course, both in the spirit of his offer and in recognition of the effort he had made to come out on such a dark night over such primitive dirt roads to see us in action. Back at Subic Bay, our troops got a big charge out of the fact that our aviator general officer took such interest in what we were doing. General Rottet gave all of us a real boost.

Our intelligence officers had briefed us on the three or four different species of poisonous snakes that we might encounter in the jungle areas where our five parachute recon teams and our amphib recon platoon were operating. When we asked our navy doctors about snake venom shots, they advised that the only serum that was effective had to be kept under constant refrigeration. Knowing, therefore, that we were unprotected against the snakes, we naturally worried the entire time our parachute recon teams were in the jungle, bashing through on their respective missions. Fortunately, though, no one received any snake bites, and only one parachute recon team reported seeing snakes.

The parachute recon team that I had gone in with carried one MAY radio for use as the radio-relay for the previously inserted four other teams. Each of those teams carried AN/PRC-10 radios with RC/292 long antennae for additional range. They used burst (abbreviated) transmissions to the radio-relay team, which in turn passed on the intelligence concerning the landing zones—clearing, confirming, amplifying, and correcting prior intelligence. Four of the five recon teams evaded overland to a small dirt airstrip at Bitulok, where they were picked up by TF-1s. We recovered them using the hasty touchdown and rapid takeoff technique that we had developed months earlier on Operation Stonewall.

Although their recovery was timely at D-2 and D-1 (two days and one day prior to the main landings) for message distribution, it was too late for the dissemination of overlays, sketches, and photographs made by the recon teams. The techniques for recovery of deep recon patrols that were later developed in Vietnam would have helped us avoid this deficiency. General Nickerson suggested in his analysis that the Fulton Skyhook recovery would have solved this as well.[7]

At the conclusion of the exercise, General Shoup recommended an earlier deployment of parachute reconnaissance teams from D-60 to D-30—that is, one to two months prior to the main landings—or earlier, with last-minute recon at about D-5 for final confirmation of intelligence gathered previously.

Pathfinder Insertion

Our four pathfinder teams came in prior to H-hour, at L-hour (scheduled landing time for the assault waves of helicopters), parachuting from two TF-1 Traders and one R4D Skytrain. Inbound, the TF-1s and the R4D crossed the Sierra Madre Mountains, and our pathfinders landed in the Coronel River valley, thirty miles inland from the landing beaches at Dingalan Bay. They immediately established two primary and two alternate helicopter landing zones for the two inbound helicopter-borne infantry battalions. One battalion was launched from the *Thetis Bay* and one from the simulated carrier, the dirt airstrip had that been renamed the *Bitulok*. This "carrier" was one of the unique artificialities of a peacetime operation—we had to "make do" with what assets were actually available. This lack of ships—which always creates the need for extensive prepositioning—was rectified in Vietnam when our navy added to the amphibious forces the LPH, or helicopter aircraft carrier. Among these specially designed amphibious assault helicopter carrier ships were the *Iwo Jima*, the *Tripoli*, and the former CVs, the *Princeton* and the *Boxer*.

Each landing zone was to be capable of handling flights of five helicopters at each landing site. Four-man pathfinder teams established initial points for each landing zone at designated terrain features. The scheme of maneuver called for two regiments of the 3d Marine Division to land abreast, battalions in column, at Dingalan Bay and to move quickly inland up the Coronel River valley to link up with the helicopter-borne assault battalions. This helicopter landing was behind the main aggressor force—the 3d Battalion, 1st Marines, reinforced with a tank company and some 1st Marine Air Wing units.

The pathfinders performed flawlessly in their insertion, jumping just thirty-minutes prior to the scheduled L-hour. Unfortunately, their "execute" had been given to them by the Tactical Air Direction Center, having been confirmed by the tactical air controller afloat. For reasons unknown, there was a lack of coordination between the two centers that caused the pathfinders to jump prior to confirmation of L-hour by the MEF commander. Atomic simulators had been placed adjacent to several of the helicopter landing zones. Because of their potential danger to inbound helicopters, it was necessary to detonate these atomic simulators prior to the landing of the helicopters but after the pathfinders had landed. General Shoup, in the critique following the exercise, praised the pathfinders for their performance and faulted the air control coordination that permitted this tactical "atomization" of our pathfinders. As an ancient Chinese proverb puts it, "The more one bleeds in peace the less in war."

Following the pathfinder landings and guidance of the assault waves to their designated sites, two of the four teams were recovered by helicopter and were flown to Cubi Point for parachute repack and possibly an additional mission. The two remaining teams recovered to the CVE *Bitulok* and were subsequently inserted by helicopter for later pathfinder missions.

Despite the artificialities of the exercise, force recon matured significantly through its participation in Operation Strongback. The general officers, from General Shoup on down, were greatly impressed by our positive performance in the operation. General Shoup's personal assessment of the parachute reconnaissance and pathfinder teams' performance was that it manifested "a professional polish and high order of achievement."[8] His critique had a salutary effect on many of our future operations. We had proven the efficacy of our tactics and methods of operation and validated our tables of organization.

We could think of no better test of a unit than to have to pick ourselves up with all of our operational gear and move six thousand miles to a foreign, jungled environment and operate with a high degree of sophistication. Perhaps this sounds a bit presumptuous of me to say, but all of us who had been involved with the idea for, and development of, the concepts of force recon and the new methods of entry were inwardly pleased that we had finally shown what we were capable of doing that went beyond the previous state of the art in submarine and recon swimming.

During our deployment to Japan and the Philippines, 1st Force Recon designed a cloth patch for itself that was not unlike the patches of the marine and navy squadrons with whom we operated. With our close affinity to naval and marine aviation, the resemblance was quite natural. Ours was an embroidered red circular patch emblazoned with silver parachute wings (gold wings came later, when they were adopted) and the flaming torch of the pathfinders—similar to both British and U.S. Army pathfinder insignia—above the parachute wings. Superimposed on these wings and pathfinder torch were the black paddles (indicative of the rubber boats of the amphibious portion of the company). Around the edge was gold embroidered "1st Force Reconnaissance Company" at the top and "FMFPac" at the bottom.

The patch was never worn on our uniforms, but it did begin to appear on the navy flight jackets that many of the officers and NCOs soon acquired. NPU awarded a "Navy Test Parachutist" patch when a jumper completed the test jumper course, and these too were added to the flight jackets. Later both the amphib recon platoon and the pathfinder platoons came up with their own patches that indicated their individual specialties. We did not actively discourage the development of these patches because we felt they were evidence of pride in unit and of an élan that the company was developing. We did order that none be worn on any items of uniform other than the jumpsuits we occasionally used for certain experimental test jumps and on the foul-weather jackets worn aboard submarine.

CHAPTER THIRTEEN
Methods of Extraction

Earlier in this history of Marine Corps force recon, I recounted two operations that took place during World War II—on Cape Gloucester, on the coast of New Britain, and at Tinian, in the Northern Marianas. On Cape Gloucester, 1st Lt. John D. Bradbeer's patrol used navy PT boats to arrive at a point just off the selected beach, where they then launched rubber boats and paddled to the shore, hiding the boats in the jungle for the ten days of the mission.

On Tinian, in Capt. Jim Jones's 5th Amphib Recon Battalion, company commanders Mervin Silverthorn and Leo Shinn used high-speed destroyer transports (APDs). The APDs took the recon teams to within a thousand yards of the beaches, where rubber boats were launched from the fantail. The rubber boats were towed in by landing craft and paddled to a safe distance off the surf zone, where swimmers went in. The team returned the same way, with their rubber boats, to the APDs.

In other World War II missions, recon teams were dropped by submarine and then rubber boats and swimmers were used in much the same manner as was done on Tinian with the APDs. Variations on the submarine drop of a patrol using rubber boats included a pickup by PBY Catalina flying boats, as Lieutenant Bradbeer, for example, experienced on one mission.[1]

The method of extracting reconnaissance personnel that was used in World War II centered on the fact that a relatively shallow insertion had been made. The beach was always behind them and became their means of extraction. Both at Marine Corps Test Unit 1 and later when we formed 1st Force Recon, it was readily apparent that the insertion of recon teams deeper into enemy-controlled territory—teams who were ten to fifty miles from friendly lines and who could not rely on having a friendly beach behind them—brought a whole new dimension to the task of getting those personnel out again.

The war in Vietnam, however, was to create the true test bed of necessity in this regard. Descriptions of helicopter recoveries of deeply inserted recon teams abound in the literature of that era, and considerable material was added to the lore of reconnaissance by the field experiences of these teams, the great majority of whom were under fire or being hunted or chased at the time of their extraction.

In Vietnam, deeply inserted teams used the Sikorsky Jolly Green Giant (USAF HH-53, USMC CH-53) when these helicopters were available. More commonly, recon teams that were within moderate distances used the Boeing-Vertol CH-46 Sea Knight, the Sikorsky H-34 Sea Horse, and the Bell UH1E Huey. If the mission was "hot" (that is, the team was receiving fire), the extracts called for all the air cover they could get. Air cover ran the gamut from F4 Phantoms, A-4 Skyhawks, marine (and sometime army) AH-1W Cobra helicopter gunships, OV-10 Mohawks, the venerable AD-1 Skyraiders—either U.S. Air Force or ARVN (Army of the Republic of Vietnam) Air Force—and the C-130 Hercules gunships or the C-47 Skytrains equipped with Gatling guns (nicknamed "Puff the Magic Dragon").[2] A recon team in trouble took all the help it could get.

Almost a decade earlier, the Marine Corps's Landing Force Development Center at Quantico was busy coordinating what we in 1st and 2d Force Recon Companies were doing with regard to team extraction, as well as monitoring what the army's Special Forces, the CIA, and the air force's Commandos were doing in that regard. Everyone realized there was a problem, and everyone was working the problem.

The Fulton Skyhook

While I was still at Test Unit 1, LFDC arranged for an inventor, Robert E. Fulton Jr., from Newtown, Connecticut, to visit us. The Development Center's Lt. Col. Bob Churley called, alerting us that Mr. Fulton had a device that we would be "most interested in." Robert Fulton, the great-great-grandson of the designer of the first successful steamboat, had come up with the idea for recovery of downed pilots on land or at sea or for CIA agents requiring extraction from distant places. The device was called the Fulton aerial retrieval system, or Skyhook.

Skyhook consisted of a droppable kit composed of three parts, similar in appearance to an aircraft wing tank divided into thirds. The tank was fitted with buoyancy so that it could be dropped by parachute to a downed pilot who was too far out at sea for helicopter recovery. One compartment of the tank contained a combination body harness and padded jumpsuit, the harness portion being comparable to a standard military parachute harness. Another compartment contained several deflated balloons, about the size of large weather balloons. Also in this compartment were two helium canisters to fill the balloon (everyone liked the 100 percent redundancy in having the two bottles and the spare balloons). In the third compartment was a five-hundred-foot pickup line. The top fifty-foot section of the line was attached to the balloon and, being made with hundred-pound-test nylon line, was designed to break away after pickup. The next ninety feet was six-thousand-pound-test tubular nylon line; the remainder of the pickup line, down to the harness, was four-thousand-pound-test tubular nylon line.

To initiate an extraction using the Fulton Skyhook system, an aircraft—at this time, a specially modified navy Lockheed P2V Neptune—would fly over and drop the tank by parachute as close as possible to the person to be picked up. The person would then don the jumpsuit and harness and then inflate the balloon and send it aloft. The aircraft would circle back in, making a run at about one hundred twenty knots, approaching from the downwind side. Centered on the nose of the special Neptune, in front of its propellers, was a twenty-two-foot yoke or "vee" made of tubular steel. The pilot would aim the plane's nose, with the two forks of the yoke immediately in front of him, at a target spot on the pickup cable that was delineated with a brightly colored piece of foil. Seizing the nylon line at that point, the yoke device would lock the line in three "triggers," creating a simultaneous lift and pull. Two of the triggers locked the line, and the third trigger spun a reel on which the line wrapped about eight turns, locking it to the airplane. The effect was to snatch the person from the surface and cause him or her immediately to rise almost two hundred feet straight up. The person would begin to trail in the air behind the aircraft and would then drop to a lower trail position, from which he or she would be winched into the aircraft using a J-hook.[3] The CIA had turned the project over to the navy in 1954, which in turn had interested the Marine Corps.

On 27 May 1958, I received a call from Maj. L. W. Parker at LFDC, asking if we were interested in personally testing the Fulton Skyhook. We immediately fired off a letter volunteering.[4] At about the same time that Parker had called me, the recently promoted Maj. Joe Taylor, CO of the newly formed 2d Force, was visiting LFDC at Quantico and, on the spot, recommended S.Sgt. Levi W. Woods from 2d Force to be the first human being to be picked up by the Fulton system. Staff Sergeant Woods had volunteered when we first began discussing such a pickup at Marine Corps Test Unit 1 nearly two years earlier. Several days later, Quantico sent a marine aircraft to 2d Force at New River, Camp Lejeune, and brought Sergeant Woods to Quantico to participate in the test.

As usually happens with a new system, it took a number of tries to work out the details. With Sergeant Woods standing by, nine of the helium balloons broke loose during one day's testing. They were then discovered to be special balloons for cold weather, not meant to be used in the one-hundred-degree heat of Quantico's summer. This batch of balloons was replaced with ones designed for warmer weather, and the testing proceeded.

In one of the last in a series of pickups using mannequins, the wind deflected the balloon outward at an angle to an altitude of only three hundred feet. The pickup was made, but the dummy initially went in one direction, and then the nylon pickup line had a slingshot effect, and the dummy, now going in the opposite direction, almost passed under the aircraft. Testing continued the next day, with another successful mannequin pickup. Before the first live pickup was attempted, however, the project officer wanted to have the P2V's systems checked over at the base.

On landing back at Quantico, the aircraft blew two tires. The Neptune's pilot admitted that he was just so excited about the prospect of picking up a human being, he had come in too "hot." The tires and some modest damage to the hydraulic lines were repaired over the weekend, and Sergeant Woods was now in the harness, ready for the first live recovery. On one of the first attempts to pick up Woods, the pilot missed the pickup cable, and the wing struck the cable at one hundred twenty knots, shearing the balloon. Sergeant Woods began to have second thoughts as five hundred feet of nylon line descended on top of him. After one more dummy pickup, on 12 August 1958, Sergeant Woods was able to go through the process of being caught by the aircraft and lifted off the ground-cable. Towed behind the Neptune for a total of twenty-two minutes, he was finally hauled into the bottom hatch, none the worse for the wear. Following the pickup, however, the navy doctor had wanted to put Woods in Quantico hospital for "observation." But Woods successfully resisted this, and all hands involved celebrated at Quantico that night.

While researching this book, I received a letter from Levi Woods in which he explained the following with respect to the plunging descent, or "arcing down," that one experiences immediately after being lifted off the ground: "The individual arcs on up [rises] until they are about the same level as the aircraft. It is at this point that [the project engineers] felt they needed an experienced parachute jumper because the individual then plunged down about 200 to 250 feet. I said I was going to try and 'Skydive' so I had spread out shortly after lift-off and was spread-eagle all the way up. As I started down I tucked into what I called the rocking chair position. I found that as long as I kept my feet spread out there was no problem. But, as soon as I let my feet dangle I flopped up and down."[5]

One of the more humorous aspects of these tests was the fact that in them, Sergeant Woods was replacing a red hog. Before these first live tests with humans, the navy and Fulton had been using a red hog. Levi Woods described it as follows: "They raised this boar from a piglet just for this project. As he grew up, before they fed him they would harness him up (in a parachute harness). So he grew up with the idea after getting the harness on he would get fed." When he got to 175 pounds, they took him out to the pickup site at Quantico, which had the not-too-reassuring name of Copps Cemetery. Here, they put the harness on the hog and proceeded to extract him with the Fulton Skyhook.

The hog was not wildly enthused about the experience. As a result, on the next pickup attempt, he gave the crew a real tussle getting him harnessed up. After the third pickup, he was one disgruntled hog. When he had been hauled in through the aircraft's hatch, he got loose in the plane and proceeded to excrete in it from one end to the other. The unhappy crew had to clean up after him. On his fourth and final pickup, it took eight marines to get the hog into his parachute harness. Somehow the term "hog-tied" comes to mind. Immediately after this last liftoff, while the hog was about thirty feet in the air, he "let loose" on a group of observing generals, admirals, senators, congressmen, and civilian counterparts. In the words of Levi Woods, "This is how I replaced the Red Boar Hog."[6]

The Quantico flight surgeon estimated an eight to eight and half G force on the liftoff of the hog—later, detailed instrumentation on some two hundred human pickups showed the average G force to be between five and eight.[7] As a precaution, Levi Woods had worn a T-7A reserve parachute on this first jump. After that pickup, however, the reserve was never considered a requirement. Sergeant Woods was later awarded the Navy and Marine Corps Medal for his actions. It is the highest noncombat medal that is awarded for heroism in saving lives, and one can indeed agree that Levi Woods's actions in these tests resulted in the saving of future lives.

Following these initial tests, the system was further developed, and ultimately, it could be used to extract three persons simultaneously. Later, both Maj. P. X. Kelley and Maj. Wesley H. "Duff" Rice were to be retrieved with the Skyhook. Pickups were also tried from the water, and one was done at altitude—a retrieval from a Rocky Mountain ridge made by a B-17 Flying Fortress at over twelve thousand feet. Eventually small lights were rigged on the balloon cable to conduct night extractions. A number of different types of aircraft were rigged for the Fulton Skyhook: the B-17, C-47, C-123, and C-130.[8]

The Fulton Skyhook retrieval system was pressed into service by the United States during the Cold War when in the Arctic, the Soviets had abandoned a meteorological station and left their instrumentation behind. Two CIA agents parachuted in and recovered the Russian gear as the ice pack began to disintegrate. Two Skyhook kits were dropped, and the agents were recovered by a Fulton-rigged B-17.[9] Use of the Skyhook in the Vietnam War was attempted on two occasions, in both North Vietnam and Laos, but on one occasion the downed pilot was moving so quickly to avoid capture that he declined to stay in one place long enough to set up the balloon, which took about fifteen minutes. He was eventually picked up by a Jolly Green from Thailand. In another case, the pilot put the balloon up in a location that would have dashed him into a mountainside. After he moved it, and before a Fulton-equipped C-130 Blackbird could make the snatch, he was overrun by the North Vietnamese Army and captured.[10]

The Trooper's Ladder

In the late 1960s Army Special Forces developed an aluminum ladder that became known in the supply system as the "trooper's ladder." By January 1969, 1st Force had scrounged several of these jungle ladders from "in-country" sources and had begun to use them on both inserts and extracts where vegetation or the steepness of terrain precluded a helicopter's touching down. A single jungle ladder was sixty feet long and four feet wide. One was attached to each side of a Huey helicopter, in a rolled-up position near the landing skids of the chopper. When the chopper reached the recovery site, the two ladders would be unrolled and deployed so that they were hung down beneath the helicopter. They could not be used on the marine Sikorsky H-34 Chocktaw helicopter because of balance problems that made directional control of the aircraft difficult to maintain. The H-34 has only one door on the right side.

Two ladders could be attached to each other side by side, making an eight-foot-wide panel. They could also be attached end-on-end, doubling the length to one hundred twenty feet, for use in heavy jungle canopy. By March 1969, 1st Force Recon Company had used the jungle ladders operationally for five extractions. The commanding general of the 1st Marine Division made a request to the Marine Corps commandant by way of the commanding general of the Fleet Marine Force, Pacific, for the addition of eight sixty-foot jungle ladders to force recon's table of organization.[11] First Force found that by "utilizing this ladder and taking advantage of the more numerous small openings in terrain and vegetation, a patrol can be inserted or extracted in seconds versus the ten to twenty minutes required by rappelling or hoisting operations."[12]

The McGuire and STABO Rigs

In Vietnam in 1969, Special Operations Group (SOG)—a joint unit that included members from the U.S. Air Force, the U.S. Navy SEALs, the U.S. Army's Special Forces, and force recon personnel—was inserting and extracting teams into Laos. SOG was having the same problems as those that 1st Force Recon had encountered in making emergency extracts of its teams. Special Forces Sgt. Maj. Charles McGuire, while serving with SOG, experimented with and developed what became known as McGuire rigs, which were one-hundred-foot nylon ropes with a six-foot loop at the lower end that contained a padded seat (much like a child's swing). Four of these rigs were carried in SOG's extract Hueys, two out of each side.

SOG used the McGuire rigs successfully. However, the team had been aware that if any of the ropes had become entangled in the jungle trees during the extract, those lines—with the extractees in them—would have had to be cut. In addition to the possibility of being cut loose by their crew chief, the team's extractees were at peril of simply slipping out of the sling due to their wounds or general weakness. There were several fatalities. In an effort to prevent such accidents, a wrist slip-loop was added to the rig, but several team members still reportedly fell to their deaths.

Necessity, as the mother of invention, led to the later development of the STABO rig by three instructors at the 5th Special Forces Group's Recondo School. The STABO harness replaced the team member's standard army web gear and was worn at all times when a team member was on an insert. When an emergency extract was needed, the patrol member unfastened two straps on his belt's back, brought them through his legs, and snapped them securely in front with a climber's snap link, called a carabiner. The Huey would hover momentarily overhead, dropping a one-hundred-foot nylon line fitted with a STABO yoke, which had two D rings at each end. The patrol member snapped into the D rings and was lifted up and flown out of the area, dangling a hundred feet below the helicopter at ninety knots.

The advantage of the STABO rig over the McGuire

was that the extractee did not have to hang on to it and could thus be firing his weapons during the extract—an advantage in suppressing fire from the Viet Cong or the NVA attempting to overrun the patrol. Later versions of the STABO harness had the carabiner in the front at all times, making it easier for a team in a pursued extract.[13]

The SPIE Rig

Aware of the McGuire and the STABO rigs that were being used by their SOG and Special Forces counterparts, 1st Force Recon Company, 1st Recon Battalion, and 1st Marine Air Wing riggers created several versions of a more simplified rig that had a greater capacity—the SPIE (special personnel insertion and extraction) rig.

The use of recon patrols made it necessary for helicopters to be capable of extracting up to twelve heavily laden team members simultaneously. The riggers took one-hundred-twenty-foot lengths of standard two-inch-wide flat nylon parachute harness webbing and sewed them together back-to-back, doubling the normally high tensile strength. At the lower end of the one line, they sewed a series of spaced reinforced D rings.

At all times when they were on patrol, every recon team member wore what parachutists call an "integrated harness," much like a standard parachute harness without a parachute attached. Each recon marine carried carabiners as well—in fact, most of them carried several. On an extract, the helicopter would drop the weighted SPIE rig through the jungle canopy to the team. All team members would then immediately hook onto the rig, attaching their harnesses to the D rings with the carabiners. Using his radio, the patrol leader would advise the pilot or crew chief when all hands were hooked up. The entire team, including any dead or wounded, would then be simultaneously lifted out—with those who were able, facing outward and firing their weapons. Marines deplore the thought of ever having to leave their dead behind on the battlefield. If someone was a "K" (KIA, killed in action), the team would snap the harness of the dead marine onto the SPIE to bring the body back with the rest of the members.

After the recon team was hooked in, the helicopter would attempt to climb as straight up as possible. This was always difficult because when a heavily weighted chopper is hovering above the jungle canopy, it is basically OGE, or "out of ground effect"—that is, it is hovering far above the ground surface that it needs to take off easily. The pilot would thus be "red-lining" his engine—pushing it to its maximum torque—in the jungle heat and the canopy-level altitude in the attempt to make the vertical liftoff. And if the extract were being attempted in a tight canopy, there was always the possibility that the team members' would be dragged through the treetops until the helicopter gained sufficient altitude to clear the canopy growth. Some injuries were sustained in these extracts, but everyone—to a man—would always opt for being banged up on trees if he knew he would be getting out of enemy territory.

The helicopter would fly back to the closest friendly area, where it would approach the ground at a high hover and, attempting to descend as gently as possible, lower the SPIE rig with its precious cargo to the ground without injury to the team hooked up below. As a method of extraction, the SPIE had tremendous advantages over the single jungle penetrator extract or the McGuire and STABO rigs. Just the knowledge that an entire recon team could be extracted in one effort, either with all members firing continuously or with their dead members hooked in, had a salutary effect on the recon marines. They all knew, too, that if they themselves were wounded, their teammates would hook them up and they would have a much higher chance of returning to behind friendly lines.

The 1st Marine Air Wing was justifiably nervous, however, about using the locally fabricated SPIE rigs without having any official authorization or any definitive testing with regard to the strength of the nylon webbing in its continued use in a tropical climate. Nylon deteriorates rapidly when exposed to bright sunlight and ultraviolet rays. In late May of 1970, the commanding general of 3d Marine Amphibious Force (who was in charge of all marine forces in Vietnam), in coordinating input from his 1st Marine Division and his 1st Marine Air Wing, sent a priority request to the commandant and to the Development Center for certification of the SPIE rig as to its safety and use.

The general cited the fact that a number of variations were being used in-country on an emergency basis for a variety of missions, search and rescue of downed air crews, medevac, recon patrols, and others: "First Recon Bn and First Force Recon Co together currently operate 26–34 recon teams daily in hostile territory, most of them in heavily canopied precipitous terrain with few LZs. In typical two-week period (7–21 May 1970) 60 extractions were conducted 13 of which were emergency extractions."[14]

Marine Corps Headquarters called out to El Centro to the National Parachute Test Range and received a distressingly laid-back answer from someone: it would take "one to two months" to do a proper evaluation. At this time, I was head of ground combat equipment—which included responsibility for intelligence and reconnaissance gear—at MCDEC at Quantico. One of the generals at Marine Corps Headquarters knew that I had been a test jumper at El Centro, so he called me with a request. In a fairly agitated state, the general informed me that the commandant was very much concerned about the request from Vietnam. "How long before you can get the SPIE rig certified?" he asked me.

All of us shared the same concern for the patrols in the bush who were having to use the locally manufactured SPIE rigs without knowing if they might be courting disaster. I felt confident of my El Centro contacts. They were all highly qualified parachute designers and engineers. I told the general that I would call back with a solid answer within several hours. I then telephoned El Centro and asked for parachute engineer Howard Fish, with whom I had worked when we did the first jumps on the TF-1 and the AJ-2 and the multiple jumps on the F3D and the A3D. Explaining the urgency of the situation, I asked for the most help he was capable of giving me.

Fish put me through to his skipper, a navy commander who was the OIC of the Naval Parachute Unit. I explained the life-and-death situation—we needed to have the SPIE rig evaluated on an immediate urgent-priority basis. Our Development Center riggers had already fabricated two of the rigs according to the 1st Marine Air Wing specifications. One of them used the simple back-to-back nylon webbing line, one hundred twenty feet long, and the second variation had two single one-hundred-twenty-foot nylon webbing lines joined by six-inch nylon-webbing cross-straps at five locations—it looked much like a long, very narrow nylon webbing ladder. So we had these two SPIE rigs on hand for immediate testing.

I told the commander that I along with another marine jumper could be on a plane to El Centro the next day. Since it was Friday, he checked the unit's schedule, and after rearranging some tests that had a lesser priority than ours, he assured me that we could do the testing within the week. I called the general back at Marine Corps Headquarters and relayed this information, and he authorized immediate TAD funding for me and Capt. Norm Hisler, a highly qualified recon marine, and we left Sunday for El Centro.

The parachute engineers did a thorough evaluation during the next two days. They went over both rigs in precise detail, examining them inch by inch and then counting the number of stitches, which dictated the strength, or carrying capacity, of the nylon webbing. The Marine Helicopter Group at El Toro provided two CH-46 helicopters for our use, and for Wednesday, we scheduled dummy pickup tests and then live tests using the rigs. Good fortune smiled on us in that one of the crew chiefs aboard had just returned from Vietnam and was familiar with the SPIE's rigging within the aircraft.

Both of the engineers and the flight surgeon at NPU were, for some reason, concerned about the physiological impact that pickup by the SPIE had on the body. Two members of the medical telemetry crew at NPU had been involved with the space program, and both of them had wired the astronauts for some of their flights. The scientists spent several hours wiring my body with sensors for respiration rate, heart rate, and other vital signs. These wires fed into a small black transmitter box that they placed immediately adjacent to my reserve parachute. And, yes, I was wearing a reserve chute. Once you are a parachutist, if you know that you are going to be hung one hundred ten feet under a helicopter flying at fifteen hundred feet above the California desert, your survival instincts kick in, and you decide to carry a reserve chute, just for the safety of it. In talking to Levi Woods, I learned that he went through the same thought process when he was the first live pickup with the Fulton Skyhook. I had the riggers fabricate a nylon cover that was fitted over my reserve parachute, covering the ripcord so that it could not be inadvertently opened. The cover could easily be removed and the parachute activated if I had to unhook and drop free during the tests.

Wednesday dawned as the usual El Centro summer day, sunny and hot. There was a light wind gusting at about eight knots when we arrived at the pickup site. We hooked up seven articulated dummies and one instrumented torso dummy for the first pickups. The use of the mannequins helped to indoctrinate the pilots on the liftoff and, more importantly, on the soft landing we hoped for. We made two dummy extractions on the single SPIE system and one extraction on the double system with flight speeds of sixty knots to an altitude of fifteen hundred feet. The mannequins were weighted at two hundred seventy pounds each.

All the dummy flights went well, and we were ready for the live pickup tests. The technicians had me wear an oxygen mask into which they had wired an instrument to record my heart rate and my voice—I was supposed to make any observations that I felt were appropriate during the various phases of the test. Later, the flight surgeon in attendance said that my pulse had been my normal fifty-eight beats per minute while sitting on the ground. But when the carabiner was hooked to the D ring on my rig, I heard the "click," and at that point my pulse went to over ninety.

Liftoff was easy. Capt. Norm Hisler and I swung against each other as we rose in the air, with four NPU test parachutists hooked in above us, singly and in pairs. Gaining altitude, the CH-46 flew several large figure eights at fifteen hundred feet over the ground-camera range to permit NPU to record the tests with ground-to-air photography. Air-to-air filming was also done from a photo plane that orbited at a safe distance.

I must say that when one is hanging a hundred and ten feet below a helicopter doing sixty to seventy plus knots, the wind has a definite impact on the body. Each of us found that we trailed backwards, facing in the direction from which we had just flown. We did determine that when the helicopter made standard turns during its figure eights, the SPIE line would make each of us move like a skater on the end of a string. We would angle back from directly below the chopper when it was in straightforward flight, but when it would make a turn, centrifugal force would hold us out at a forty-five-degree angle to the ground. While this was occurring, I was attempting to express my observations for the navy flight surgeon, recording them in my face-mask microphone. The digital tapes indicate that at the point where I was describing the sensation of being towed at the forty-five-degree angle in the turns, my heartbeat went up over one hundred thirty. So much for trying to be cool and nonchalant.

Our touchdown landings—that is, landing while still hanging the full one hundred ten feet beneath the helicopter—were relatively easy. When multiple extractees are coming down in pairs, the lowest pair touches down first, and they try to move out from under the next pair immediately above them. Since Norm and I were the low men on the totem pole, we moved several times, and as the last pair dropped in on top of us, we all ended up in more or less a football pile, with no injuries and everyone happy about the flight.

The tests were successful; the NPU engineers approved the SPIE rig as designed. They computed the tensile strength of the doubled nylon webbing as having about 300 percent more lift capacity than would ever be required. We were all pleased to hear that. The next morning Captain Hisler and I flew back to Quantico with the two SPIE rigs. We immediately briefed Maj. Gen. Al

Armstrong, who was the commanding general of MCDEC and our boss, and the rest of his staff. General Armstrong, as a marine aviator, took a keen interest in our reports on this gear. He was leaving shortly for an air wing assignment in Vietnam and took particular note of the results.

Together, the skipper at the newly designated Naval Aerospace Recovery Facility (the old NPU) and I drafted an immediate-priority message clearing further use of the SPIE rig. The message was sent in June 1970 to the commander of the Naval Air Systems Command, the chief of naval operations, the Marine Corps commandant, the commanding general of Fleet Marine Force, Pacific, and the commanding general of the 3d Marine Amphibious Force. The engineers did caution that when not in use, the rigs should be stored away from any sunlight to avoid ultraviolet deterioration.

This was my last effort on behalf of reconnaissance during my twenty-eight-year Marine Corps career. I was pleased to have had the opportunity to provide some input into ensuring the recovery of the patrols who were then operating deep beyond our lines.

CHAPTER FOURTEEN
Combat Parachuting

A number of force recon's early critics faulted us for developing HALO and other parachuting techniques for insertion of small teams behind an enemy's lines. They felt it would be unrealistic to think that these methods could actually be used in armed conflict. And indeed, our predecessors in the paramarines of World War II, who were disbanded in February 1944, never had the opportunity to make a combat jump.[1] The war in Vietnam, however, proved the efficacy of operational parachute insertion of force recon teams in combat situations.

The first-ever combat parachute jumps in Marine Corps history—a total of three—were made by marine recon over a three-year period in Vietnam, from 1966 to 1969. All three of the jumps were static line, using the T-10 parachute with the T-7A reserve parachute. In each instance the jumps were for the purpose of inserting a recon team.[2]

The First Combat Parachute Jump

On 14 June 1966, a thirteen-man recon team from 4th Platoon, 1st Force Recon, exited an army DeHavilland CV-2 Caribou (virtually identical to the air force's Fairchild C-123 Provider), dropping the stick from the lowered after-ramp at eight hundred feet above the jungle. Their target DZ was some thirty-five miles north and west of Chu Lai in South Vietnam. This first-ever Marine Corps combat jump was a night jump. Led by Capt. Jerome T. Paull, the team exited at approximately 0205. Staying in a tight stick, they landed in a small (five-hundred-meter) area on a grassy hillside.[3]

Their training in keeping a tight stick coupled with the slow (seventy-knot) drop speed of the CV-2 paid off. They all landed within one hundred fifty meters of one another, from first to last. Burying their parachutes, they set up a nearby observation post, from where they began to report troop movements. Late the second day, a dog that was following two Vietnamese woodcutters discovered and dug up several of their parachutes. Shortly thereafter the marines observed a Viet Cong unit, obviously alerted, searching the area. Knowing that the enemy was now aware of their presence, the marines requested and received an emergency extract at dusk by marine H-34 helicopters back to Chu Lai.

The Ill-Fated Second Jump

In September 1967, Gy.Sgt. Walter M. Webb Jr. took a nine-man recon team into western Happy Valley, south and west of Da Nang, in South Vietnam. The mission was an attempt to verify the presence of 300-mm Russian rockets, reportedly with nuclear capability. Again, it was a night jump from a Caribou. The pilot had been briefed to drop the team at eight hundred feet, but when their canopies popped, they were between fifteen hundred and two thousand feet. Severe winds aloft immediately separated the stick, causing linkup problems. The heavy jungle canopy where they landed had been hit by previous B-52 air strikes. The trees had been badly damaged, their splintered limbs resembling giant punji stakes. Several of the team hung in their harnesses in the top of the canopy for a number of hours until they could tell how high they were above the jungle floor. Two marines received sprained ankles on landing.

Gunny Webb, injured in the groin, hung in his harness, listening. In the darkness he dropped his helmet and timed the distance to the ground: three seconds, over seventy feet. He heard it hit rocks and then splash into a stream. At dawn he finally made it to the ground, where he briefly contacted teammate Sgt. James W. Hager. They separated moments later when they were spotted by an armed three-man Viet Cong patrol. In attempting to evade the VC, Webb became separated from the rest of his team. He was urinating blood, and with his testicles aching, he was barely able to walk. He made the decision to use his pilot's RT-10A survival radio to call for an extract. Webb was picked up about 1830 by a Jolly Green and returned to base.

Using clickers reminiscent of those used by the army paratroopers in the hedgerows of Normandy, Sgt. M. D. McNemar—who had been badly cut on the back of his head in landing—was able to join up with Cpl. R.J. "Pappy" Garcia. Garcia had wrenched his knee in his tree landing. They in turn joined up with two more of the team, Cpl. John W. Slowick and S.Sgt. Thomas J. Vallario, the assistant patrol leader. Realizing it was now a case of survival and evasion, the four planned to look for the others and then get out. With plenty of water in the area, they drank all of their own water that they could. Keeping two canteens apiece, they then buried all of their excess food. A medevac Jolly Green was called, and at noon the two injured marines (Garcia and McNemar) were hoisted out using a jungle penetrator rig.

By using pencil flares and radio directions from one of

the helicopters overhead with two Huey gunships standing by, five of the remaining six team members were able
to rendezvous: Staff Sergeant Vallario, Sergeants Woo
and Hagar, Corporal Owens, and Lance Corporal Slowick. Sgt. D. M. Woo had a badly sprained ankle and could
not walk. He too was medevaced by a Jolly Green at
about 1830. Harboring up for the second night, the last
four were recovered the next day by marine H-34 helicopters. The team's corpsman, HM2 Michael Louis
"Doc" LaPorte, was never found and is still carried as
MIA (missing in action).

This second combat jump was a pure disaster, considering the number of jungle-canopy landing injuries and
their early discovery by the enemy, requiring evasion and
later evacuation. Some team members conjectured that
Doc LaPorte had been impaled on one of the splintered
trees when he was landing. Because of Gunny Webb and
Sergeant Hager's encounter with the three-man VC patrol, others thought that Doc may have parachuted in on
top of a VC patrol and had been killed or taken prisoner
immediately on landing. Several in the company considered a third possibility: It was later determined in the investigation that Doc LaPorte had both a Vietnamese wife
and a child in Saigon, and it was reported that he had
jumped in carrying an inordinate amount of medical supplies. After the prisoner exchange and the end of hostili-
ties, LaPorte's name did not turn up on any of the lists of
the names of those who had been taken prisoner or those
who had died in captivity. Several who served with him
feel that he may still be in Vietnam. We will never know.[4]

The intended DZ for this jump was, in hindsight,
faulted because of its proximity to the high ridges and
corridors on the edge of Happy Valley. This terrain is
probably what funneled in the unusually high winds aloft
that dispersed the jumpers and carried them some two

kilometers out of the DZ into the high canopy at the eastern edge of Happy Valley.

The Final Jump

Two years passed following the devastating results of the Happy Valley jump. The final jump in Vietnam was made on 17 November 1969 by 1st Lt. Wayne Rollings with his six-man "Team 51." Rollings was joined by Staff Sergeant Chamberlain, Sergeant Moorman, Corporal Smith, Lance Corporal Lyons, and Hospital Corpsman Noble. Jumping at night, this time from a marine Boeing-Vertol CH-46 Sea Knight, they were headed for a DZ that was a grassy area two hundred meters inland from a beach off the South China Sea near the village of Nui Tran. Exiting the darkened after-ramp at one thousand feet at a ninety-knot drop speed, the recon patrol was inserted into a suspected VC supply and staging area located on a small peninsula.

In the past, major marine infantry units had been unable to capture any VC or supplies in the area because of the open ground. The flat, grassy terrain provided the VC with plenty of advance warning on the approach of any major unit moving toward the peninsular haven. Tactically, the thought was that, by making night parachute entry, the recon marines would give the VC no inkling of their insertion and would thus possibly be able to accomplish what the larger units had not. Everyone carried preset compasses that guided them back to the beach for rendezvous after they had landed. Assembly of the team went like clockwork, and they immediately moved out on patrol. After four days of intensive patrolling of the entire peninsula, they found no major VC or significant caches. They did find and search three caves, which were empty.

Despite its lack of apparent success, the jump had a very positive effect on the pride of the marines in force recon: they now knew that they could conduct a night parachute entry into enemy territory and successfully assemble and patrol without detection. The "negative intelligence" actually turned out to be quite positive—their actions had determined that neither the VC nor the NVA were using the peninsula as a supply collection and forwarding area, as had previously been thought.[5]

Combat Use of HALO in Vietnam

Despite the fact that this book is about the formation of force reconnaissance, it is most appropriate to give recognition here to army Special Forces parachutists, who were able to implement HALO for the first time in combat. Indeed, force recon and Special Forces have always had a close relationship. This goes back to World War II in Gen. Bill Donovan's Office of Strategic Services (OSS), when marine officers such as Capt. Sterling Hayden (a movie actor both before and after the war) went into Europe and worked closely with the OSS predecessors of Special Forces. Force recon marines and the army's Special Forces trained together, jumped and dived together, and on occasion, died together. In addition, both Special Forces and 1st Force Recon (and later, 2d Force) were doing developmental HALO work together as early as 1957. "Three-Finger Louie" (Maj. Lou Conein) of Special Forces and I had been exchanging technical information for several years. And Sgt. Bob Zwiener and I had done some early HALO work from marine F3Ds in 1957 and 1958.

It is with this background that I briefly describe here the first combat HALO jumps in U.S. parachuting history. For further reading, I refer the reader to a book that I believe will become a major resource in the history of special operations in Vietnam, *SOG: The Secret Wars of America's Commandos in Vietnam*, by Maj. John L. Plaster, USA (Ret.). Major Plaster describes the Special

Forces' participation in the CIA's SOG HALO operations
into Laos and South Vietnam. It is only the passage of
time and declassification of these secret missions that
permits telling their story now.

In October 1970 the decision was made to use HALO
to emplace a SOG reconnaissance team into Laos. "Recon Team Florida" was chosen. It was composed of three
Americans and three indigenous individuals: S.Sgt. Cliff
Newman, Sgt. Sammy Hernandez, Sgt. Melvin Hill, one
ARVN officer, and two Montagnards. Hernandez was a
graduate of the Special Forces HALO school at Fort
Bragg, where Hill had been an instructor. Though all
were experienced SOG recon team members, they did rehearsal jumps on Okinawa for a month.

During the early morning hours of 28 November 1970,
the team took off in a completely black C-130 Hercules
(appropriately named Blackbird). The area targeted for
reconnaissance in Laos was the site of a major North
Vietnamese road complex that had one Vietnamese division located within ten miles of it. The armament the recon team carried was impressive. Each team member
carried an Eagle Arms CAR-15, while the team weaponry
included several sawed-off M-79 (40-mm) grenade
launchers, a sawed-off shotgun, a Colt Cobra airweight
snub-nosed revolver, and some .22-caliber suppressed
Hi-Standard pistols, as well as a brace of assorted
grenades. Rucksacks were stowed and tied beneath their
reserve parachutes. The backs of their main chutes had
been sprayed with a temporary luminescent paint that was
supposed to facilitate each member's following down the
jumper preceding him below.[6]

Inbound, the blackened C-130's red lights were on. All
hands were breathing oxygen for the eighteen-thousand-
foot altitude. No oxygen bail-out bottles were to be used
during the actual drop. At 0200 the rear ramp went down

and the red lights went off. It was a rainy, dark night, and the C-130 was above the clouds. The HALO jumpers had rehearsed the seventy-one-second free fall many times. They would exit, take up stabilized free-fall positions, and open at fifteen hundred feet. The men's blackened faces made their hulking forms look grotesque.[7]

When the "Go!" signal was given, each American, with his hand on the shoulder of one of the indigenous men, stepped off into the rain and darkness. Within five seconds of exit, they entered the rain-filled clouds. They lost all sight of each other until they met on the ground when they assembled so that they could all be accounted for. Immediately after assembly, they split up into three groups, each having a discrete mission. After five days in the jungles of Laos, they rejoined and were recovered by a Jolly Green helicopter from Thailand. They had done what they had come for. And they had proved the efficacy of the HALO penetration for insertion of reconnaissance teams.[8]

A number of subsequent HALO insertions were made into Laos and into the border areas of South Vietnam. The teams went into areas where heavy ground and antiaircraft fire had made reconnaissance impossible heretofore. It was not until twenty-five years later, however, that the U.S. Army acknowledged the fact that its Special Forces jumpers (while serving with SOG) had made these combat jumps at all. In 1995, S.Sgt. Cliff Newman and the other HALO parachutists were given special HALO wings affixed with a gold star, indicative of a combat jump.[9]

Because this book is intended to cover the ideas leading to the formation and establishment of force recon within the Marine Corps, tales of force recon's exploits in Grenada, Panama, the Persian Gulf, and Africa will be left to other historians. We of the Marine Corps can look with pride on those officers and men of 1st and 2d Force Recon Companies. They sowed the seeds of new ideas and nurtured and brought these new methods, tactics, and equipment to fruition. May those within the reconnaissance community continue to be innovative and daring, always rising to future challenges. Our current force recon assets bear the results of those who have gone before.

AFTERWORD

In the era of Marine Corps history covered by this book, each marine division had its own reconnaissance battalion whose mission was to conduct recon both for its parent division and for its subordinate elements. If there were more than one marine division in a marine amphibious force (MAF) or a marine expeditionary force (MEF), however, these forces' specialized reconnaissance needs were to be fulfilled by the higher level force reconnaissance company. To continue the logic of this rather simple delineation of missions, there have been amalgamations in the more recent past in which a force recon company was attached to the division recon battalion so that it became essentially just another recon company. This loss of independence caused a deterioration in mission capabilities in the opinion of a majority of experienced reconnaissance officers.[1] This kind of amalgamation was done in both the 1st and the 3d Marine Divisions from 1966 through 1969 with tacit approval of the commanding generals of III Marine Amphibious Force.[2]

Reconnaissance, like any specialty within the military, must be responsive to change. Such change is on occasion dictated by new developments in tactics and in methods of employment, by new technologies, or by the national interest—as was the case with the increase in overseas deployments, which were called "pumps" by the marines and "peacekeeping" missions by the State Department. And pathfinders, for example, were an entity within force recon that largely disappeared as a result of technological developments, particularly global positioning satellite navigation.

Until early 1970, each marine division had its own organic recon battalion, directly under the operational control and direction of the major general who was the division commander. At force level, each of the four force reconnaissance companies (one with each of the active-duty MEFs and one with the reserve) was under the operational control of the MEF commander's SRIG (surveillance, reconnaissance, intelligence group). Thus 1st Force Recon Company was under 1st SRIG, 2d Force Recon under 2d SRIG, and so on.

The SRIGs were an institutionalized outgrowth of the Vietnam-spawned Surveillance and Reconnaissance Center (SRC). The first SRC was instituted under Lt. Gen. Herman Nickerson in August 1969. The brainchild of Lt. Col. Al Gray and Lt. Col. Gerald Polakoff, the SRC was designed to function as a "dynamic, integrated intelligence/surveillance and reconnaissance capability" for the III Marine Amphibious Force commander. It would fulfill this role by using the assets of the 1st and 3d Force Recon Companies, which had previously been attached to (and in some minds, misused by) the division recon battalions within their respective marine divisions.[3]

The blending of force recon into the division recon battalion was done again in October 1997 at Camp Lejeune in II Marine Expeditionary Force at the direction of its commander, Lt. Gen. Charles Wilhelm. Initially all recon assets of force troops and the 2d Marine Division were consolidated into 2d Recon Battalion, 2d Marine Division. Three letter companies were then created: Alpha Company, which was previously 2d Marine Division Recon

Company; Bravo Company, which had elements of the prior 2d Marine Division Recon Company and 2d Force Recon Company; and Charlie Company, which became the MEF force recon asset. A and B Companies were to support the requirements of the Direct Action Platoon, which habitually deployed with the marine expeditionary units (MEUs) for overseas assignments.

This test restructuring went through another permutation in January 1998 when B and C Companies were reestablished as the "new" 2d Force Recon Company. Currently the 2d Marine Division Recon Battalion is structured with a battalion headquarters company, a single division recon company, and a force recon company. The force recon company now has a headquarters element and six operational platoons.[4] The restructuring has been explained as the result of the recent high tempo of operational deployments of East Coast FMF units. For example, now one force recon platoon deploys, along with a division recon battalion platoon, with each MEU. Every MEU now deploying carries the designation SOQ (special operations qualified).

Part of the difficulty faced by the reconnaissance community in its increasing operational commitments is the relatively long period of time that is required to train marines for force recon duty. After graduating from the School of Infantry, prospective recon marines are sent to Basic Recon School, either at Little Creek, Virginia, or at Coronado, California. (It is anticipated that these two schools will be consolidated at one location in order to reduce personnel and increase the number of marines that Basic Recon School can turn out.) Graduates of Recon School then go on to seek qualification as basic divers at the new Marine Corps Combat Diving School, located at Panama City, Florida. The diving school was established in recognition of the uniqueness of training required for Marine Corps divers. From all reports, the school appears to be a great success. After completion of dive school, the young recon marine goes to Fort Benning, Georgia, to become parachute qualified. Then, once the recon marine reports to his company and platoon, he continues with more specialized training such as SERE, HALO, survival, ranger, and jumpmaster courses.

In creating a recon MOS (military occupational specialty), 0321, the Marine Corps finally recognized the compendium of these specialized skills. This should help, but the long lead time for recon replacements is still causing manning problems within force recon as well as in the division recon companies.

In March 1998, representatives from each of the elements of the reconnaissance community met at Quantico at the Marine Corps Combat Development Command as a working group to review current doctrine, organization, training, and manning of Marine Corps reconnaissance assets. The participants reached the following four conclusions. First, force recon companies of fourteen officers and 169 enlisted personnel, organized into a company headquarters and five force recon platoons, were to operate within I and II Marine Expeditionary Forces (T/O 4718D). Second, a division recon company of fourteen officers and 231 enlisted personnel, organized into a company headquarters and nine division recon platoons, was to operate within I and II Marine Expeditionary Forces (T/O 1423P). Third, III Marine Expeditionary Force's force recon company was to be structured for nine officers and 129 enlisted personnel, with a company headquarters and four platoons (T/O 4719C). And fourth, the 3d Marine Division's recon company was to be structured for seven officers and 118 enlisted personnel, with a company headquarters and four platoons (T/O 1423Q).[5] The recon conference/workshop also institutionally reaffirmed the practical sequence of training of recon marines—from the School of Infantry through Basic Recon, diving, and finally parachute training—as it was crafted by the respective force recon companies.

In restructuring and consolidating 1st Force Recon as just another company within the division's organic recon battalion, the commanders of 1st Marine Division and II Marine Expeditionary Force were in essence replicating the amalgamation that had been done with Northern I Corps in the 3d Marine Division in Vietnam thirty years before.

Lt. Col. Alex Lee's book *Force Recon Command* ably relates the extreme difficulty he encountered in attempting to extract 3d Force Recon from the clutches of the 3d Marine Division Recon Battalion commander. It was only through the intercession of Lt. Gen. Herman—affectionately called "Herman the German"—Nickerson Jr. as commanding general of III Marine Amphibious Force, that Alex was able to accomplish his goal.[6] Under General Nickerson's forceful leadership presence, 3d Force was placed under the control of a newly created SRC for the coordination and operations for all deep reconnaissance and special operations within the MEF's tactical area of responsibility.

The SRC concept grew and developed with the experience of its personnel. Initially in Vietnam the SRC was run by a lieutenant colonel. It became institutionalized and expanded into SRIGs, which were commanded by colonels. The SRIG has now been replaced by the "intelligence and electronic warfare" battalion, which has most of the same assets (intelligence companies and radio battalion) and functions that its predecessor had. The "intelligence and electronic warfare" battalions have become the coordinators for all "special operations"—a term that, in this context, embraces raids, sabotage, hostage rescue, and SAR (search and rescue) and downed pilot rescue. Generally, these battalions exceed the training and equipment of the division's organic reconnaissance companies.

In the past, the recon companies of the marine division

recon battalion were tasked with reconnaissance of areas to the front and the flanks of their division and its regiments within the artillery fan (the area that can be covered by the fire of the artillery group serving with a particular division). Today, in contrast, the development of offset bombing beacons, laser range-finders, pulse emitters, and more sophisticated sensors and infrared and night-vision devices permits force reconnaissance teams to operate at far greater distances behind enemy lines, as was done by force recon in the Persian Gulf in Operation Desert Storm.[7]

The American press has well documented the plight of all of our armed forces in the drawdowns dictated by fund shortages created by our frequent and extensive "peace-keeping" missions, such as those in Bosnia, Haiti, and Africa.[8] It would seem that on occasion, within the Marine Corps, we can become our own worst enemies and hasten to repeat the costly mistakes of the past.

Maj. Gen. Wayne E. Rollings, former commanding general of the III Marine Expeditionary Force, went on record at a 1997 SRIG conference expressing his opposition to placing force recon anywhere other than under the direct control of the MEF commander. (In his earlier days as a first lieutenant in Vietnam, as I recounted earlier, General Rollings parachuted his force recon team in on one of the Marine Corps's three combat parachute jumps.) Among Marine Corps general officers, there were some expressions of displeasure with how the SRIGs operated during Desert Storm. Several G-3s felt that the SRIGs were a little "too independent" in their operation of the intelligence assets. Their irritation is understandable. There is an ongoing territorial conflict between the intelligence community (G-2s) and the operations officers (G-3s), each group feeling that it should have control over all operational assets. Scores of articles in the *Marine Corps Gazette* over the years have examined the need to strengthen the G-2s and the intelligence community and not to leave them in their traditional role as subservient to the G-3 operations officers.

Lt. Gen. James "Jungle Jim" Masters was one general who felt that there was no inherent conflict in having strong G-2s whose primary responsibility was for the intelligence assets, to complement the decisions of the G-3 operations officers of the marine division. Lt. Gen. Herman Nickerson Jr., as commanding general of III Marine Amphibious Force in Vietnam, felt the same way when he established the SRIG predecessor intelligence coordinating organization in the SRCs. As frequently happens, the personalities of the incumbents (the SRIG colonels) may have rubbed the G-3 types a bit too strongly.

I respectfully submit that this high-priority coordination of all of a unit's intelligence and reconnaissance assets should not be considered a logical reason for virtually eliminating a vital force-level intelligence asset. It would seem that the commanding general of the MEF could surely provide appropriate command guidance to avoid this apparent conflict between G-2s and G-3s over turf and return the MEF organization to a smoothly running command staff, using all elements, both operational and intelligence assets, to their fullest—ideally where the intelligence community works closely with the operational community.

One must wonder what Lt. Gen. "Howling Mad" Smith would have said if someone had tried to take his force-level V Amphibious Corps's recon battalion away from him during the some one hundred eighty operations in which they performed so brilliantly during World War II. Ask a former commandant, Gen. Paul X. Kelley or Gen. Al Gray, both of whom had extensive reconnaissance and intelligence tours during their early careers. Ask the former commander of III Marine Amphibious Force, Lt. Gen. Herman Nickerson Jr. I am confident that all of these distinguished combat leaders would fight tenaciously against the MEF or MAF commander if they were in danger of losing their own organic deep reconnaissance unit.

We who have worked in reconnaissance are keenly aware of the dictates of reduced budgets and downsizing. But a unit does not have to be disestablished simply because it is utilized to a very great extent. If the actual reason for disestablishing 2d Force Recon Company is overcommitment, then rather than dissipating force recon's unique strength and expertise and relegating the unit to the level of a functionary within the marine division's recon battalion, our leaders need to recognize the increased requirements created by the current rate of deployments and increase the reconnaissance assets accordingly. Reports from the 1998 recon working group indicate movement toward this solution: increasing the manpower available for force recon so that it can meet the obvious increase in its commitments. It is hoped that this recognition of force recon's extensive utilization will continue.

Only time and future operational deployments will determine the wisdom of these decisions. I strongly feel that maintaining force recon at force level (as is currently in I MEF and III MEF) is the sound solution. The reduction of force recon from an independent unit to "just another company" within the 2d Marine Division's recon battalion is a structural error. If history repeats itself, as it is wont to do, when the requirement for deep, force-level reconnaissance arises, the force or the MEF commander will again demand his own dedicated force recon company. One thing that I know will remain a constant in this sorting-out: the dedication, devotion to duty, and spirit of the officers, marines, and corpsmen of units performing reconnaissance missions in our Marine Corps, wherever they are located. To them and to all marines who will participate in deep reconnaissance in the future this treatise is respectfully dedicated.

NOTES

Chapter 1

1. Marine Corps dispatch 102102, 11 April 1944, cited in Lanning and Stubbe, *Inside Force Recon*, 21, n. 19.

2. Morison, *Breaking the Bismarck's Barrier*, 378.

3. McMillan, "Scouting at Cape Gloucester," 26. Coleman, "Amphibious Recon Patrols," 25.

4. "Citation for Soldier's Medal," dated February 1944. Maj. John Bradbeer, interview by author, at Amphibious Reconnaissance School, TTUPac, Coronado, California, 20 April 1954.

5. Morison, *New Guinea and the Marianas*, 353.

6. Pratt, *The Marines' War*, 290–92. Hoffman, *The Seizure of Tinian*, 24–25.

7. Pratt, *The Marines' War*, 291.

8. As Fane and Moore write in *The Naked Warriors*, "The early 'Assault Personnel Destroyers' (APDs) were four-stack destroyers from World War I, remodeled for troop transport by removal of two boilers and fireroom to give additional troop space" (86).

9. "Northern Troops and Landing Force Operations Order 27–44," dated 9 July 1944 (copy in Archives Section, Marine Corps Historical Center, Washington, D.C.).

10. "K-Bar" is the marine term for the Ka-Bar fighting knife trademarked by Ka-Bar Knives of Olean, New York. The Fairbairn is a stiletto-design fighting knife that was initiated by 4th Marine captain Samuel Sylvester Yeaton in the 1940s in Shanghai and later jointly developed with the Shanghai police officers W. E. Fairbairn

and E. A. Sykes. Known as the Fairbairn-Sykes commando knife, it was introduced into Marine Corps raider, paramarine, and amphibious reconnaissance units during World War II. It gradually replaced the Ka-Bar and was used by commandos, some U.S. Marine Raiders, and some marine recon personnel.

11. Harwood, *A Close Encounter*; 1. Hoffman, *The Seizure of Tinian*, 22.

12. McMillan, "Scouting at Cape Gloucester," 26. Coleman, "Amphibious Recon Patrols," 25.

13. Col. Merwin H. Silverthorn, telephone interview by author, 3 November 1996. See also Williams, "Amphibious Scouts and Raiders," 153.

14. Silverthorn, interview, 3 November 1996.

15. In the book he coauthored with Percy Finch, General Smith describes this rather acrimonious discussion between himself and the admirals, which ultimately led to adoption of White 1 and White 2 (see Smith and Finch, *Coral and Brass*, 205–7).

16. Smith and Finch, *Coral and Brass*, 207. Pratt, *The Marines' War*, 292. Cates, foreword to Hoffman, *The Seizure of Tinian*, iii.

17. Smith and Finch, *Coral and Brass*, 207.

18. Hoffman, *The Seizure of Tinian*, 21. Cates, foreword to Hoffman, iii. Smith and Finch, *Coral and Brass*, 207–12.

19. Lanning and Stubbe, *Inside Force Recon*, 21–22.

Chapter 2

1. Musicant, *The Banana Wars*, 215–19. Sgt. Herman Hannekan and Cpl. William R. Button (who both received the Medal of Honor for their actions) painted their bodies with burnt cork and crept through six concentric rings of guards, wherein Hanneken shot Haitian guerrilla leader Charlemagne Perault. They fought their way out, bringing with them Perault's body on a mule, for identification and last rites. This action brought the guerrilla movement under control in the area.

2. *The Games of the Xth Olympiad Committee*, Los Angeles

1932: Official Report (Los Angeles: Xᴛʜ Olympiad Committee, 1933), 625.

3. Davis, *Marine*, 394.

4. Wayne Morris (1914–59) was a navy pilot during World War II and had a distinguished combat record, shooting down seven enemy aircraft and flying fifty-seven combat missions.

5. See Reber, "Pete Ellis."

6. Col. Merwin H. Silverthorn, telephone interview by author, 6 May 1997. Col. Joseph Z. Taylor, USMCR (Ret.), telephone interview by author, 11 June 1997.

7. The Amphibious Reconnaissance School frequently embarked together with UDT. Usually this was on the USS *Perch*. Whenever the *Perch* was unavailable (in overhaul or on another mission), we would be assigned to one of the other fleet boats: the *Ronquil*, *Bream*, or *Queenfish*, for example.

8. See Fane and Moore, *The Naked Warriors*.

9. A. R. Sears, "Beach Jumper Units," Naval War College lecture, 3 November 1955 (copy in the archives at the Marine Corps Historical Center and at the Naval Historical Center in Washington, D.C.).

10. Davis, *Marine*, 67–69.

Chapter 3

1. "Parachute Delivery of Special Forces Personnel Utilizing Free-Fall Techniques (HALO)," interim report by Lucien E. Conein, Quartermaster, Research and Engineering, 17 December 1957.

Chapter 4

1. Cushman, "Amphibious Warfare Tomorrow," 32.

2. Pierce and Hough, *The Compact History*, 301–2. Montross, *Cavalry of the Sky*, 77, 156–206.

3. Commandant Shepherd's letter of instruction establishing Marine Corps Test Unit 1, 10 August 1954 (copy in Archives Section, Marine Corps Historical Center).

4. Ibid.

5. Aide memoir to Lemuel C. Shepherd Jr., CMC, 16 July 1954 (copy in Archives Section, Marine Corps Historical Center).

6. "Notes for . . . Briefing," in aide memoir to Lemuel C. Shepherd Jr., CMC, 16 July 1954.

7. Edward N. Rydalch, "Briefing for SecNav Thomas Gates on Marine Corps Test Unit One," 16 October 1956.

8. See Suhoskey, "Test Unit One," 30.

9. Edward N. Rydalch, CO, Marine Corps Test Unit 1, letter to Lemuel C. Shepherd Jr., CMC, 12 May 1955.

10. Suhoskey, "Test Unit One," 31.

11. "Request for Specialized Training for Reconnaissance Platoon," Edward N. Rydalch, CO, Marine Corps Test Unit 1, letter to Lemuel C. Shepherd Jr., CMC, 3 October 1955.

12. Edward N. Rydalch, CO, Marine Corps Test Unit 1, letter to Randolph M. Pate, CMC, 13 February 1956.

13. See Lanning and Stubbe, *Inside Force Recon*, 33.

14. Randolph M. Pate, CMC, letter to Edward N. Rydalch, CO, Marine Corps Test Unit 1, 21 June 1956.

15. Captain Kittinger exited over New Mexico on 16 August 1960, making a free fall of 16.04 miles (McWhirter, *Guinness Book*, 298).

16. Johnstone, *United States Marine Corps Parachute Units*, 7.

17. BUPERS (Bureau of Naval Personnel) Notice 111020, 12 July 1963.

Chapter 5

1. Dated 14 June 1956, the document report that I prepared for the commandant explaining our findings was titled "Memorandum for the Record, Grumman TF-1: Potential Use of TF-1 Transport Aircraft for Parachute Recon and Pathfinding Units in the Helicopter Assault."

2. Lt. Cdr. Roy Taylor, quoted in Ken Earle's report, "TF-1 Bailout Evaluation," 9 July 1956.

3. "Investigation to Inquire into and Report on the Circumstances Attendant to the Injury of Maj. Bruce F. Meyers," Lewis T. Vinson, OIC, Naval Parachute Unit, 10 October 1956.

4. Geer, *The New Breed*, 19–20.

Chapter 6

1. Operations Ballistic Armor, Kentucky, Napoleon, Lancaster II, Saline, Fortress Attack, Napoleon, and Saline II.

2. "Quota for Assignment to Airborne Training," Lewis B. Puller, CG TTUPac, letter to Lemuel C. Shepherd Jr., CMC, 1 April 1953.

3. Maj. Gen. Clayton Jerome wrote in 1956 that "the lack of proper navigational equipment stimulates a need for a dependable terminal guidance system . . . that could be employed by reconnaissance personnel in or near the [helicopter] landing zone."

4. Commandant's letter of instruction establishing Marine Corps Test Unit 1, 10 August 1954.

5. Stubbe, *Arugha!*, 91, n. 424.

Chapter 7

1. Capt. Donald L. Koelper, testimony, "Record of Proceedings, Board of Investigation . . . to Inquire into the Circumstances Surrounding the Death and Injuries Sustained by Personnel of the Reconnaissance Platoon, Headquarters and Service Company, Marine Corps Test Unit # 1, on 17 January 1957, Ordered on 17 January 1957," 179.

2. Lt. Cdr. Lloyd Hardy, testimony, "Record of Proceedings," 147.

3. Capt. Joseph Z. Taylor, testimony, "Record of Proceedings," 14, 16, 21.

4. Capt. Roy M. Taylor, testimony, "Record of Proceedings," 152. Capt. Joseph Z. Taylor, testimony, "Record of Proceedings," 21.

5. Pvt. Thomas N. Szymanski, testimony, "Record of Proceedings," 51.

6. Capt. Joseph Z. Taylor, testimony, "Record of Proceedings," 22.

7. Cpl. Frank Kies, testimony, "Record of Proceedings," 61.

8. Capt. Joseph Z. Taylor, testimony, "Record of Proceedings," 17.

9. Opinion 8, "Record of Proceedings," iii.

Chapter 8

1. Our report to the commandant, "Final Summary Report of Marine Corps Test Unit #1 for Period 1Jul55 to 30Jun57," is on file in the Archives Section of the Marine Corps Historical Center in Washington, D.C.

2. "Report on Progress in Preparing Recommended T/Os and T/Es for the Reconnaissance Elements," Edward N. Rydalch, CO, Marine Corps Test Unit 1, letter to Edward Snedeker, G-3 HQMC, 13 February 1957.

3. Brig. Gen. Donald "Buck" Schmuck, USMC (Ret.), interview by author, 10 March 1997.

4. "Report on Progress," enclosure 2.

5. Ibid.

6. Ibid. The term "mount-out" refers to the deployment overseas for operational missions. It is used frequently to describe equipment that is packed and stored especially for such an operation. In the case of force recon, mount-out gear includes spare parachutes and rubber boats, as well as diving and other specialized equipment not usually in current standard supply stocks.

7. See "Comments and Recommendations Regarding Applicability of 'Sky-diving' Parachute Techniques to Parachute Reconnaissance and Pathfinding Activities of the Fleet Marine Force," Edward N. Rydalch, CO, Marine Corps Test Unit 1, letter to CG FMFPac, 7 May 1957.

8. "Marine Corps Test Unit 1, Test Project 6H; Final Report," Edward N. Rydalch, CO, Marine Corps Test Unit 1, report to Randolph M. Pate, CMC, 15 June 1957.

9. Lanning and Stubbe, *Inside Force Recon*, 40–41.

10. "Base Plate McGurk" was later determined to have been the pseudonym of Lt. Gen. William K. Jones, the brother of Maj. Jim Jones, of 5th Amphib Recon Battalion in World War II, and the uncle of the current commandant of the Marine Corps, James L. Jones.

Chapter 9

1. See United States, Chief of Naval Operations, *Landing Operations Doctrine*, "Reconnaissance Patrols," sec. 6. par. 442. See also Shinn, "Amphibious Reconnaissance."

2. "Report of Operations during Puerto Rico Campaign, 2–3Mar38," W. H. McKelvy Jr., CO, Company F, 2d Battalion, 5th Marines, report to CO, 2d Battalion, 5th Marines, 4 February 1938; and enclosure C, "Attack Force Order of 2Feb38," to Commander, U.S. Fleet Training Detachment, the USS *New York*.

3. Smith, "The Development of Amphibious Tactics," 47.

4. *Amphibious Reconnaissance*, USMC Amphibious Manual 15 (HQMC, 1951) appendix A, A-1-A-5.

5. United States, Chief of Naval Operations, *Dictionary of American Naval Fighting Ships*, 5:263.

6. See *Dictionary of American Naval Fighting Ships*, 5:263.

7. "Report of First War Patrol," R. D. Quinn, CO, the USS *Perch*, report to Chief of Naval Operations, 6 October 1950, enclosure 1 (originally classified Secret).

8. Col. Joseph Z. Taylor, interview, 11 June 1997. *Dictionary of American Naval Fighting Ships*, 5:262, 415–19. Capt. Paul Keenan, USN (Ret.), telephone interview by author, 11 June 1997.

9. M.Sgt. Bobby J. Patterson USMC (Ret.), telephone interview by author, 11 June 1997. Capt. William McKinstry, interview by author, 11 June 1997.

10. Ens. John Grobe, USNR, interview by author, 31 July 1998. "Report of Operation RECONEX 58D," Bruce F. Meyers, CO, 1st For Recon, report to Vernon E. McGee, CG FMFPac, 14 January 1958.

11. Col. R. H. Daugherty, USMC (director of aviation safety at

Naval Safety Center, Norfolk, Virginia), letter to author, 10 October 1957.

12. A common misperception is that scuba divers are breathing oxygen. It is never oxygen, however. It is always compressed breathing air—the same as what one ordinarily breathes.

13. Closed-circuit rebreathers are "closed" in the sense that no expelled air leaves the system, as it does in normal open-circuit scuba. The diver simply rebreathes oxygen to and from a breathing bag, putting the oxygen through a carbon dioxide absorbent along the way. When there is no longer sufficient oxygen in the bag, more oxygen is bled into it, and the new oxygen is scrubbed by the carbon dioxide absorbent (see Conference for National Cooperation in Aquatics, *The New Science of Skin and Scuba Diving*, 57–58).

14. Capt. P. X. Kelley, the executive officer of 2d Force Recon, provided a very lucid analysis of 2d Force's operations in submarine recovery in his report to the commandant, "Employment of Buoyant Ascent Techniques by Amphibious Reconnaissance Personnel," dated 26 November 1958, which was comparable to our 1st Force report on the same subject, dated 29 September 1958.

Chapter 10

1. The Momsen lung was used only once in combat in World War II, by nine crew members of the legendary submarine *Tang* (SS-306) in October of 1944. After a successful attack on a Japanese convoy near the north end of Formosa Strait in the vicinity of Turnabout Island, the twenty-third torpedo from the USS *Tang* broached, striking the vessel in the after torpedo room and sinking her. The skipper, Cdr. Richard Hetherington O'Kane, and eight others used their Momsen lungs, ascended, and were captured. They were the only survivors. Commander O'Kane received the Medal of Honor for his actions. See Mooney, ed., *Dictionary of American Naval Fighting Ships*, 7:37–39.

2. See Silverstein, "Escape," 16. CWO Richard Gerten, USN, interview by author, OIC Submarine Escape Training Facility, Submarine School, Groton, Connecticut, 4 March 1997. I had the op-

portunity to don (not to use) a Steinke aboard the USS *Michigan* (SSBN-747) underway, submerged, from Naval Submarine Base Bangor, in Washington state, on 20 March 1997.

3. Today most submarines do not carry a physician aboard; there is only an experienced navy corpsman, normally a chief petty officer.

4. At the submarine school in New London, Connecticut, there was another submarine escape tower identical to the one at Pearl Harbor. Both towers have now been decommissioned and replaced with shallower yet equally effective facilities for teaching submarine escape. The one at New London was torn down, but the one at Pearl Harbor was designated as a national historical site. Comparable tower facilities are in operation today at Coronado, California, and at the Naval Diving and Salvage Training Center (NDSTC), which serves as the center of U.S. Navy diving, in Panama City, Florida.

5. See United States, Navy Department, *Diving Manual* 7-1-7-50; and Graver, ed. *Advanced Diving*, 40–44.

6. Hyperventilation is breathing more than you need before submerging. It has little effect on the body's oxygen supply per se but "blows off" carbon dioxide from the normal stores. The practical effect is that the diver has more breathholding time, since it takes longer for the carbon dioxide to build up to its break point. See Conference for National Cooperation in Aquatics, *The New Science*, 56.

7. A diver should not fly for twenty-four hours after any significant amount of bottom time. During this interval, any compressed gasses that are still in suspension in the circulatory system will dissipate properly. But since our bottom time had been relatively brief, we had no problems in this regard. See the U.S. Navy's *Diving Manual*.

8. CG, 1st MarDiv, letter to ComSubRon 3, 9 May 1958; referenced in "Employment of Buoyant Ascent Techniques by Amphibious Reconnaissance Personnel," Bruce F. Meyers, CO, 1st Force Recon, report to Randolph M. Pate, CMC, 29 September 1958.

Chapter 11

1. "Amphibious Reconnaissance, Parachute Reconnaissance and Parachute Pathfinding Matters, Recommendations Concerning," Edward N. Rydalch, CO, Marine Corps Test Unit 1, letter to Randolph M. Pate, CMC, 28 March 1957, enclosure 2, "Austerity T/O and T/E."

2. See Johnstone, *United States Marine Corps Parachute Units*, 11.

3. "Blank Gore Parachute Evaluation and Stabilized Free-Fall Parachuting Instruction," written by Capt. Joseph Z. Taylor, signed by Bruce F. Meyers, CO, 1st Force Recon, report to Randolph M. Pate, CMC, 1 April 1958.

4. For the actual jump figures, see "Blank Gore Parachute Evaluation," 3.

5. These data are shown in "Blank Gore Parachute Evaluation," enclosure 1, 1–4.

6. See "Blank Gore Parachute Evaluation," 1–10.

7. "Parachute Delivery of Special Forces Personnel," interim report by Conein.

8. P. X. Kelley, letter to William Weise, inspector instructor, 3d Force Recon, Mobile, Alabama, 23 May 1963.

9. Col. Robert N. Burhans, USMC (Ret.), interview by author, 9 April 1997.

10. "Investigation to Inquire into Circumstances Surrounding Death of Capt. Peter J. Johansen Which Occurred at Fountainhead, NC, on 16Jan63," CG, Force Troops, FMFLant, letter to David M. Shoup, CMC, 7 February 1963 (copy in Archives Section, Marine Corps Historical Center).

11. "Recommended Adoption of HALO and the Maneuverable T-10 for Use by Force Recon Companies," P. X. Kelley, Marine Corps Landing Force Development Center (LFDC), letter to David M. Shoup, CMC, 15 October 1963 (copy in Archives Section, Marine Corps Historical Center).

Chapter 12

1. See Nickerson, "Force Recon."

2. "Reassignment of the Parachute Pathfinder Platoon, Force Reconnaissance Co. into the Marine Aircraft Group (Helicopter)," CO, MAG 26, letter to CG FMFLant, 28 April 1960.

3. Years later in the Mediterranean, while I was serving as landing force commander of a Sixth Fleet BLT, we had the 2d French Foreign Legion Parachute Battalion attached to us for operations on Corsica. Working with the Foreign Legion parachutists, we learned that French parachutists customarily yell "Merde!"—which is translated in English as "Shit!"—as they exit their aircraft.

4. L.Cpl. Dennis Boyle (now a civilian), interview by author, February 1997.

5. "Unusual Incident during Parachute Operations," J. S. Mc-Callister, CO, 1st Force Recon, report to David M. Shoup, CMC, 3 May 1962.

6. Maj. Bob McKenzie, interview by author, June 1997.

7. Nickerson, "Force Recon," 48.

8. Maj. Gen. David Shoup, cited in "1st MEF Critique Report, PHIBLEX 58M, Operation Strongback," March 1958, 2–3.

Chapter 13

1. Bradbeer, interview.

2. See Norton, *Force Recon Diary, 1969* and *Force Recon Diary, 1970*; Lee, *Force Recon Command*; and Lanning and Stubbe, *Inside Force Recon*. See also Plaster, *SOG*.

3. This process and its mechanism are described by Robert Fulton Jr. in "Fulton Air-to-Ground Pickup System for Caribou Aircraft," U.S. Army Transportation Research Command Technical Report 64–17, February 1964, a copy of which is available in the Archives Section at the Marine Corps Historical Center.

4. Bruce F. Meyers, CO, 1st Force Recon, to C. W. Parker, LFDC, 27 May 1958.

5. M.Sgt. Levi W. Woods, USMC (Ret.), letter to author, 1 June 1997.

6. Woods, letter to author. See also Fulton, "Fulton Air-to-Ground Pickup System," 31.

7. See Fulton, "Fulton Air-to-Ground Pickup System," 31.

8. "Fulton Air-to-Ground Pickup System," 15.

9. Robert Fulton Jr., telephone interview by author, 3 May 1997. See also the Naval Institute Press book *Project COLDFEET: Secret Mission to a Soviet Ice Station*, by William M. Leary and Leonard A. LeSchack (Annapolis, 1996); and Plaster, *SOG*, 72.

10. See Plaster, *SOG*, 72, 282, 287.

11. CO, 1st Recon Battalion, 1st MarDiv, message to Leonard F. Chapman Jr., CMC, 20 April 1970.

12. The commanding officer of 1st Recon Battalion sent three letters to the commandant regarding the "trooper's ladder": 10 March 1967, 1 February 1970, and 8 April 1970.

13. See Plaster, *SOG*, 148–49. STABO is an acronym formed from the names of the three innovators, Maj. Robert Stevens, Capt. John Knabb, and SFC Clifford Roberts.

14. "Emergency Insertion and Extraction of Personnel by a Hovering Helo," CG, III MAF, 29 May 1970.

Chapter 14

1. See Johnstone, *United States Marine Corps Parachute Units*, 7.

2. My primary sources of information regarding these three Marine Corps combat jumps are audio tapes (222, 307, 1598, and 4668) in the Archives Section of the Marine Corps Historical Center.

3. The only enlisted parachutists on this jump who are identified on the tapes are Gy.Sgt. Maurice Jacques, Sgt. Johannes Haferkamp, and a Sergeant Martin, whose first name is not given.

4. See Lanning and Stubbe, *Inside Force Recon*, 125–26.

5. *Inside Force Recon*, 126.

6. Plaster, *SOG*, 298–99.

7. Ibid., 299.

8. Ibid., 301.

9. Ibid., 312, 342.

Afterword

1. "Comments Concerning Reconnaissance Structure Study," James P. O'Donnell, director, Intelligence, Surveillance and Reconnaissance Branch, Marine Corps Development and Education Command, report to Special Study Group, Reconnaissance Structure Study, 17 October 1971.

2. For a complete chronicling of this amalgamation, see Lee, *Force Recon Command*, esp. 24–31.

3. Gray, foreword to Lee, *Force Recon Command*, xiii.

4. Gregory Gordon, 2d Force Recon, "Report to 'Sitrep,'" *Force Recon Newsletter* 1, no. 17 (April 1998): 5–10.

5. James P. O'Donnell, "Preliminary Report of Reconnaissance Working Group," 14 April 1998; repr. in "Report to 'Sitrep,'" *Force Recon Newsletter* 1, no. 17 (April 1998): 8.

6. Gray, foreword to Lee, *Force Recon Command*, xiii. See also Lt. Gen. Herman Nickerson Jr., "Commanding General's Comments," in Lee, *Force Recon Command*, ix–x.

7. Jon R. Anderson, "The End of Force Recon?" *Navy Times*, Marine Corps edition, 17 March 1997, 12–14. See also O'Donnell, "Preliminary Report of Reconnaissance Working Group."

8. Anderson, "The End of Force Recon?" 12–13.

GLOSSARY

A3D The Douglas Skywarrior, a carrier-based strategic bomber used for insertion of marine recon teams by free fall.

AD The Douglas Skyraider, a carrier-based bomber used for antisubmarine surveillance missions and close air support.

airborne A generic term applied to army-type parachute operations or units.

air officer Marine aviator assigned to assist ground commander in appropriate use of air support including helicopters.

AJ2 The North American Savage, a carrier-based prop-jet, capable of use for insertion of recon teams by free fall.

amphib recon A unit or the personnel of a unit whose primary mission is to conduct amphibious reconnaissance. Also a generic term describing the conduct of reconnaissance of a beach area by seaward means—e.g., rubber boats, swimmers, or scuba divers from a parent vehicle at sea.

APD   High-speed destroyer transport. Developed at the start of World War II. Used for transport of marine recon, UDT, and small special warfare forces.

APSS   Transport submarine. Modified fleet diesel submarines, carries up to one hundred ten troops. Examples are the USS *Perch* (APSS-313) and the USS *Sealion* (APSS-315).

ASR   Submarine rescue ship. Used for rescue and salvage of submarines.

ASSP   The early designation for transport submarines. The USS *Perch* was designated ASSP-313 from January 1950 to October 1956, when it was redesignated APSS-313. The USS *Sealion* was ASSP-315 from January 1950 to March 1955, when its designation was changed to APSS-315.

ASW   Antisubmarine warfare.

battalion   A marine tactical unit composed of a number of companies. Named for primary element, e.g., infantry battalion. Size varies, but approximately twelve hundred marines.

Beach Jumpers   Personnel specially trained for deception by use of spurious communications, pyrotechnics, and the like, during an amphibious operation. Established during World War II.

blown panels   A situation where component panels of a parachute are damaged either by opening or by burns in nylon caused by a line over the canopy. Usually requires pulling reserve parachute.

BLT Battalion landing team. A balanced reinforced marine infantry battalion with tanks, artillery, reconnaissance, and logistic support. Contains approximately two thousand marines.

board of inquiry/board of investigation Designated by senior naval commanders to ascertain facts regarding incidents of death and injury to determine if negligence were involved. May make recommendations for changes in tactics and/or equipment.

boat A term used by naval personnel to refer to a submarine. Also applied to landing craft and other small craft that can be hoisted aboard a ship.

boondockers Marine field shoes used in World War II and the Korean War.

buoyant ascent The technique of ascending from a submerged submarine where the diver uses a Mae West and "blows and goes" by continually exhaling air during ascent to surface.

C-119 U.S. Army and Air Force designation for the Fairchild Flying Boxcar, a twin-engine prop transport used for dropping of cargo and parachutists in the 1950s. Designated R4Q by the Marine Corps.

canopy The main supporting surface of a parachute. Previously made of silk, now of rip-stop nylon. Connected to harness by suspension lines.

Capewell release A metal fitting on parachutes that permits disengagement of the parachute canopy, risers, and shroud lines from the harness to prevent the parachutist from being dragged along the ground.

CG AirFMFPac Commanding general, Air Fleet Marine Force, Pacific. Headquartered originally at MCAS El Toro and now at MCAS Miramar in California.

CG FMFPac Commanding general, Fleet Marine Force, Pacific. Headquartered in Honolulu, Hawaii.

chief of the boat Senior chief petty officer aboard a submarine. Considered the executive officer's right-hand man in the administration of the crew.

"clean" A slang term used by recon parachutists and divers to refer to any action that is performed without equipment.

CMC Commandant, Marine Corps. The general officer commanding the Marine Corps, member of the Joint Chiefs of Staff.

CNO Chief of naval operations. The senior officer of the navy, member of the Joint Chiefs of Staff.

CO Commanding officer. The person in command of a ship. Also used as a designation for "commander," the person in charge of a unit or a fleet or force.

combat swimming A term applied to the techniques of reconnaissance entry by underwater swimmers and water survival. The designation fell into disuse after World War II.

ComNavAirPac Commander, Naval Air Force, Pacific Fleet. Headquartered at NAS North Island, San Diego, California.

ComNavFE Commander, Naval Forces, Far East. Headquartered at Yokusuka, Japan.

conning tower The large superstructure midships on fleet submarines from which the vessel is steered when on the surface. Below the open bridge.

corps A term referring to the Marine Corps and also to the next higher unit above a marine division, commanded by a lieutenant general.

CPO Chief petty officer. Senior enlisted rank.

CV Aircraft carrier.

CVA Attack aircraft carrier.

CVB Large aircraft carrier.

CVE Escort aircraft carrier.

CVHA Assault helicopter aircraft carrier. Replaced by designation LPH.

CVN Aircraft carrier, nuclear propulsion.

CWO Chief warrant officer. A commissioned officer in the navy or marine corps ranking immediately below an ensign or a second lieutenant.

DD Navy destroyer.

D-day The particular day on which a military operation is to commence. A means of providing a time-line for any specific operation. Measured in days—e.g., D-45, D-30, and so on. Also "pre-D-day."

DE   Destroyer escort.

delay   A period of time before the rip cord is pulled in a free-fall parachute jump. Usually timed in seconds of delay from exit to opening, e.g., a sixty-second delay.

deployment bag   A nylon container for the canopy of a troop-type parachute that is connected to aircraft by a static line.

depth gauge   A wrist instrument worn by divers that displays the depth in feet. Usually luminescent.

diving planes   Horizontal surfaces on a submarine, bow and stern, used to control the motion of the vessel in a vertical plane.

dogs   Metal cleats that swivel against a seat to tighten a hatch against its watertight seat. To "dog the hatch" is to tighten all the cleats after the hatch has been closed.

DZ   Drop zone. An area for the landing of parachutists.

DZ control   Administrative personnel who run the drop zone prior to and during a parachute operation.

E&E   Escape and evasion.

escape trunk   A special chamber, usually above the forward or after torpedo rooms, designed for escape from the submarine by rescue bell from the surface. Also used for submerged exit and entry by marine recon, UDT, and SEAL swimmers.

"exec"   A slang term for the second in command of a ship, unit, battalion, squadron, company, and so on.

FAC/A   Forward air controller/airborne.

Face mask   Face piece used by divers to be able to see underwater. Worn with a strap over the head, with the nose enclosed but the mouth open to the sea.

fantail   The aftermost deck area topside on a ship or submarine. On a submarine it is the weather deck aft of the conning tower.

flaps   Horizontal control surfaces on aircraft wing which are angled down by the pilot to slow an aircraft down for slow flight as for landing or for dropping parachutists.

force recon   A generic term referring either to personnel within a force reconnaissance unit or to the unit itself, whose mission is to conduct deep reconnaissance operations in support of a landing force and its subordinate elements. Does recon for the force or corps commander (above the marine division level).

foredeck   Forward section of the weather deck. On a submarine it is the weather deck forward of the conning tower.

forward air controller   Marine aviator assigned to an infantry unit as advisor and coordinator of all use of air support and air assets.

free fall   A parachute jump in which the jumper activates the chute by pulling the rip cord—in contrast to a static-line jump, in which the rip cord is pulled automatically as the parachutist exits the aircraft.

G-2 Intelligence officer of a division.

G-3 Operations officer of a division.

G force, G load Gravitational force, gravitational load. The measurement of the force of gravity on an object in relation to the weight and the acceleration of that object.

"grunts" A slang term for marine infantry, who are also called "ground-pounders."

HAHO High-altitude, high-opening. A term that refers to a parachute jump made from ten thousand to thirty thousand feet, with high-altitude opening of the chute. Done with oxygen, cold-weather equipment, and steerable parachutes.

HALO High-altitude, low-opening. A term that is applied to free-fall parachuting, where the parachutist jumps at a high altitude and the parachute opens at low altitude, around two thousand feet.

harness Nylon straps that attach the parachute to the body of the jumper.

hatch Access opening in the hull or a bulkhead of a ship.

H-hour The specific hour on D-day that a particular operation is to commence.

HQMC Headquarters, Marine Corps.

hydrography   The science of determining the underwater configuration of a beach or harbor area. Important to UDT and marine recon swimmers.

infrared   Light source and receivers of low end of color spectrum that are invisible to the human eye. Used for ship-to-ship communications and by reconnaissance swimmers.

JT sonar   A type of sonar for sound-ranging aboard a submarine. Allows an experienced operator to obtain location, range, and bearing from the sound source.

jump log   The official documentation of military parachute jumps. Shows the date, location, type of jump, type of aircraft, and any special conditions or equipment used.

jumpmaster   The senior parachutist on a jump. Coordinates the plane's approach, the jump altitude, the drop location, and the time and conduct of the jump.

jump wings   The insignia of a military parachutist. Gold jump wings, awarded only by naval or marine units requiring parachuting as a mission, represent a level of qualification beyond the basic (silver) jump wings.

L-5   The army Stinson Sentinel. Virtually identical to the marine Convair OY-1 Sentinel. A small utility aircraft, used for aerial reconnaissance, artillery spotting, and so forth.

L-20   The DeHavilland Beaver, a large single-engine utility aircraft used for liaison, medical evacuation, and parachute drops.

LFDC Landing Force Development Center.

line-crossers Indigenous agents who are used to cross a forward edge of the battle area to gather information and return behind friendly lines. Used extensively in Korea.

line-over A parachute malfunction in which one or more suspension lines are positioned over the top of the canopy after the chute opens.

LPH Amphibious assault ship, helicopter. Aircraft carrier specially designed to carry marine amphibious units and assault helicopters as an integrated unit.

LVT Landing vehicle, tracked. An amphibious tractor.

LZ Landing zone for helicopters. Within the zone are landing sites, which are composed of one or more landing points for individual helicopters. Landing zones are named for objects, animals, and colors— e.g., LZ Crow, LZ Red.

Mae West Inflatable life preserver. Smaller than regular aviator or troop-type flotation devices. Fits over the head, with adjustable straps for around the back and arms.

MAF Marine Amphibious Force.

MAGTF Marine air-ground task force. Now called a marine expeditionary force (MEF).

marine division A force of four or more regiments with supporting arms and logistics support. Commanded by a major general. Usually about twenty thousand marines. Generally teamed with a marine air wing (comparable command of aircraft and aircraft support) into a MAGTF. Two or more marine divisions form a corps.

MAY A portable ground-to-air 225–390 MHz receiver-transmitter. Used by pathfinders for guidance of helicopters and fixed-wing aircraft.

MCAS Marine Corps Air Station.

McGuire rig An extraction device consisting of nylon line with a seating sling for one person at the bottom. Dropped from helicopter for retrieval of personnel from triple canopy jungle or other remote locations. Used primarily from Huey helicopters in Vietnam.

Momsen lung A submarine escape device. No longer in use, it was replaced by the Steinke hood.

NAB Naval amphibious base.

NAF Naval air facility. Provides operating and some maintenance facilities for naval aviation.

NAS Naval air station. Provides operating, testing, overhaul, training, and personnel facilities for naval aviation. Larger than a naval air facility (NAF).

NPU The Naval Parachute Unit. Located at the National Parachute Test Range at El Centro, California, it was once the largest joint parachute testing facility of the armed forces. Primarily navy and air force with some army representation. The facility's name is now the Naval Auxiliary Air Station (NAAS).

O-1 The Cessna Bird Dog, a single-engine liaison utility aircraft. Used for aerial observation and transport. Used in Vietnam by FAC/A.

OIC Officer in charge. A generic term describing those officers who are not COs but who have responsibility of directing special units or activities.

OSS Office of Strategic Services.

P2V The Lockheed Neptune, a multiengine aircraft used primarily for ASW work. Used as utility parachute aircraft at El Centro.

P5M The Martin Marlin, a twin-engine amphibian that largely replaced the PBY Catalina after World War II. Used for ASW work and reconnaissance and for drop and pickup of recon teams.

parachute reconnaissance Reconnaissance of an area made by a small team inserted by parachute, usually from a carrier-launched aircraft.

paramarines Elite parachute units of battalion size that were organized during World War II. Fought with distinction as infantry units in South Pacific. Ceased operations in 1944.

pathfinders Personnel with specialized equipment and training for guidance of follow-on assault units landed by parachute or helicopter.

PBY The Lockheed Catalina, a twin-engine amphibious flying boat. Used in World War II for patrol and limited attack and on occasion for surface drop and pickup of reconnaissance personnel.

periscope   The optical device of mirrors and prisms that projects above the conning tower of a submarine.

PLF   Parachute landing fall. The manner in which a parachutist lands on the ground. A term also applied to the technique of landing in such a manner as to reduce chance of injury.

PT   Motor torpedo boat. Used in Solomon Islands on occasion to transport amphibious reconnaissance personnel.

R4D-8   The Douglas Super Skytrain, the most recent version of twin-engine utility transport. Used for dropping of cargo and parachutists.

rifle company   A marine tactical infantry unit composed of a number of rifle platoons and a small headquarters.

rubber boats   A generic term applied to inflatable boats of varying sizes. Specified as LCR(L)—landing craft, rubber, large (nine-man)—and LCR(S), landing craft, rubber, small (four-man). Also called "inflatable boats" (IBs).

S-2   An intelligence officer for a unit below the division level—e.g., regimental S-2, battalion S-2.

S-3   An operations officer for a unit below the division level.

SEAL Sea, air, land. A special U.S. Navy warfare unit capable of overt actions in littoral areas. SEALs use methods of entry similar to those of marine recon, the army's Special Forces (Green Beret) unit, and the air force's Air Commandos.

SERE Survival, evasion, resistance, and escape. Program of training for aircrew or personnel operating behind enemy lines.

slipping The term that refers to a jumper's manipulation of the suspension lines and the canopy of his or her parachute in order to steer the chute in a particular direction.

SOC Special operations capable. A term used in reference to a unit (usually a BLT) whose personnel qualify under a strict program for specialized operations in hostage rescue, downed-pilot rescue, and embassy relief.

SOG Special Operations Group. In the Vietnam War, a highly classified unit, an outgrowth of OSS from World War II that conducted clandestine penetrations and reconnaissance of areas throughout Vietnam, Cambodia, and Laos.

sonar Sound navigation and ranging. Underwater sound equipment for submarine detection and navigation.

Special Forces Elite U.S. Army unit trained in antiguerrilla operations, popularly known as the Green Berets. Marine force recon frequently trains with, and occasionally operates with, Special Forces and exchanges information on methods of entry.

SPIE rig Special personnel insertion and extraction rig. A long nylon line with D rings for eight persons that is lowered to the ground from a helicopter for recovery.

STABO rig Special parachute gear developed during the Vietnam War for the air rescue of reconnaissance troops by allowing them to be picked up by the harness. Replaced the McGuire rig for most extractions by SOG.

static line A nylon webbing line permanently attached to a troop-type parachute (T-10A). Also attached to the aircraft to allow for the type of jump in which the chute is automatically opened after the jumper clears the aircraft.

Steinke hood Modern submarine escape system utilizing a hood worn over the top of the head. Replaced the Momsen lung.

stick A group of parachutists who exit an aircraft in sequence.

surf zone The term used in hydrography and in amphib recon to designate the area of breaking surf, from the waterline to the outermost line of breakers.

suspension lines Thin nylon lines extending around top of a parachute canopy and down from edge of the canopy to connector links attaching the chute to the harness.

T-7A The standard military reserve parachute. Twenty-eight-foot diameter. Partial hemispherical configuration.

T-10 The standard military parachute with thirty-four-foot nominal diameter, static line actuated. May be modified to permit free-fall use. Designed for safe descent of heavy parachutist with equipment. Oblate spheroid in shape.

T/E Table of equipment. The list of all major items of equipment, weapons, radios, specialized equipment, and so forth, authorized for a particular marine unit.

test parachutist Highly trained parachutist used to test and evaluate new parachute equipment or usage.

TF-1 The Grumman Trader, a twin-engine, high-performance carrier-based utility aircraft used for COD (carrier onboard delivery). Capable of carrying crew of two and nine parachutists in off-carrier operations. Redesignated C-1A in the early 1960s, following the standardization of aircraft nomenclature.

T/O Table of organization. The list of all personnel authorized for a particular unit in carrying out its standard mission.

TOE Table(s) of organization and equipment.

torpedo room The compartment in a submarine where the torpedo tubes are located and operated. When such a vessel is reconfigured for carrying troops, the area is used as berthing space and is still referred as the "torpedo room."

UDT Underwater demolition team. A specially trained team for conduct of inshore hydrographic reconnaissance and for demolition of beach obstacles.

UDU Underwater demolition unit. Composed of a number of UDTs.

USA United States Army.

USAF United States Air Force.

USMC United States Marine Corps.

USMCR United States Marine Corps Reserve.

USN United States Navy.

USNR United States Navy Reserve.

utilities Marine dungarees or field uniform.

VMF(AW) Night all-weather fighter squadron.

VMF(N) Night-fighter squadron.

"whipping silk" A slang term used by parachutists to describe the act of repacking parachutes.

White Beach, Yellow Beach, etc. Color designations of beaches used to distinguish landing sites during amphibious operations—e.g., White Beach 1, White Beach 2, Yellow Beach 1, and so on.

winds aloft A term referring to the speed of wind in the air, particularly at the level of an aircraft in flight. Important for aerial navigation and for parachutists from the time they exit the aircraft until they reach the ground.

BIBLIOGRAPHY

Angelucci, Enza, and Paolo Matricardi. *World Aircraft, Military, 1945–1960*. Chicago: Rand McNally, 1980.

Bartlett, Merrill L., and Dirk A. Ballendorf. *Pete Ellis: An Amphibious Warfare Prophet, 1880–1923*. Annapolis, Md.: Naval Institute Press, 1996.

Buerline, Robert A. *Allied Military Fighting Knives and the Men Who Made Them Famous*. Richmond, Va.: American Historical Foundation, 1984.

Coleman, William F. "Amphibious Recon Patrols," *Marine Corps Gazette* 29, no. 12 (1945): 22–25.

Conference for National Cooperation in Aquatics. *The New Science of Skin and Scuba Diving*. Illustrations by Andre Ecuyer. Rev. ed. New York: Association Press, 1962.

Cushman, Robert C. "Amphibious Warfare Tomorrow." *Marine Corps Gazette* 39, no. 4 (April 1955): 30–34.

Davis, Burke. *Marine! The Life of Lt. Gen. Lewis B. ("Chesty") Puller*. Boston: Little Brown, 1962.

Fall, Bernard B. *Street without Joy: Indochina at War, 1946–54*. Harrisburg, Pa.: Stackpole, 1961.

Fane, Francis Douglas, and Don Moore. *The Naked Warriors*. New York: Appleton-Century-Crofts, 1956.

Geer, Andrew Clare. *The New Breed: The Story of the U.S. Marines in Korea*. New York: Harper, 1952.

Graver, Dennis, ed. *Advanced Diving: Technology and*

Techniques. Montclair, Calif.: National Association of Underwater Instructors, 1989.

Harwood, Richard. *A Close Encounter: The Marine Landing on Tinian*. Washington, D.C.: History and Museums Division, Headquarters, U.S. Marine Corps, 1994.

Hoffman, Carl W. *The Seizure of Tinian*. Washington, D.C.: Historical Division, Headquarters, U.S. Marine Corps, 1951.

Johnstone, John H. *United States Marine Corps Parachute Units*. Marine Corps Historical Reference Series 32. Rev. ed. Washington, D.C.: Historical Branch, G-3 Division, Headquarters, U.S. Marine Corps, 1962.

Lanning, Michael Lee, with Ray William Stubbe. *Inside Force Recon: Recon Marines in Vietnam*. New York: Ivy Books, 1989.

Lee, Alex. *Force Recon Command: A Special Marine Unit in Vietnam, 1969–1970*. Foreword by Al Gray. Annapolis, Md.: Naval Institute Press, 1995.

McMillan, George. "Scouting at Cape Gloucester." *Marine Corps Gazette* 30, no. 5 (May 1946): 24–27.

McWhirter, Norris, ed. *Guinness Book of World Records: 1977 Edition*. Enfield, Conn.: Guinness Superlatives, 1978.

Meyers, Bruce F. "Force Recon." *Marine Corps Gazette* 45, no. 5 (May 1961): 48–53.

———. "Jungle Canopy Operations." *Marine Corps Gazette* 53, no. 7 (July 1969): 20–26.

———. "Malaya Jungle Patrols." *Marine Corps Gazette* 44, no. 10 (October 1960): 28–35.

Montross, Lynn. *Cavalry of the Sky: The Story of U.S. Marine Combat Helicopters*. New York: Harper, 1954.

Mooney, James L., ed. *Dictionary of American Naval Fighting Ships*. Vol. 7. Washington, D.C.: Naval Historical Center, Dept. of the Navy, 1970.

Morison, Samuel Eliot. *Breaking the Bismarck's Barrier, 22 July 1942–1 May 1944.* Vol. 6 of *History of United States Naval Operations in World War II.* Boston: Little Brown, 1961.

———. *New Guinea and the Marianas, March 1944–August 1944.* Vol. 8 of *History of United States Naval Operations in World War II.* Boston: Little Brown, 1961.

Musicant, Ivan. *The Banana Wars: A History of United States Military Intervention in Latin America from the Spanish-American War to the Invasion of Panama.* New York: Macmillan, 1990.

Nickerson, Herman, Jr. "Force Recon: By Sea and Air." *Marine Corps Gazette* 43, no. 2 (February 1959): 44–48.

Norton, Bruce H. *Force Recon Diary, 1969.* New York: Ivy Books, 1991.

———. *Force Recon Diary, 1970.* New York: Ivy Books, 1992.

Pierce, Philip N., and Frank O. Hough. *The Compact History of the United States Marine Corps.* New York: Hawthorn Books, 1960.

Plaster, John L. *SOG: The Secret Wars of America's Commandos in Vietnam.* New York: Simon and Schuster, 1997.

Pratt, Fletcher, *The Marines' War: An Account of the Struggle for the Pacific from Both American and Japanese Sources.* New York: W. Sloane, 1948.

Reber, John J. "Pete Ellis: Amphibious Warfare Prophet." *U.S. Naval Institute Proceedings* 103 (November 1977): 53–64.

Shinn, Leo B. "Amphibious Reconnaissance." *Marine Corps Gazette* 29, no. 4 (April 1945): 50–51.

Silverstein, Jeffrey. "Escape." *Sub Aqua* 45 (1997): 16–17.

Smith, Holland *M. The Developments of Amphibious Tactics in the U.S. Navy.* Preface by Edwin H. Simmons. Washington, D.C.: History and Museums Division, Headquarters, U.S. Marine Corps, 1992.

———. "The Developments of Amphibious Tactics, Part IV: Six Fleet Landing Exercises, 1934–1941." *Marine Corps Gazette* 30, no. 9 (September 1946): 43–47.

Smith, Holland M., and Percy Finch. *Coral and Brass.* New York: C. Scribner's Sons, 1949.

Stubbe, Ray W. *Arugha!: Report to Director, Historical Division, Headquarters, Marine Corps, on the History of Specialized and Force-Level Reconnaissance Activities and Units of the United States Marine Corps, 1900–1974.* Washington, D.C.: U.S. Marine Corps, 1981.

Suhoskey, Robert A. "Test Unit One." *Leatherneck* 39, no. 7 (July 1956): 28–32.

Taylor, Michael. "Elite Forces Operate behind Enemy Lines." *San Francisco Chronicle*, 1 February 1991.

United States. Navy Department. *Diving Manual.* Washington, D.C.: Government Printing Office, 1996.

———. Division of Fleet Training. *Landing Operations Doctrine, United States Navy.* Fleet Training Publication 167 (1938).

———. Naval History Division. *Dictionary of American Naval Fighting Ships.* Washington, D.C.: Government Printing Office, 1959–81.

Williams, Ralph Chester. "Amphibious Scouts and Raiders." *Military Affairs: Journal of the American Military Institute 13*, no. 3 (1949): 150–157.

Woods, Levi W. "Doing a Recon on Skyhook: The Fulton Aerial Retrieval System." *Gung-Ho* 11 (1985): 22–26, 76–81.

INDEX

Page references in italics refer to maps and illustrations.

A3D. *See* Douglas A3D
  Skywarrior
A-4 Skyhawks, 217
absolute pressure, 169
accidents: free-fall parachuting,
  194; Operation Ski Jump,
  81–82, 83–84; tail hook, 206
A Company (VAC), 6–8
AD. *See* Douglas AD Skyraider
Adak Island: RECONEX 58D
  phase 2, 132–33, 138–41
Advanced Infantry Officer's
  Course, 32
Africa, 241, 248
AGLEX (air-ground landing
  exercise) 57-D, 100
AGLEX (air-ground landing
  exercise) 57-E, 77
AGLEX (air-ground landing
  exercise) 57-I, Operation Ski
  Jump, 81–82, 100
AH-1W Cobra, 217
air cover, 217
aircraft carrier, 55; COD
  (carrier on-board delivery),
56; jet, 60–63; types used,
  55. *See also specific aircraft*
aircraft carrier (CVs): assault
  helicopter (CVHAs), 269;
  attack (CVAs), 269;
  designation for, 269; escort
  (CVEs), 13, 269; large
  (CVBs), 269; nuclear
  propulsion (CVNs), 269; *See
  also specific carriers*
Aitken, Ken, 166
AJ-2. *See* North American AJ-
  2 Savage
"Alabama," 19
alcohol consumption, 177,
  210
Alderholt, Harry "Heinie," 35
Alford, Noble S., 193–94
Allen, Weldon, 110
Alpha Company, 244
Amos, Herschel, 110
amphibious assault ship,
  helicopter (LPH), 274
amphibious assault ship,
  helicopter (LPH-2), 71

amphibious reconnaissance, xiii, 128, 265; first marine unit, 1; inherent dangers, 28–29; Pacific operations, 2; scuba use, 161; submarine finding, 154–57; training, 44–51. *See also specific operations*

2d Amphibious Reconnaissance Battalion, 110

Amphibious Reconnaissance Battalion, I Amphibious Corps, 4

Amphibious Reconnaissance Battalion, III Amphibious Crops, 4

Amphibious Reconnaissance Battalion, V Amphibious Corps (VAC), 1, 110; A Company, 6–8; B Company, 6–8; Tinian Island operations, 4–12, *11*, 216

Amphibious Reconnaissance Battalion Fleet Marine Force, 12

1st Amphibious Reconnaissance Company, xiv, 116–17

Amphibious Reconnaissance School, 13–31, 44–45, 72, 253 n. 7; beach reconnaissance, Hokkaido, Japan, 18–23; Far East deployments, 18; training

Chinese Nationalists, 13; training with UDT, 24–27

Amphibious tractor. *See* landing vehicle, tracked (LVT)

Anderson, George W., 51–52

AN/PQC-1 radio, 154–56

AN/PRC-10 radio, 211

antennae, RC-292, 79

APDs. *See* destroyer transports, high-speed (APDs)

APSS. *See* transport submarines (ASSPs)

arctic overshoes, 134

Arman, Phil, 119–22

Armstrong, Al, 232–33

Army Advanced Infantry School, xvi

24th Army Division, 17

77th Army Division, 5

Army of the Republic of Vietnam (ARVN) Air Force, 217

ASR. *See* submarine rescue ship (ASR)

assault helicopter aircraft carrier (CVHA), 269

assault personnel destroyers (APDs): early, 251 n. 8. *See also* destroyer transports, high-speed (APDs)

ASSP. *See* transport submarines (ASSPs)

Atomic Energy Commission, 40

attack aircraft carrier (CVA), 269

Averill, Gerald P. (Gerry), 186

Avery, Neil, 85, 90, 95, 108, 111, 184–86

B-17 Flying Fortress, 223

Bahrain Island: beach reconnaissance, 22–23

Bailey, Chuck, 42

Ball, Kenneth (Ken), 46, 84–85, 87–94

"ball-buster" openings, 63

Barnes, Harry, 123

Barnett, Lonzo M., 65, 109–11

Barnhill, Claude "Barney," 42

"Base Plate McGurk" series, 125

Basic Recon School, 245

2nd Battalion, 7th Marines, 135

3rd Battalion, 1st Marines, 82

battalion landing team, 267

B Company (VAC), 6–8

beaches: color designations for, 281; over-the-beach landings in Vietnam, 70–71

Beach Jumpers, 27–28, 266

Beach Jumper Unit 1 (BJU 1), 27, 29

beach reconnaissance: Hokkaido, Japan, 18–23; Kuwait and Bahrain Island, 22–23

Beakley, Wallace M., 198, 199

Beany (small directional antenna), 154

bears, 135

Bell, Kenneth R., 59, 110–11

Bell UH1E Huey, 217

"the bends," 152

Bennington (CVA-20), 59

Bitulok, 197, 212

Bledsoe, Willmar "Bill," 40

Block, Bill, 119

blown panels, 54, 266

BLT. See battalion landing team (BLT)

Blue Angels, 48

board of inquiry/board of investigations, 267; Operation Sky Jump, 96–98

boats, 267; inflatable (IBs), 277; patrol torpedo (PTs), 3, 216, 277; picket-boats, 8; rubber, 127, 141–46, 277

Boeing-Vertol CH-46 Sea Knight, 217, 230, 238

Bohn, Dewy "Bob," 40–42

Bondurant, Nick, 203

boondockers, 7, 13, 267

Bosnia, 248

Boxer, 82, 212

Boyd, L.G., 97

Boyle, Dennis, 206–8

Bradbeer, John D., xxi, 2–4, 216

Bradley, Omar, 31

Brandon, Joe, 74

bravery, xix

Bravo Company, 245
Bream, 130, *156,* 176, 253 n. 7
breathing air, compressed, 258
   n. 12
Broadnax, John, 207
Broderick, Jim, 166
Bronze Star, xxi
broomsticks, 68
buoyant ascents, 159–79;
   "Employment of Buoyant
   Ascent Techniques by
   Amphibious Reconnaissance
   Personnel" (Kelley), 258 n.
   14; "Employment of Buoyant
   Ascent Techniques by
   Amphibious Reconnaissance
   Personnel" (McKeever and
   Meyers), 177–78; first from
   U.S. submarines, 173–79
Burhans, Robert N. (Bob), 55,
   194
Burke, Richard F., 6
Buse, Henry W. "Bill," xvi
Button, William R., 252 n. 1

C-1A. *See* Grumman C-1A
   Trader
C-47 Skytrains, 217, 223
C-119. *See* Fairchild C-119
   Flying Boxcar
C-123, 223
C-130 Hercules, 55, 217, 223
C-130 Hercules "Blackbird,"
   223, 240–41
caisson disease, 152

Caldwell, Frank, 32–33
Camp Del Mar, California,
   109, 122, 125, 141
Camp McGill, Japan, 18, 26
Camp Pendleton, California,
   ix, xiv, 14, 26, 40, 41,
   79–80, 184, 186; Chappo
   Flats, 79; Operation Ski
   Jump, 81–82, 83–84
Cape Gloucester operations
   (September 1943), 1–4,
   216
Capewell canopy-release
   assembly, 37, 98, 267
Carlusi, "Lug," 15
Carothers, Pat, 54
Case Springs, Camp Pendleton,
   California: Operation Ski
   Jump, 81–82, 83–84
Cashion, Dana, 16
Cavallaro (APD-128), 199,
   202, 209
1st Cavalry Division, 17
Central Intelligence Agency
   (CIA), 34; extraction
   methods, 218; Fulton
   Skyhook retrieval system,
   223; SOG HALO
   operations, 240
Cessna OE-1 Bird Dog, 102,
   276
Chanticleer (ASR-7), 165,
   173–74
Chappo Flats, 79
Charlie Company, 245

Chinese Nationalist Army and Navy, 13
Chipp, Bill, 166
Chitose Air Force Base, 18
Chocktaw (H-34). *See* Sikorsky H-34 Chocktaw
Churley, Bob, xvi, 218
claustrophobia, 150
"clean," 268
closed-circuit rebreathers, 258 n. 13
Cobra (AH-1W), 217
The Cockleshell Heroes (film), 104
COD (Carrier onboard delivery) aircraft, 56
Cold War, 19, 223
cold weather submarine operations, 132–41
color designations for beaches, 281
Colt Cobra, 240
combat parachuting, 234–42; final jump, 238–39; first jump, 234–35; second jump, 235–38
combat swimming, 268
Commandos, 218
communications, 75–79; 31MC, 142, 149; AN/PQC-1 radio, 154–56; AN/PRC-10 radio, 211; MAY radios, 75–78, 84, 211, 275; PRC-6 and PRC-10 organic radios, 78; PRC-25 organic radios,

78; RC-292 antennae, 79; SCR300 radio, 8; sound signals, 155; underwater, 155–56
compasses, wrist, 151
Conein, Lucien E. "Three-Finger Louie" (Lou), 35–36, 190–91, 239
conning tower, 141, 269
coordination of intelligence and reconnaissance assets, 248–49
Corboy, Leo, 18
Corie, Orie, 65
Coronado, California: submarine escape tower, 259 n. 4
COWLEX (cold-weather landing exercise), 132–33
Cronkite, Walter, 68
cross-service schooling, 34–36
cross-training, 128, 180
Culebra, Puerto Rico, 127
Cushman, Robert, 37, 38
CV. *See* aircraft carrier (CV)
CVA. *See* aircraft carriers, attack (CVAs)
CVB. *See* aircraft carriers, large(CVBs)
CVE. *See* aircraft carriers, escort (CVEs)
CVHA. *See* aircraft carriers, assault helicopter (CVHAs)
CVN. *See* aircraft carriers, nuclear propulsion (CVNs)

Dailey, Dan, 24
D'Arco, Anthony, 119
D-day, 269
DDs. See destroyers (DDs)
DEs. See destroyer escorts (DEs)
deep submergence rescue vehicles (DSRVs), 147
DeFazio, Ernie "the Seal," x, 118, 123–24; buoyant ascents, 166, 171–73; cold weather operations, 133–36, 139; Operation Strongback, 208–9
DeHavilland CV-2 Caribou, 234–35
DeHavilland L-20 Beaver, 55, 273
Del Mar Officers' Club, 125
depth gauges, 151, 270
Desert Rock VI, 40–41
destroyer escorts (DEs), 270
destroyers (DDs), 269
destroyer transports, high-speed (APDs), 127, 216, 266
Dickinson, Dennis, 111
diesel submarines (SSs), 130
Direct Action Platoon, 245
divers: parachutists, 128; scuba, 146–54, 160–61; submarine escape tower instructors, 168
diving: buoyant ascents, 159–79, 258 n. 14, 267;

Marine Corps Combat Diving School, 245; scuba, 161–62, 258 n. 12
diving planes, 270
diving watches, 125, 151, 205
DMOs (doctors), 162–63
"doghouse," 142
dogs, 270
Dominican Republica: Operation Dom-Rep, 82
Donovan, Bill, 35
Douglas A3D Skywarrior, ix, xx, 55, 265; Operation Strongback, 199; simultaneous jumps from, 67–68
Douglas AD Skyraider, 13, 217, 265
Douglas Aircraft Corporation, 57–58
Douglas F3D-2 Skyknight, ix, xx, 36, 55, 103, 106; first jumps from, 58–61; Operation Strongback, 199, 210; simultaneous jumps from, 67
Douglas R4D-6 Skytrain, 55; Operation Strongback, 199, 212
Douglas R4D-8 Super Skytrain, xx, 105, 182, 277
drop and pickup, 26
drop zone (DZ), 270
Drug Enforcement Agency, 103
dry-deck launch, 143–44, 146

dry launches, 141–46
DZ. *See* drop zone (DZ)

E-1 parachutes, 185, 187–89
E-2A Hawkeyes, 71
Eagle Arms CAR-15, 240
Earle, Ken, 57
E&E (escape and evasion) training, 45–46
Electric Boat Company, 130
Ellis, Pete, 20
El Toro Marine Corps Air Station, 15
"Employment of Buoyant Ascent Techniques by Amphibious Reconnaissance Personnel" (Kelley), 258 n. 14
"Employment of Buoyant Ascent Techniques by Amphibious Reconnaissance Personnel" (McKeever and Meyers), 177–78
engines, 56
equipment: first full equipment jumps, 62–65; improvements, 98; jump helmets, 61, 91–92; mount-out, 256 n. 6; pathfinders, 76–77; scuba diver, 160–61; special, 119; table(s) of organization and (TOE), 111–13, 280
escape and evasion (E&E) training, 45–46

escort aircraft carrier (CVE), 269
Evans, George F., 16–17
exposure suits, 151
extraction: drop and pickup, 26; by Fulton Skyhook, 218–23; by McGuire rig, 225–26, 275; methods of, 216–33; by SPIE rig, xv, 226–33, 279 by STABO rig, 225–26, 279; swimmer pickup, 26; by trooper's ladder, 223–24

F4 Phantoms, 217
face masks, 151, 271
Fairbairn, W.E., 251 n. 10
Fairbairn fighting knives, 7, 251 n. 10
Fairbairn-Sykes commando knife, 251 n. 10
Fairchild C-119 "Flying Boxcar," 191, 267
Fall, Bernard, 71
Fane, Francis Douglas, 24–25
fantail, 271
fatalities, 225; parachute, 91–93, 98, 194
FBI. *See* Federal Bureau of Investigation (FBI)
Federal Aviation Administration (FAA) regulations, 80
Federal Bureau of Investigation (FBI), 103

Ferrer, José, 104

Finn, Robert C. "Bob," 77, 123

fins, 151

Firm, R.B., 3

Fish, Howard, 57, 82, 229

flaps, 271

Fleet Landing Exercise 4, 127

Fleet Marine Force (FMF), xiv, xvi. *See also specific exercises, groups, operations.*

Fleet Marine Force (FMF), Pacific, 12

Fleet Training Publication 167, 127

Fleet Transport Squadron VR-5, 56

flu shots, 138

Flying Fortress (B-17), 223

Folsom, Oscar, 84, 87

force reconnaissance, 44, 271; battalion, 109–11; extraction methods, 216–33; organization of, 244; parachute fatalities in, 194; restructuring, 244; and Special Forces, 239; training, 245–46. *See also* reconnaissance.

1st Force Reconnaissance Battalion, 228

1st Force Reconnaissance Company, xi, xiv; amphib recon platoon, 112, 123, 180, 198, 202; buoyant ascents, 159–79; cold weather operations, 132–41; communications platoon, 112; deployment overseas, 197–215; extraction methods, 216–18, 223, 226–27; first combat parachute jump, 234–35; formation xvii–xxi, 100–113; HALO work, 239; housing, 122; jump logs, 54–55; jumpmaster training, 105–9; maintenance shop, 122; mandate, 180–81; mission, 129; MT dispatch, 122; nucleus, 44; officers and enlisted personnel, 119; operational elements, 123; Operation Stonewall, 182–84; Operation Strongback, 197–215; organization of, 119; parachute loft, 122; parachute recon platoon, 112, 123, 180, 198; 4th Platoon, 85–86; recovery of pathfinder teams, 101–5; restructuruing, 247; scuba divers, 146–54; selection process, 119–22; shaking down, 180–96; special equipment, 119; supply and service platoon, 112; support for, xvi–xvii; tables of organization and equipment,

111–13; tactical capability, 181; tactical missions, 180; training, xvi–xix; wet and dry launches, 132–41

2nd Force Reconnaissance Company, xi, xviii, 191, 244; disestablishment of, 250; extraction methods, 218; formation, 111, 122, 184, 198; free-fall accident, 194; Fulton Skyhook testing, 219–21; HALO work, 239; new, 245

3rd Force Reconnaissance Company, 247

Fornier, J.P., 4

Fort Benning, Georgia, 30–36, 73, 246

Fort Bragg, North Carolina, 34, 98, 190–91

forward escape trunk, 147–48, 158

free-fall parachuting, 113, 195, 271; accident, 194; highest, 47; stabilized, 187

Freitas, John, 166

2d French Foreign Legion Parachute Battalion, 261 n. 3

Fuller, Régan, ix, xvi, xvii, 41–44, 59, 89, 104, 110; as father of force reconnaissance, 44

Fulton, Robert E., Jr., 218

Fulton aerial retrieval system. See Fulton Skyhook

Fulton Skyhook, xv, 218–23; first live pickup with, 219–22

G-2s. See intelligence officers (G-2s)

G-3s. See operations officers (G-3s)

Gallihugh, Roy, 111

Garcia, Dionicio, 87, 109–11

Garcia, R.J. "Pappy," 236

Gatling guns ("Puff the Magic Dragon"), 217

Gato-class diesel submarine, 156

Geiger, Roy S., 5

German navy, 161

G force, G load, 272

Gilmer (APD-11), 7

Gipe, A. E., 3

gliders, 72

gold jump wings, 52

Gonzales, Cy, 123

GP bag jumps, 108

GPS (global position satellite) navigation systems, 70

Gray, Al, vii–xi 244, 249

"grease gun" (M3A1), 63, 104

green table time, 98

Grenada, 241

grenade launchers (M-79, 40-mm), 240

Grobe, John, 138

ground pounders, 74

Grumman Aircraft Corp.,
      57–58, 59
Grumman C-1A Trader, 194
Grumman TF-1 Trader, ix, 13,
      55–59, 103, 105, 182, 280;
      first jumps from, 57–58, 59;
      first problem with, 206–8;
      insertion of pathfinders with,
      79; Operation Stonewall,
      183; Operation Strongback,
      199, 206, 212; parachute
      jumps from, 36; primary
      pilot, xx; simultaneous
      jumps from, 67–68
Grumman TF-1 Trader "Vitalis
      772," 85, 89
Grumman TF-1 Trader "Vitalis
      777," 85, 89, 95
grunts, 272
gunnery sergeant (rank), 17
Guttierrez, Robert L. "Guts,"
      118, 124, 133–35, 140,
      154–56, 166; as bear
      shooter, 135

Haferkamp, Johanne, 118
Hager, James W., 236–37
HAHO (high-altitude, high-
      opening) parachute, 272
Haiti, 248
HALO (high-altitude, low-
      opening) parachute, 35, 196,
      272; combat jumps in
      Vietnam, 239–42
Hamber, John, 107, 200–202

Hannekan, Herman, 14, 252 n.
      1
Hardy, Lloyd, 84, 87
harness, 272; integrated, 226
hatch, 272
HATRON (Heavy Attack
      Squadron) 2, xx, 199
HATRON (Heavy Attack
      Squadron) 6, xx
HATWING 6(heavy attack
      wing) fleet, 67
Hawkeye (E-2A), 71
Hayden, Sterling, 239
Hejna, Stanley, 166
helicopter drops, 27, 218
helicopters: landing zone for,
      274; over-the-beach
      landings, 70–71; pathfinding
      for, 72–73. See also specific
      types
HELILEX (helicopter landing
      exercise) IV, 82, 100
heli-teams, 43
helmets, 61, 91–92
Henry, Charles E., 206
Hercules (C-130), 55, 217, 223
Hercules "Blackbird" (C-130),
      223, 240
Hernandes, Sammy, 240
H-hour, 272
high-speed destroyer transports
      (APDs), 127, 216, 266
Hilborn-Hamburger, 52
Hill, "Handsome Harry," 8–9
Hill, Melvin, 240

Hisler, Norm, 230; SPIE rig testing, 231–32

Hi-Standard pistols, 240

Hokkaido, Japan: beach reconnaissance, 18–23

Honsowitz, Russ, 124

Hooker, Harold, 111

Hooker, Joseph, 85, 92–93

Houghton, Kenny J., xvi, 16, 31, 118

Howard, Jimmy, 118

Howard, Trevor, 104

Htelter, F.C., 198

Hunt, Robert, 193–94

hydrographic surveys, 24–25, 273

hyperventilation, 259 n. 6

hypothermia, 138, 141, 177

IBs. See inflatable boats (IBs)

immersion foot, 137

infantry school, 30–31

inflatable boats (IBs), 277

inflatable life jackets (Mae West), 148, 151, 274

initiative, 45–46

injuries, 62–64, 94–95, 186, 227

insertion: by buoyant ascent, 159–79; by HALO entry, 239–43; by helicopter drop, 27, 218; Operation Stonewall, 182–84; by parachute entry, 29–30, 199–211, 234, 276; by

submarine and rubber boat, 216; techniques of, xvii–xix; via water, 129–30

insignia, 214; parachutist, 51–52

inspirational signs, 42

integrated harness, 226

intelligence: from across enemy lines, 13; coordination of, 248–49

intelligence and electronic warfare battalions, 247

intelligence officers (G-2s), 248, 272

intelligence officers (S-2s), 277

Istell, Jacques, 35–36, 114–15, 185–86, 190, 198

Iwo Jima: reconnaissance from Perch, 132

Iwo Jima, 71, 212

Jackson, Gilder, 31

jackstaff, 143

Jaskilka, Sam, 42

Jernigan, Curtis "Red Dog," 42

jet aircraft: first jumps from, 60–63

Johansen, Peter J., 194

Johnson, Walter, 166

Jolly Green Giant (USAF HH-53, USMC CH-53). See Sikorsky Jolly Green Giant (USAF (HH-53, USMC CH-53)

Jones, James Logan (Jim), 1, 6, 101, 110, 216
JT sonar, 273
jump helmets, 61, 91–92
"jumping junkmen," 82, 181
jump logs, 53, 273; 1st Force Recon, 54; Test Unit 1, 54–55
jumpmaster checkouts, 107
jumpmasters, 273; training for, 32–34, 103–9
jump pay, 124
jump school, 30, 33, 47, 73, 246; pre-jump school, 46; for test parachutists, 49
jump wings, 273; gold, 52
Justrite (approach light), 76

Kaufman, Draper, 7
"K-Bar" knives (Ka-Bar fighting knives), 7, 155, 251 n. 10
Keenan, Paul, xx, 132, 164
Kelley, Paul Xavier, xi, xviii, 191, 195–96, 199, 223, 249; "Employment of Buoyant Ascent Techniques by Amphibious Reconnaissance Personnel," 258 n. 14
Kies, Frank, 85, 93–94
King, Frank T., 137–38
King, Neal, xi, 85, 90, 94–95, 106, 110, 116
Kittinger, Joseph "Kitt," 47
Knorring, Bob, 166

Kodiak island: RECONEX 58D phase 1, 132–38
Koelper, Donald E. (Don) "Mr. Pathfinder," ix, 59, 106, 110–16, 116–17; as assistant S-3, 119; Operation Ski Jump, 87–89; Operation Strongback, 198, 202; Test Unit 1, 46, 75–76
Kraince, Francis X. "Bull," x, 22
Kuwait: beach reconnaissance, 22–23

L-5. See Stinson L-5 Sentinel
L-20. See DeHavilland L-20 Beaver
LaCoursier, Gerald L., 65, 85, 95, 111
Laine, "Chuck," 191
Lamb, Mike, 208
Lambert, Larry, 47
landing craft, rubber (LCR): large (LCR(L)), 277; small (LCR(S)), 277
landing exercises, 77–78; AGLEX (air-ground landing exercise) 57-E, 77; AGLEX (air-ground landing exercise) 57-I, Operation Ski Jump, 81–82, 100; COWLEX (cold-weather landing exercise), 123; fleet, 127; HELILEX (helicopter landing exercise) IV, 82,

100; PHIBLEX 58M, Operation Strongback, 66, 123, 184, 197–215

Landing Force Development Center (Quanitco, Virginia), 218

landing vehicle, tracked (LVT), 274

landing zone marking lights (SE-11), 76

LaPorte, Michael Louis "Doc," 237

large aircraft carrier (CVB), 269, 269

Larson, James, 111

LCR. *See* landing craft, rubber (LCR)

Lee, Alex, 247

Lee, Bill, 85, 94–95, 110, 116

Lefthand, Harry R., 45, 80–81, 111

life jackets, Mae West, 148, 151, 274

line-overs, 53, 274

Livingston, Bill, 65, 106, 110, 116–17, 184; as operations officer, 119

Lockheed P2V Neptune, 55, 276; Fulton Skyhook pick up with, 219

Lockheed PBY Catalina, 15, 216, 276

Lockwood Hall, 167

LPH. *See* amphibious assault ship, helicopter (LPH)

Lundemo, Gerald, 110

LVT. *See* landing vehicle, tracked (LVT)

M3A1 "grease gun," 63, 104

M-79 (40-mm) grenade launchers, 240

Mae West life jackets, 148, 151, 274

MAF. *See* marine amphibious force (MAF)

MAG(HR)-16 (helicopter air group), 73

MAGTF. *See* marine air-ground task force (MAGTF)

Maiden, Robert "Mumbles" (Bob), 16–17

1st Marine Air-Ground Task Force, 81–82, 83–84

marine air-ground task force (MAGTF), ix, 274

Marine Air Group 16 (MAG-16), 199

Marine Air Group 36 (MAG-36), 78

Marine Air Repair Squadron 37. *See* MARS-37 R4D-8

1st Marine Air Wing, xx, 65, 75–76, 198, 226–28

3rd Marine Air Wing, xx

III Marine Amphibious Force, 243

marine amphibious force (MAF), 243, 274

Marine Corps Combat Diving School, 245

Marine Corps Development and Education Command (MCDEC), 110

Marine Corps Gazette, 125

Marine Corps Test Unit 1, xiv–xviii, 37–52; activation, 39–40; air elements, 39; broad mission objectives, 39; disbanding, 100, 115–18; endorsement of Capewell canopy-release assembly, 98; exercises and field tests, 77–78; extraction methods, 216–18; focus, 127–28; heli-teams, 43; inspirational signs, 42; jump logs, 54; Operation Ski Jump, 81–82, 83–84; organization, 39; pathfinding, 70–82; plans and development (P&D) section, 41–42; recommendations for 1st Force Recon, 109–11; reconnaissance platoon, 44–45; reconnaissance training, 44–51; reorganization, 41; war room, 42

1st Marine Division, 1–4, 22, 128, 243

2nd Marine Division, 5, 9–10, 22, 244–45

3rd Marine Division, 27, 73, 198, 212, 243, 246

4th Marine Division, 5, 9

27th Marine Division, 5

I Marine Expeditionary Force, 246

II Marine Expeditionary Force, 244–46

III Marine Expeditionary Force, 246

marine expeditionary force (MEF), 243, 247

MARS-37 R4D-8 (marine air repair squadron), 80

Marshall, George C., 31

Marte, Gary, 67

Martin P5M Marlin, 103, 276

Massaro, John R., 118

Masters, James "Jungle Jim," 249

MAY radios, 75–78, 84, 228, 275

31MC (communications), 142, 148

McGuire, Charles, 225

McGuire rigs, 225–26, 275

McKeever, Elmer V. "Mac," xx, 164, 175; "Employment of Buoyant Ascent Techniques by Amphibious Reconnaissance Personnel," 177–78

McKinstry, William E. (Bill), 118, 123–24, 133–41, 166,

171–73; Operation Strongback, 208–9

McNemar, M.D., 236–37

"mechanical mules," 40

Medal of Honor winners, xxi

MEF. *See* marine expeditionary force (MEF)

McGee, Vernon E., 197–99

Meritorious Mast, 82

Meyers, Bruce F., 104; army training, 32–36; as assistant G-2, 13; buoyant ascents, 159–79; as CO, 1st Force, 34, 118, 164, 190; as CO, SLF Alpha, 71; as division parachute officer, 51; "Employment of Buoyant Ascent Techniques by Amphibious Reconnaissance Personnel," 177–78; first buoyant ascents from U.S. submarine, 173–79; first jet aircraft jumps, 60–63; first off-carrier jump, 59–60; first simultaneous jumps, 64–67; Fulton Skyhook testing, 219–21; gold jump wings, 52; HALO work, 239; as head of ground combat equipment, 228; as helicopter assault airborne techniques officer, 42; and Istell, 114–15; as jumpmaster, 106; as landing force commander, Sixth Fleet BLT, 261 n. 3; as lieutenant colonel, 36–52; as major, 46; as midshipman, 13; as OIC, Amphib Recon School, 13, 16, 17, 143, 153; Operation Ski Jump, 81–82, 83–84; Operation Strongback, 197–215; orders to Fort Benning, 30–31; parachutist training, 30; pelvic fracture, 62–64; as platoon commander, 10; pranks on, 108–9; as reconnaissance/pathfinder project officer, xiv, 42; as rifle company commander, 13; SPIE rig testing, 228–33; Steinke hood use, 258 n. 2; as swimmer, 15–16; as test parachutist, 49; Test Unit 1 service, viii–ix, 41, 115–16; at UDT scuba school, 159–60

Michigan (SSBN-747), 258 n. 2

military occupational specialty (MOS), 246

Miller, John C., 18

Mills, Stan, 85, 95

Mitchell, William "Bill," xvi, 75

Mohawks (OV-10s), 217

Momsen, Charles, 162

Momsen lung, 162, 258 n. 1, 275

Moore, Don, 24
Moorman, Sgt., 238
Morris, Wayne, 17
Morrison, Tiz "King of the Frogmen," 25–27
MOS (military occupational specialty), 246
motor torpedo boats. *See* patrol torpedo boats (PTs)
mount-out equipment, 256 n. 6

NAAS. *See* Naval Auxiliary Air Station (NAAS)
The Naked Warriors (Fane and Moore), 24
NAS. *See* naval air station (NAS)
National Parachute Test Range (El Centro, California), 275
naval air station (NAS), 275
Naval Air Station (NAS) Adak, 139
Naval Amphibious Base (Coronado, California), 13
Naval Auxiliary Air Station (NAAS), 47, 275
Naval Diving and Salvage Training Center (NDSTC), 259 n. 4
Naval Parachute Facility (NPF), 186
Naval Parachute Loft, 30
Naval Parachute Unit (NPU), 47, 275
Naval Station Kodiak, 138

navigation: pathfinding, 70–82; pressure-proof wrist compasses, 151
Navy Cross, xxi
"Navy Test Parachutist" patch, 214
Navy Underwater Sound Laboratory, 154
Neff, Donald, 8
Negritos, 203–4
Neipling, Larry, 58–59
Nelson, Stanley, 40
Nereus (AS-17), 162
New London, Connecticut: submarine escape tower, 259 n. 4
Newman, Cliff, 240–41
"The New Recon Marine," 68
Ngo Dinh Diem, 36
Nickerson, Herman, Jr. "Herman the German," xvi, 211, 244, 247–48
night all-weather fighter squadron (VMF(AW)), 281
Night All-Weather Fighter Squadron VMF(AW)-513, 199–200
Night All-Weather Fighter Squadron VMF(AW)-542, 65
night fighter squadron (VMF(N)), 281
Night Fighter Squadron VMF(N)-513 "The Flying Nightmares," xx, 200

Night Fighter Squadron
VMF(N)-532, xx
"night soil," 201
Norman, Clint, 34
North American AJ-2 Savage,
55, 67, 265
NPU. *See* Naval Parachute Unit
(NPU)
nuclear blast simulation, 86
nuclear weapons testing, 40–41

OE-1. *See* Cessna OE-1 Bird
Dog
off-carrier capability, 53–69
Office of Strategic Services
(OSS), 35, 239
Ogata, Kiochi, 5
O'Kane, Richard Hetherington,
258 n. 1
Oliver, Donald (Don), 84, 87
O'Neill, Matthew J., Jr., 85,
93–94
Operation Desert Storm, xx,
23, 248
Operation DomRep, 82
operations: Cape Gloucester,
1–4, 216; cold weather,
132–41; Pacific, 1;
submarine, 130; Tinian
Island, 4–12, *11*, 216
Operation Ski Jump, 81–82,
83–84, 100
operations officers (G-3s), 248,
272
operations officers (S-3s), 277

Operation Stonewall, 182–84
Operation Strongback
(PHIBLEX 58M), 66, 123,
184, 197–215
Opsal, John W., 17
organic radios: PRC-6 and
PRC-10s, 78; PRC-25s, 78
OSS. *See* Office of Strategic
Services (OSS)
OV-10 Mohawks, 217
oxygen rebreathers, 153, 258 n.
13
oxygen toxicity, 153

P2V. *See* Lockheed P2V
Neptune
P5M. *See* Martin P5M Marlin
Pacific operations, 1
Panama, 241
Panama Canal, 117–18
Panama City, Florida:
submarine escape tower, 259
n. 4
parachute canopy, 267;
Capewell canopy-release
assembly, 37, 98, 267;
collapsing, 90–91
parachute landing falls (PLFs),
33, 277
parachute operations schedules
(operations orders), 80
parachutes, 113–15; canopy,
90–91, 267; Capewell
canopy-release assembly, 37,
98, 267; conical, 49; E-1,

parachutes (*continued*)
185, 187–89; QAC (quick attachable, chest) packs, 49; QFB (quick fit, back) , 49; seat packs, 49; "Sky Diver" blank-gore, 36, 184–93, 198; steerable, 185–90; T-7A, 50, 234, 279; T-10, 89–92, 186–90, 192, 195, 234, 280; testing, 191–92; "Tojo," 185, 188–89, 192; "whipping silk," 281

Parachutes, Inc., 35, 114, 190

parachuting, 276 "ball-buster" openings, 63; with blown panels, 54, 266; by canyons, 95–96; combat, 234–42; on the edge, 53; entry capability, xvi; from F3D Douglas Skyknight, 36; fatalities, 93–94, 98, 194; first full equipment jumps, 62–64; first jet aircraft jumps, 60–63; first multiple simultaneous jumps, 64–68; first off-carrier jumps, 59–69; free-fall, 47, 79, 187, 194, 271; GP bag, 108; from Grumman TF-1, 36; HALO (high-altitude, low-opening), 35, 196, 239–42, 272; insertion by, 29–30; jump logs, 53–55, 273; jump pay, 124; jump school, 30, 33, 46–50, 73, 246; line-overs,

53–54; Operation Ski Jump, 81–82, 83–84; Operation Strongback, 198–211; pay for marines on jump status, 124; simultaneous jumps, 68–69; space-suit jumps, 49; stacking jumps, 50; static line, 279; stick, 279

parachutists: divers, 128; French, 261 n. 3; insignia, 51–52; "jumping junkmen," 57, 181; jumpmasters, 32–34, 105–9, 273; losing half, 185–94; Special Forces, 239, 241; swimmers, 180; test, 48–49, 280

paramarines, 51, 276

Parker, L. W., 219–20

patches, 214

pathfinders, 72, 243, 276 atomization of, 212; first operational use of, 78; insertion of, 80, 211–13; "jumping junkmen," 82, 181; last Marine Corps use of, 82; methods of operation, 78–79; necessity of, 72–82; Operation DomRep, 82; Operation Stonewall, 183; Operation Strongback, 211–13; "rag jumpers," 182; weapons and equipment, 76

pathfinder teams, 101–5, 182–83

pathfinding: in Test Unit 1,
    70–82; in Vietnam, 70–71
Patinetti, L.V., xvii
Patrick, Charles "Pat," 8
Patrol Squadron VP-19, 140
patrol torpedo boats (PTs),
    216, 277; PT-110, 2; PT-325,
    2; PT-327, 2
Patterson, Bobby Joe, 118, 124
Paull, Jerome T., 235
payment: jump pay, 124
PBY. *See* Lockheed PBY
    Catalina
peacekeeping missions, 244,
    248
Pearl Harbor, Hawaii:
    submarine escape tower,
    167, 259 n. 4
Perault, Charlemagne, 252 n. 1
Perch (APSS-313), x, xx, 117,
    129–31, 146, *156*, 253 n. 7,
    266; buoyant ascents from,
    164, 166, 173–79; cold
    weather operations, 132–41;
    (re)commissioning, 129–31;
    hangar, 132; Iwo Jima
    reconnaissance from, 132;
    "Report of First War Patrol,"
    131; specifications, 130
Perch (ASSP-313), 266
periscope tows, 144–45
Persian Gulf, 241, 248; beach
    reconnaissance, 20–23;
    Operation Desert Storm, xx,
    23, 248

PHIBLEX 58M. See Operation
    Strongback (PHIBLEX
    58M)
Philippine Army Regimental
    Combat Team, 198
Philippine Marine Corps, 198,
    209
Philippine Navy, 198
Philippines: Operation
    Strongback, 197–215
physicals, 166
physicians, 259 n. 3; DMOs,
    162–63; talking doctors, 166
picketboats, 8
Pioneer Parachute Company,
    114, 187, 190–91
Plain, Lewis, 30
Plaster, John L., 239
4th Platoon, 1st Force Recon,
    234–35
PLFs. *See* parachute landing
    falls (PLFs)
Pliny the Elder, xix
poisoning: oxygen toxicity,
    153; snake, 210–11
Polakoff, Gerald, 244
Potts, Elmer, 3
pranks, 108–9
PRC-6 and PRC-10 radios, 78
PRC-25 radios, 78
pre-jump school, 46
pressure, absolute, 169
pressure-proof wrist
    compasses, 151
Princeton, 212

Pringle, Master Sergeant, 81
prisoners, 28
1st Provisional Marine Brigade, 4
1st Provisional Reconnaissance Battalion, 27
PTs. *See* patrol torpedo boats (PTs)
Puerto Rico, xiii, 127
Puller, Lewis B. ("Chesty"), xvi, 16, 30–31, 72–73
pumps, 243–44
Punsalang, Rudolfo, 209
Purple Heart, xxi

QAC (quick attachable, chest) packs, 49
QFB (quick fit, back) chutes, 49
Queenfish, 130, *156*, 176, 253 n. 7

R4D-8. *See* Douglas R4D-8 Super Skytrain
"rag jumpers," 181
Ramsey, David "Dave," 106, 123, 181
RC-292 antennae, 79
Recondo School, 225
RECONEX (reconnaissance exercise) 58D, 132–41
reconnaissance: air cover, 217; amphibious, xiii, 1, 28–29, 44–51, 265; beach, 18–23; coordination of, 248–49;

extraction methods, 216–33; force, 44; insertion xviii–xix, 182–83; insertion by buoyant ascent, 159–79; insertion by HALO penetration, 239–43; insertion by helicopter drop, 27; insertion by parachute entry, 29–30, 198–211, 234, 276 insertion via water, 129–30; organization of, 243; Test Unit 1 training, 44–51. *See also* force reconnaissance; *specific operations*
1st Reconnaissance Battalion, 226
2d Reconnaissance Battalion, 2d Marine Division, 244–46
reconnaissance divers. *See* scuba divers
Recon Team Florida, 240
Red Boar Hog, 221–22
Redfish, 130, *156*
Rennel, Paul, 4
Rice, Wesley H. "Duff" (Wes), 67, 223
Rochester (CA-124), 198
Rollings, Wayne E., 238, 248
Ronquil, 130, *156*, 176, 253 n. 7
Rottet, R.K., 210
Royal Marines, 104
rubber boats, 127, 277; dry-deck launch, 143–44, 146;

landing craft, rubber, large (LCR(L)), 277; landing craft, rubber, small (LCR(S)), 277; periscope tows, 144–45; wet and dry launches, 141–46; wet-deck launch, 142–43, 146

Runnells, Milton E., 118, 124, 133–35, 140, 154–56, 166

Rupertus, William H., 2

Russians, 19

Ryan, Robert, 15

Rydalch, Edward, ix, xvi, 41–44, 96, 110

S-2s. *See* intelligence officers (S-2s)

2-3s. *See* operations officers (S-3s)

safety procedures, 53–54

Sanborn, Lew, 36, 190

Schmuck, Donald "Buck," 111

schooling. *See* training

scouts, 4

SCR300 radio, 8

scuba divers, 146–54

scuba diving, 160–61, 258 n. 12; underway recovery without, 178

SE-11 signal lights, 76

Sea Horse (H-34). *See* Sikorsky H-34 Sea Horse

Sea Knight (CH-46), 217, 230, 238

Sealion (APSS-315), x, xx, 130, 132, 146, *156*, 266

Sealion (ASSP-315), 266

SEALs, 278

seat packs, 49

self-evaluations, 180–96

SERE (survival, evasion, resistance, and escape) training, 45, 278

Sexton, Martin J. "Stormy," 27

Shepherd, Lemuel C., Jr., ix, 38

Shinn, Leo B., 7, 216

Shoup, David M. (Dave), xvi, 51, 123, 198, 211–13

Sikorsky H-35 Chocktaw, 224

Sikorsky H-34 Sea Horse, 55, 217, 238

Sikorsky HRS-1s, 74

Sikorsky Jolly Green Giant (USAF HH-53, USMC CH-53), 217, 224, 236

Silver Star, xxi

Silverthorn, Merwin H. "Silver," 6–8, 22–23, 216

Simpson, Ben, 85, 93–94

Skimmer, 131–32

"Sky Diver" parachutes, 36, 184–93, 198

skydiving, 113–15

Skyhawks (A-4), 217

Skytrains (C-47), 217, 223. *See also* Douglas R4D-6 Skytrain; Douglas R4D-8 Super Skytrain

Slowick, John W., 236–37
Smith, Harold "Dutch," 15
Smith, Holland M. "Howling Mad," 5, 8, 128, 249
Smith, Kirkwall, 2, 3
Smith, Oliver, P., 31
Smoke Bomb Hill, 34
Snedeker, Edward, xvi, 110, 123, 166
SOC unit. *See* special operations capable (SOC) unit
SOG. *See* Special Operations Group (SOG)
SOG: The Secret Wars of America's Commandos in Vietnam (Plaster), 239
Soldier's Medal, 4
Solomon Islands, *10*; Tinian Island operations, 4–12, *11*, 216
sonar, 278
SOQ (special operations qualified) designation, 245
sound signals, 155
space-suit jumps, 49
Spanjer, Ralph "Smoke," xvi
Spark, Michael (Mike), xiv, 117–18, 128
Special Forces, 190–91, 218, 223–24, 239–42, 278
5th Special Forces Group, 225
10th Special Forces Group, 55
77th Special Forces Group, 190

Special Forces Warfare Center, 34–35
Special Landing Force (SLF) Alpha, 71
special operations capable (SOC) unit, 247, 278
Special Operations Group (SOG), 224; 278; *SOG: The Secret Wars of America's Commandos in Vietnam* (Plaster), 239
"Special Projects," 184
SPIE (special personnel insertion and extraction) rig, 226–33, 279
SRC. *See* Surveillance and Reconnaissance Center (SRC)
SRIGs (surveillance, reconnaissance, intelligence groups), 244, 247
SSs. See diesel submarines (SSs)
stabilized free fall, 35, 187
STABO rig, 225–26, 279
stacking jumps, 50
Standard Oil Company, 23
static line, 279
Steinke, Harris E., 162
Steinke hood, 162, 258 n. 2, 279
stick, 279
Stillwell, Joseph, 31
Stinson L-5 Sentinel, 19, 273

Stringham (APD-6), 6–8
submarine escape, 162
submarine escape tower
  instructors, 168
submarine escape towers, 259
  n. 4; Pearl Harbor, 167
Submarine Flotilla 1, 24
submarine physicals, 166
submarine rescue, 147–48
submarine rescue ship (ASR),
  266
submarines, 127–57; cold
  weather operations, 132–41;
  conning tower, 141; diesel
  (SSs), 130; escape trunk,
  147–48, 270; finding,
  154–57; first buoyant ascents
  from, 173–79; forward
  escape trunk, 147–48, *158*;
  jackstaff, 143; periscope
  tows, 144–45; physicians
  aboard, 259 n. 3; sail, 141;
  torpedo room, 280; transport
  (ASSP), 266; wet and dry
  launches, 141–46
surf swimming, 127
Surveillance and
  Reconnaissance Center
  (SRC), 244, 247
suspension lines, 279
Suzuki, 131
Swanda, Donald, 22–23
swimmer pickup, 26
swimmers, 180, 216. *See also*
  divers

swimming: clandestine, 153;
  combat, 268; surf, 127
Sykes, E.A., 251 n. 10
Szymanski, Thomas, 89,
  92–93

T-7A parachutes (standard
  troop reserve), 49, 234, 279
T-10 parachutes, 90–92,
  187–90, 192, 234, 280;
  modified free-fall, 195
table(s) of organization and
  equipment (TOE), 280; for
  1st Force Recon, 111–13
tactical missions, 180
tail hook accidents, 206
Tang (SS-306), 258 n. 1
Task Force 72 (Seventh Fleet),
  198
Taylor, Joseph Z. (Joe), ix, xiv,
  xvii, 34, 55, 184–86, 190,
  199; as executive officer of
  1st Force Recon, 106, 111,
  118, 121; Fulton Skyhook
  testing, 219–21; and Istell,
  114–15; Iwo Jima recon
  command from *Perch*, 132;
  Operation Sky Jump, 85,
  87–89, 95–96; Operation
  Strongback, 198; Test Unit
  1, 43–44, 46–47, 116–18
Taylor, Kenneth T., 82
Taylor, Roy, xx, 58, 85, 87
"Team 51," 238
technical sergeant (rank), 17

terrestrial reconnaissance training, 44

test parachutists, 48–49, 280

6511th Test Squadron, 47

Test Unit 1. See Marine Corps Test Unit 1

TF-1. See Grumman TF-1 Trader

Thermo (boot), 134

Thetis Bay (CVHA-1), 197–98, 202, 212

Thomas, Gerald C., 31

Tinian Island operations (July 1944), 4–12, 11, 216

TOE. See table(s) of organization and equipment (TOE)

"Tojo" parachute, 185, 188–89, 192

torpedo boats. See patrol torpedo boats (PTs)

training, 245–46; amphib recon, 13–31, 44–51; with army, 32–36; buoyant ascent, 167–73; at Camp McGill, 18, 26; at Camp Pendleton, 26; of Chinese Nationalists, 13; cross-service, 34–36; cross-training, 128, 180; E&E (escape and evasion), 45–46; jumpmaster, 33–34, 105–9; jump school, 30, 33, 46–50, 73, 246; of marine and navy units, 27–28; pathfinder, 72;

reconnaissance, 44–51; SERE, 45; specialized, 245–46; terrestrial recon, 44; for Test Unit 1, 44–51; with UDT, 24–27

transport submarines (ASSP), 266

Treleven, Lew, 119

Tripoli, 212

trooper's ladder, 223–24

Troop Training Unit, Atlantic (TTULant), 16, 22

Troop Training Unit, Pacific (TTUPac), 16; Amphibious Reconnaissance School, 13–31

Tucker, Chester, 65

Turney, Conrad, 85, 95, 110, 185

UDT. See underwater demolition team (UDT)

UDU. See underwater demolition unit

underwater communications, 155–56

underwater demolition team (UDT), 22, 24–27, 159–60, 253 n. 7, 280

Underwater Demolition Team 3 (UDT 3), 24

Underwater Demolition Team 5 (UDT 5), 7, 24

Underwater Demolition Team 7 (UDT 7), 7–8, 24

Underwater Demolition Team 11 (UDT 11), 24
underwater demolition unit (UDU), 281
Underwater Demolition Unit 1 (UDU 1), 24
underwater sound telephone, 155–56
Underwater Warrior (film), 24
underway recovery without scuba, 178
uniforms, 134
U.S. Air Force, 191–92
U.S. Army, 32–36
U.S. Army Airborne, 120
U.S. Border Patrol, 103
U.S. Immigration and Naturalization Service, 103
U.S. Marine Corps (USMC). *See specific companies*
U.S. Navy: Transport Squadron VR-5, xx; unit training, 27–28
U.S. Submarine Base, Pearl Harbor, Hawaii: submarine escape tower, 167–70, 259 n. 4
utilities, 281

VAC. See Amphibious Reconnaissance Battalion, V Amphibious Corps (VAC)
Vallario, Thomas J., 236–37
Vandegrift, Archibald, 37

Vietnam War, 217; combat HALO jumps, 239–42; combat parachuting, 234–37; extraction methods, 228; Fulton Skyhook retrieval system, 223; helicopter assaults and over-the-beach landings, 70–71; pathfinding, 70; *SOG: The Secret Wars of America's Commandos in Vietnam* (Plaster), 239
Vigil, Charles, 85, 93–94, 109–11
Vinson, Lewis T. "Lew," xvii, 47, 57, 58, 64, 68, 97–98
VMF(AW). *See* night all-weather fighter squadron (VMF(AW))
VMF(N). *See* night fighter squadron (VMF(N))
VR-5 (fleet transport squadron), 55
VR-21 (fleet transport squadron), 56

Walters, Harry, 52
watches, 125; diving, 125, 151, 205
water buffaloes, 205
water-induced hypothermia, 177
weapons, 7
Webb, Walter M., Jr., 235–36
Weiss (APD-135), 138
wet-deck launch, 142, 146

wet launches, 141–46
wet suits. See exposure suits
"whipping silk," 281
wild boar hunting, 203
Wilhelm, Charles, 244
Winchester Model 70 rifle, 135
"wind dummy," 79
winds aloft, 97, 281
Wociesjes, A. M., 3
Woods, Levi W., 110, 133, 184, 230; first live pickup with Fulton Skyhook, 220–22
World War II, 1–12; extraction methods, 216–18; Pacific operations, 1

Wright R-1820-82 engine, 56
wrist compasses, 151
wrist watches, 125, 151, 205

Yeager, Chuck, 68
Yeaton, Samuel Sylvester, 251 n. 10

Zwiener, Robert (Bob), 55, 65–67, 184, 191; forming 1st Force Recon, 108, 110–11, 122; HALO work, 239; Operation Ski Jump, 85, 94; Test Unit 1, 46, 49, 52